Pelican Books
Moving Goods and People

Peter Gilmour gained his early education at a Victorian
country state school and later attended Scotch College,
Melbourne. He holds a Master of Business Administration
from Cornell University, a Diploma of Education from
Monash University and a Ph.D from Michigan State
University. During 1977-8 he was a Research Fellow at
Harvard University. He is the editor of *Physical Distribution
in Australia* and co-author of *Ticket to Nowhere*. He teaches
in the Faculty of Economics and Politics at Monash
University.

Peter Gilmour
Moving Goods and People

Transport in Australia

Penguin Books

Penguin Books Ltd,
Harmondsworth, Middlesex, England
Penguin Books,
625 Madison Avenue, New York, N.Y. 10022, U.S.A.
Penguin Books Australia Ltd,
Ringwood, Victoria, Australia
Penguin Books Canada Ltd,
2801 John Street, Markham, Ontario, Canada
Penguin Books (N.Z.) Ltd,
182-190 Wairau Road, Auckland 10, New Zealand

First published 1978

Made and printed in Australia by
Hedges & Bell Pty Ltd, Maryborough, Victoria

Set in Plantin by The Dova Type Shop, Melbourne

CIP

Gilmour, Peter, 1942-.
Moving goods and people.

Index.
Bibliography.
ISBN 0 14 022052 6.

1. Transportation – Australia. I. Title.

380.5'0994

For my family:
Mary Herrick Gilmour
Jonathan Herrick Gilmour
Caroline Padgett Gilmour

Contents

Figures

Tables

Tables

Chapter 1
The Need for Mobility

The industrial revolution brought to an end the position of the household as the prime business and economic entity. Large-scale manufacture and the specialization of skills which accompanied it required that more people lived together in cities. Easy access to work was still important to people, but now many worked at the same physical location and as a result cities grew.

Prior to the industrial revolution merchants and household industries lived together in a city primarily for protection. City walls provided defence against warring neighbours. Within the walls the city developed in a manner to minimize the problems of internal transportation. Land transportation was still a scarce resource: either man or animal provided the power. In the first case the power source was relatively weak and in the second relatively unreliable. So the medieval city developed in a circular pattern. The characteristic crooked streets minimized the distances required in internal movements. In fact transportation requirements rather than cultural similarities determined the development pattern of early cities. Amsterdam and Osaka are strikingly similar. Both are on rivers which empty into the ocean and both have extensive canal structures to increase access to the port. Warehouses line the river and the canals and behind them are residential and business areas which are not differentiated by status.

In these cities transportation was by animal-drawn vehicle or by walking. As the home was the economic as well as the cultural centre for the family, walking was used for relaxation rather than for business. Walking provided a means to escape the over-crowding of the home.

Development of trains and street-cars in the nineteenth century changed all this. Factory owner and worker no longer had to live in the same area. Access to the place of work was now possible from many areas of the city. Transportation development was a direct cause of the social stratification of cities. While factory owners and managers could move away to more pleasant and less polluted neighbourhoods, workers could only afford to live close to the factory. Industrial slums grew.

The horse-drawn omnibus was the first street public transportation method of the nineteenth century. In order to reduce friction and reduce the number of horses needed the wheels were large. In order to ensure passenger safety the carriage was wide and the wheels far apart for stability. The result was a large, cumbersome vehicle which was very difficult to manoeuvre through medieval streets. Mounting the vehicle on rails provided far greater stability and enabled the carriage to be reduced in size. Reduced friction also enabled fewer horses to be used. During the 1870s and 1880s steam-powered cable cars replaced the horse-drawn omnibus, but with a few exceptions these were replaced by electric powered streetcars in the last decade of the century. In Europe and the United States lightweight railways mounted above or below the street provided a solution to the unreliability of the streetcar due to traffic congestion. Steam also proved to be a relatively unsatisfactory power source for the underground and elevated railway systems, primarily because of extensive pollution. But with electricity came a subway boom in the 1890s. At the same time as steam-powered streetcars and subways were being developed the 'penny-farthing' bicycle appeared as did the steam-powered automobile. The gasoline-powered internal combustion engine and the pneumatic tyred bicycle were developments of the last years of the century. Motorized trucks appeared around 1905. The first bus operated in London in 1904. In 1908 Henry Ford produced the Model T Ford. Considerable street paving activity during the first decades of the twentieth century completed the essential developments of the current transportation system.

Because the white settlement of Australia occurred in the period of the post-industrial revolution a strong need for establishing cities existed from the first. This is one reason for the existence of a strange paradox: Australia is one of the most highly urbanized countries in the world while at the same time having one of the lowest population densities. This situation creates considerable transportation difficulties. In the cities, on the one hand, are all the classical symptoms of the modern 'transportation problems': congestion, pollution, poor service, high costs. In the rural and provincial areas, transportation services and facilities are poor because the population sparsity does not provide the required markets and passenger and freight volumes. Mobility is difficult and expensive in both areas but for completely different reasons.

For the first half of the nineteenth century the Australian colonies were so small and relatively localized that horse-drawn carriages and waggons provided a reasonably satisfactory mode of transportation. In 1854 the first railway was completed in Australia – a 2½-mile (4 km) link between Melbourne and Port Melbourne. The next year a 14-mile (22 km) line between Sydney and Parramatta opened. Lines from Newcastle to East Maitland and from Melbourne to Geelong followed. In the 1860s once the difficulty and expense of crossing the coastal ranges had been overcome, several lines were opened linking ports with pastoral areas inland. Railways from Melbourne to the goldfields at Bendigo and from Geelong to the goldfields in Ballarat were completed in 1862. In all cases private ventures to build and operate railways in Australia failed despite government land grants and government guarantees to investors against loss. The reason for this was that rail could not compete economically against sea carriage and so rail lines had to go inland. But no population centres existed inland. During this time only the railways linking Adelaide and Melbourne with their ports were profitable ventures.

Planning for the first railways in New South Wales, Victoria and South Australia began in the early 1850s. At that time the engineer who designed Sydney's first railway, Wentworth Shields, rejected British government advice to build on the English gauge of 4 feet 8½ inches and selected instead the 5 feet 3 inch Irish gauge. Planners in Victoria and South Australia followed his lead and also chose the wide gauge. But Shields resigned and his successor advocated the English gauge. The Sydney to Parramatta line was built 4 feet 8½ inches wide while Victoria and South Australia continued with the 5 feet 3 inch gauge. Once the principle of standardization was broken a variety of different gauges developed: Queensland chose a 3 feet 6 inch gauge which was popular in Norway and India, as did Western Australia and Tasmania. South Australia in 1870 decided to build a series of narrow-gauge lines into its wheat belt.

It was not until late in the century that the different gauge widths caused a problem. Until then all the rail networks in Australia linked an inland area with the nearest port. Australia had a series of isolated systems. In 1883 the railway had extended to join Australia's two largest cities, Melbourne and Sydney. With the increased ability of rail to compete with sea during the twentieth century the different rail gauges have become a much more serious problem.

Australia has only one major internal waterway – the Murray River and its tributaries, the Darling and Murrumbidgee. In 1853 the first paddle steamer entered the Murray near Adelaide to service the wool-growing areas of Victoria and New South Wales and later the gold-fields of north eastern Victoria. Passage of wool to Melbourne by paddle steamer was less expensive than by bullock teams despite the fact that by water it was ten times the distance. But the paddle steamer could not compete with rail and the line linking Echuca with Mel-bourne, which was completed in 1864, truncated the route of the paddle steamer. Eventually the paddle steamer became merely a shuttle service between the rail heads linking the river with Mel-bourne.

The twentieth century in Australia, as elsewhere, has seen the domi-nance of the gasoline-powered internal combustion engine, the decline of rail-and water-based systems and the emergence of air travel. But there is serious question as to whether the infrastructure required and provided during the first half of the twentieth century for the car and the train has not seriously limited the extent and devel-opment of future transportation options. Cartoons drawn by Virgil Partch of the United States Steel Corporation question with hindsight the value of major twentieth century transportation developments. His banker is talking to Henry Ford:

Do you realize, sir, that if your invention should gain popular acceptance – which I do not for one moment believe it will – we should have to provide paved roads throughout the length and breadth of the country, thousands of pumping stations to supply ready access to fuel, and innumerable vacant lots in every city in which to park vehicles? Take my advice and forget this folly, Henry.

In another cartoon the same banker is talking to a row of railway men standing in front of Stephenson's Rocket:

The whole business is economically unsound, gentlemen. With a train of this length and forty miles of track, we find that only 0.0568 per cent of the track will be in use at any given time, representing a constant idle investment of 99.9432 per cent.

But such investment did take place and we are now faced with a 'transportation problem'.

In Australian urban areas congestion on the roads is steadily increasing whether for the journey to work or for the weekend trip out of the city. High levels of air pollution and noise exist. Car drivers show hostility and a willingness to break the law at levels never contemplated in other normal daily activities. The criss-cross of paved roads carrying high-speed traffic has segmented and isolated the community. Children can no longer roam with safety any distance from their homes, certainly not far enough to mingle with children of markedly different socio-economic characteristics. Housewives in splendid suburban isolation on their own quarter-acre building blocks but without use of the family car or access to adequate public transportation develop myriad neuroses. Each day in Australia more than 10 people die and more than 245 are injured on the roads.

The direct cost of obtaining this mobility is a considerable portion of the total expenditure by Australian households. In a survey by the Australian Bureau of Statistics of household expenditure in 1974–5 the category 'transport and communication' absorbed $26.29 (or 17 per cent) of $157.01 total average weekly expenditure. This of course does not include the share of tax revenue paid for land acquisition, track laying, road construction, rolling-stock purchase and reimbursement to public transportation systems and road construction authorities for operating deficits. Neither is the indirect cost of fatal traffic accidents and disabling injuries included in this amount.

Australians are willing to pay this high cost because mobility is important to any modern community because it provides access. Access to a wide variety of jobs within the person's ability range. Access to a wide variety of living styles. Access to a wide social network of friends. Access to a wide variety of cultural and recreational activities. In fact modern Australia would be unrecognizable without this high level of access.

But mobility is not evenly spread throughout the community. In the large cities white-collar jobs tend to concentrate in the central

Figure 1.1   Socio-economic status zones in Sydney

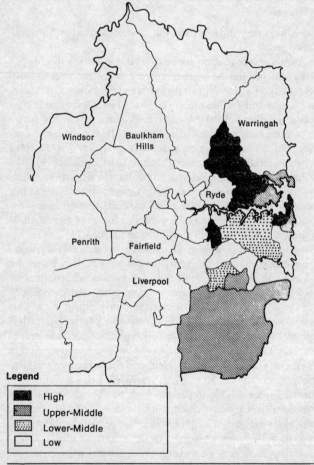

Legend

■	High
▨	Upper-Middle
▦	Lower-Middle
□	Low

Source   John Paterson Urban Systems, *Transport Services Available to and Used by Disadvantaged Sections of the Community*, Commonwealth Bureau of Roads, Melbourne, June 1974, p. 23 and p. 25

Figure 1.2   Socio-economic status zones in Melbourne

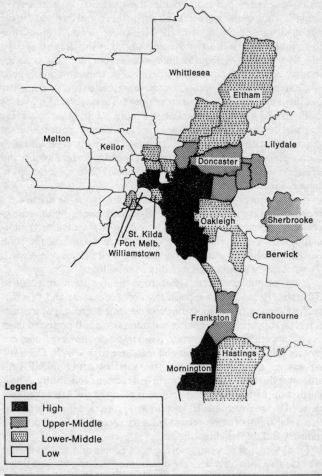

Legend

■	High
▨	Upper-Middle
▧	Lower-Middle
□	Low

Source   John Paterson Urban Systems, *Transport Services Available to and Used by Disadvantaged Sections of the Community*, Commonwealth Bureau of Roads, Melbourne, June 1974, p. 23 and p. 25

city area while blue-collar jobs tend to be more numerous in outer areas where the supply of potential labour is better. Most Australian cities have developed radial public transportation systems serving well the white-collar worker for his trip to the central business district but inadequately coping with the blue-collar worker on his cross-town journey. This situation is compounded by the fact that in cities like Sydney and Melbourne high socio-economic status areas are located close to the city centre where public transportation is good while areas of low socio-economic status are located further out where public transportation services are not good. This is shown for Sydney in Figure 1.1 and for Melbourne in Figure 1.2. In order to achieve an equal degree of mobility those living in the outer urban areas must purchase a car out of a wage which is far less able to cope with such a large expenditure. Higher percentage expenditures for mobility and greater distances to travel for the same benefits of access create questions of inequity.

For the minority of Australians who do not live in the urban areas mobility disadvantages also exist. Freight and passenger public transportation services are expensive to provide to rural areas even at minimal levels. Per capita road construction requirements for rural Australians also run much higher than for their urban counterparts. To what extent should rural mobility be subsidized?

Issues of public concern also shroud the movement of goods in Australia. Because of few population concentrations and vast distances all modes of transportation receive some degree of government financial support. In most states rail transport is still protected from open competition with the truck. Road transport, however, does not pay for the full extent of wear and tear done to the roads. Domestic air services are limited by law to two carriers, Ansett and T.A.A., who snuggle together in government-guaranteed profitability. A proportion of the total shipping volume is reserved for Australian carriers. Massive governmental support and protection is also provided to several transportation-related industries, notably the automobile industry and shipbuilding.

Transportation services (moving both people and goods) should provide all Australians with the opportunity to improve their living standards by increasing the availability of goods and services, jobs, social exchange and cultural and recreational activities. Mobility should not act as a bridge for some sections of the community and a wall for others.

Chapter 2
The Future of the Car

Modern cities have had a long romance with the motor car:

... as we improve our standard of living ... we must place greater emphasis on those forms of transport which prove most efficient under present-day conditions. In this regard motor transport is proving itself, and its use must be considered synonymous with prosperity.[1]

It is only relatively recently that advocates such as Ralph Nader have been able to have the opposite view seriously considered by government decision makers. 'The self-defeating consequences of trying to adapt cities to cars have become more and more widely recognized in the past decade.'[2] Where does the car fit into effective planning for transportation in Australian urban areas?

The nature of movement in Australian cities has changed significantly with the changing nature of the cities themselves over recent years. During the early years of the century most commercial activity was concentrated in the central business district. As a result fixed-track public transportation systems were established on a radial basis to serve this centre of activity. But as the cities became larger much of the activity moved out. Over the few years between 1961 and 1972 in the central business district of Melbourne shopping space decreased by 7 per cent and manufacturing space by 29 per cent. Widespread residential development and increased car ownership have led to the development of large regional shopping centres. Industrial parks in the outer suburban areas have also flourished.

These developments have left the fixed-track public transportation system, primarily serving the central business district, with rapidly declining patronage. By 1970 in the capital cities of Australia between 53 per cent (in Sydney) and 70 per cent (in Adelaide) of all trips to work were made by private car. Of those who worked in the central business district (where the best public transportation service exists together with the most congestion for the private car) 23 per cent travelled by private car in Sydney, 28 per cent in Melbourne and 58 per cent in Perth.

The current malaise of public transportation in Australia is highlighted by the amazing fact that 93 per cent of all people living in Sydney are within half a mile of a public transportation route. Well over two-thirds of the people living in Adelaide and Perth live within a quarter mile of a bus service.

The overall form of the city has had a major influence on this development. A transportation system developed when the city had certain characteristics is unlikely to be satisfactory when significant changes occur in the form of the city. Australian cities developed as centralized cities with financial and commercial activity concentrated in the central business district and with manufacturing nearby. A radial public transportation system suited well this type of city. At the opposite pole to the centralized city is the dispersed city – a city with houses, flats and places of work distributed quite uniformly throughout the city and its suburbs. Modern Australian cities are tending in this direction but have not reached the extremes of this type of city. In between are the nucleated city and the system city. A nucleated city still has a central business district, but a lesser degree of concentration occurs there. Other centres with the characteristics of smaller central business districts are developed within the suburban areas. High-speed line-haul transportation links are established between the nucleii. Some interest has been shown in the possibility of extensive development of Dandenong which would convert Melbourne into a nucleated city. System cities are similar to nucleated cities except that the new centres are planned outside the existing area of development. Corridor development, as proposed for Perth and Melbourne, is a form of system-city development.

Less than 20 per cent of metropolitan employment is provided in the central business district of Sydney. In Melbourne less than 15 per cent of metropolitan jobs are in the central business district with another 15 per cent in the St Kilda Road area. These jobs are predominantly white-collar jobs; the blue-collar worker must make cross-town trips by car or suffer from the poor co-ordination and frequency of public transportation for this type of trip. Often people earning low incomes are required to pay high journey-to-work costs. This is particularly true when household location is restricted either by the inability to afford accommodation in a large number of areas or because the individual is receiving subsidized housing from the Housing Commission. Concern for this segment of the urban community led the Commonwealth Bureau of Roads to conduct a study into the areas which most needed improvements in public transportation on social welfare grounds. Sydney was the initial choice and the data and traffic zones of the 1971 Sydney Area Transportation Study (published in 1974) were used. The key variables in the analysis were journey-to-work costs (both money and time) and income. These were taken as an average for each zone. Also calculated for each zone was an index relating the present cost of using public transportation to the average cost of all public transportation users in Sydney. By this method disadvantaged zones were identified; contiguous zones at Green Valley, Mt Druitt and Penrith being worst served in that order. As expected, average journey-to-work costs increased with the distance from central Sydney. Highest transportation costs relative to income occurred in the western and south-western growth corridors with, as mentioned, the worst situation occurring in the Housing Commission areas of Green Valley and Mt Druitt. The study also examined in detail the work trips for those living in Green Valley. For 25 per cent of Green Valley workers, travel time adds the equivalent of two extra days to their working week. Most workers from the area travel between 40 and 80 kilometres to and from work each day. Sixty per cent of the families do not own a car and even if they did it would take half a day in travelling for a trip to the beach or zoo. A sizeable proportion of trips to work are to Bankstown with bus-rail-bus connections over 21 kilometres or three bus legs over 13 kilometres. Direct bus service, a section of bus-only lane and a priority turn signal for buses were evaluated as possibilities for significantly improving public transportation facilities for this segment of the community. These alternatives would be relatively easy to implement within a short space of time.

The situation at Green Valley is repeated to some extent in every capital city in Australia. Part of the problem is that there has never been proper integration between the two major types of urban movement systems: the random-route system and the fixed-route system.

Roads are the infrastructure of the random-route system and cars are the major vehicle. As the name 'random-route' suggests there are no fixed origins and destinations for trips made by this system; neither are trips made at regular times. Cars are free to move at any time in any direction over the road network.

Fixed-route transportation systems are commonly thought of as trains running on metal wheels on a metal track down their own right-of-way. But the fixed-route system also uses the road network. Buses use the roads but cannot deviate from a specified route nor collect passengers at other than predetermined stops. This is the case also for the tram network in Melbourne while ferries in Sydney and Hobart also operate a fixed route on another variable-route medium – water.

Additional differences which are considerable in consequence but less obvious to the casual observer, exist between the two systems. Essentially the random-route system moves vehicles while the fixed-route system moves people. This fact creates one of the greatest problems of the random-route system. When the random-route vehicle reaches its destination space must be found for both the occupants of the vehicle and for the vehicle itself. Parking in congested areas, such as central business districts, is a major urban problem of the twentieth century. Land in these areas is scarce and many alternative uses for the land compete with its use as a parking lot. At current values a car parked in a cleared lot in the golden mile of Melbourne is occupying around $10 000 worth of land while its owner is at work. Apart from the cost of parking spaces, the number of spaces is never adequate to service the peak needs of the central business district. Even at suburban shopping plazas, with acres of parking area, parking spaces are often not easy to find. Parking at the other end of the journey, at the conventional suburban residential estate, is not a problem, although the expense of garage construction and road paving is not inconsequential.

Another considerable difference between the two systems is the amount of land space required. A two-lane subway requires a cross-sectional width of about 10 metres while an eight-lane freeway requires a 60-metre right-of-way. The subway with trains stopping at all stations can carry 40 000 passengers per lane per hour while the freeway carries 2625 people per lane per hour. Also for the random-route system vast amounts of additional land are used up by petrol stations, garages, parking lots and car washes. One-third of the total land area of the city of Los Angeles is taken over by the requirements of the random-route transportation system. In the central business district of Los Angeles this figure rises to two-thirds. Obviously a much more pleasant urban environment would exist if only a percentage of this land were converted into parks and gardens.

Traffic flow in the random-route system is only under partial control by means of a maze of traffic lights and police officers. The fact that a large percentage of Australia's law enforcement officers are used to control traffic indicates a major misallocation of resources. Traffic lights and police officers do not prevent the death and destruction which occur on the roads. In comparison total control of traffic flow can operate on a fixed-route system.

Most recent engineering developments in urban transit have been for the fixed-route system, as in the automatic train control where the system is operated automatically from a centralized location with the aid of a computerized master board. Some of the automatic train control systems already in operation are the Metro in Montreal, Line II of the Paris Metro, the B.A.R.T. system in San Francisco and the Municipal Subway II in Barcelona. An essential element in these systems is the gathering of information about the desired destination of entering passengers, which is done automatically either when the ticket or token is purchased or when the passenger goes through the turnstile into the station. Automatic scheduling and sizing of trains should respond directly to this information.

Some proposals for future urban transportation systems have the same vehicle use both the random-route and the fixed-route networks. Typical of these proposals is the 'automaton' which would act as a robot and follow guidance devices in the roadbed or mount rails and proceed to the destination which the rider had keyed into it. Such proposals would substantially reduce the accident rate, but would greatly under-utilize very expensive capacity and not greatly affect the road congestion problem.

With the enormous and well-publicized rate of technological and social change in the twentieth century the motor car stands out as the major aberration to this exponential trend. The motor car of 1977 is essentially the same as the motor car of 1910. Because the cost of owning and operating a motor car does not seem to be a significant variable in the decision to buy a car, it will take some major change, such as the virtual depletion of the world's oil reserves (not merely considerable price increases of petroleum), to change the essential form of the 1910 motor car. International automobile manufacturers and oil producing and marketing companies also exert considerable influence to maintain the status quo. So it will not be surprising if the motor car of 1980, 1990 or even 2000 is still, underneath its sophisticated gadgetry, the motor car of 1910.

For these reasons, together with the enormous amounts invested in the road system (in Australia expenditure on roads is estimated to be about $500 million per year for the next five years), technological advances in the past decade have been and for the next few decades will be concentrated on the fixed-route system. For the immediate future the most realistic policy options are for making the existing fixed-route system work better rather than trying to change it physically.

A combination of factors have interacted to result in the complete dominance of the random-route system. Every holding of land in Australia must by law have access to the road system. Urban development, especially over the past two or three decades, has assumed that the random-route transportation system is adequate. Everyone is hooked into it; few consider access to the fixed-route system. Social status has also played a key role: on the random-route system the user has purchased the vehicle, while on the fixed-route system the user has merely purchased the particular ride. Modern mobile societies attach great status to vehicle ownership. Indeed the status attached to the car often outweighs the status attached to any other possession, including the house.

Fixed-route systems developed during the pre-motor car era when competition for passengers was not strong. Efficiency and economy were much more important than comfort and service to the customer. Then cars with their personalized comfort and flexibility developed with a rush. Public funds were poured into road building while the rail-based transportation systems did not receive sufficient public funding to upgrade their facilities to a competitive level.

The stage of development of these two main urban transportation systems, the random-route and the fixed-route systems, is such that politicians and urban planners must evolve strategies that work within these technical constraints and select in the short and medium term the most appropriate level of utilization of both systems. Technological change can occur in urban transit systems but any worthwhile change must be massive and involve an enormous expenditure and commitment over many years. At present this is a remote possibility, despite the fact that many interesting technologies have already been developed. It is remote because of the inherent weaknesses in the politically-based urban transportation planning process and also because the financially disastrous experiences of such projects as the automatic train control systems in San Francisco (B.A.R.T.) and Washington D.C. (Metro) influence basically conservative politicians to remain conservative.

The new town of Stevenage about 50 kilometres north of London provides a good example of how a road-based combination of the random-route and fixed-route systems can be made to work. A thorough study undertaken by the Stevenage Development Corporation evaluated many transportation alternatives for the new city including mono-rails, guided track hovercraft, moving pavements and mini-buses. Eventually a system based on the standard modern bus was selected and planned to work on the existing road network. Professor Nathaniel Litchfield, who directed the study, advocated that the £4½ million available should be spent on improving the bus services rather than on elevated road works '. . . a combination of an enhanced bus service and the ground-level road system is better than building the elevated road works and supplying a reduced or residual bus service'.[3] This decision was an important one because it was the first time in the United Kingdom that road building funds were diverted to passenger transportation services.

Stevenage has an industrial section located on the side of the central business district opposite to the residential section. Main roads link the two sectors, by-passing the town centre. Frontal development onto these roads has been restricted to reduce the amount of traffic generated by the roads themselves. This, together with the prohibition of parking at all times, has resulted in these roads having very high capacities of up to 2000 vehicles per lane per hour. Bus routes to the town centre and industrial estate, with a small number of pick-up and discharge points linked by a high-speed line haul, were established. Progressively improved service (a bus every five minutes by day and every ten minutes at night), together with conversion from two-man to one-man operation, provision of separate exits and a reduced flat fare completed the transformation. This service resulted in an increase in passengers carried on the first new route from 19 700 per week to 41 500. Car usage to the town centre and the industrial estate decreased by 4 per cent. At a later period the weekly number of off-peak passengers increased from 15 850 to 26 700. Transport planners are often critical of improvements to urban transit systems which do not convert car passengers to public transportation at the same rate as people who previously did not travel at all are attracted to the public transportation system. This was the case at Stevenage. But such criticism does not account for the fact that sectors of the community who were previously denied mobility now have access to it.

Quite a different method of converting car movements into bus movements has been tried in Nottingham. The similarity with Stevenage is that in both cities traffic management methods have been substituted for motorway construction.

In the city centre of Nottingham many of the footpaths have been widened to encourage pedestrians, on-street parking has been prohibited and two free, high-frequency circular bus services introduced. Up to 100 000 passengers use this service each week and after operation for one year the additional passengers attracted to the remainder of the bus system generated enough revenue to almost cover the free inner-city service.

Nottingham has also introduced a system of zones and collars as a progressive experiment in traffic control. A series of 'no entry' and 'buses only' signs limits the rate at which cars can enter main roads. Special traffic lights operating during the peak period, but which bus drivers can turn green by an electronic gun, also limit congestion on the main roads. Movement in the zones where these controls are operating is encouraged for buses but retarded for cars.

Collars operate on main roads at about 2½ kilometres from the city centre. Typically these roads have three lanes – two operating in the peak direction, one for buses, bicycles, and emergency vehicles and the second for all other vehicles. At the collar, lights force the cars to queue if a risk of traffic congestion in the city centre occurs. An outer collar at the outskirts of the city prevents out-of-town commuters from congesting the main roads into the city. At both collars car parks are provided from which rapid bus services operate to the city centre. As a final aid to the efficiency of the system additional buses have been provided and more stringent control of city-centre parking has been implemented. Electronic linkage between all parts of the system enables it to be effectively monitored and controlled.

In the United States, also, several attempts have been made to increase the importance of the bus. In Los Angeles some of the key entry ramps to freeways have two lanes, one exclusively for buses and the second for all other vehicles. If the traffic flow on the freeway slows, this second lane can be closed by hydraulically operated vertical rubber tubes which have the appearance of primed metal pipes. Other entry ramps are controlled by traffic lights.

The Shirley Highway in Washington D.C. is another example where rapid bus service is possible by avoiding the congestion caused by cars. Two additional lanes, to be used exclusively by buses, were built down the centre of a 10-kilometre stretch of interstate highway linking Virginia with Washington D.C. Both lanes operate inwards during the morning peak and outwards during the evening peak. When the buses leave the interstate highway for the last part of the journey into the city centre, their progress is aided by bus-only lanes on the city streets and computerized traffic lights biased in their favour. An increase in bus patronage of more than 100 per cent occurred on this service over its first 18 months of operation. Time savings were vividly demonstrated by a much publicized race between a car and a bus over 22 kilometres including the 10-kilometre Shirley Highway stretch. Both vehicles started at eight o'clock in the morning with the bus arriving at the finishing point near the White House at 8.35 a.m. and the car at 9.05 a.m.

For the layman car driver it is difficult to think about taxis in charitable terms. Taxi drivers are the menaces who stop in the middle of a moving flow of traffic to let off a passenger or who charge across traffic and stop to pick up a fare. But the taxi should be regarded as part of the public transportation system and as such be given priority over cars. Opposition to any special favours for taxis often stems from the view that they are the means of mobility employed by the rich and as such should not have priority over the cars driven by the middle classes. This view is erroneous. Not only is the taxi the means of mobility for the rich but it is to a larger extent the means of mobility for the non car-owning poor.

The Transport Commission of Western Australia recognized the potential importance of the taxi in metropolitan passenger transport and planned a detailed study for 1976, but the study was never carried out because of lack of funding. During 1974 the Victorian Ministry of Transport commissioned a firm of consultants to investigate taxi services in Melbourne. The report was completed early in 1975 but has never been released.

While there are solid arguments for trying to convert as many as possible of the journey-to-work trips from the private car to public transportation, there are also equity arguments for providing the option of owning a car or not owning a car to the entire community. Access to many cultural and recreational activities will then be widely provided and not restricted on the basis of mobility. Car ownership could be a realistic alternative for many more individuals and families if everyone had the option to use their car for private purposes or for hire. In this manner the very high fixed costs of owning a car could be subsidized by even a very small amount of for-hire operation.

Taxis operate in the middle-ground between the bus and the car. Utilized capacity of a taxi is similar to a bus and far greater than a car, although of course a taxi cannot carry the absolute number of passengers that a bus can. Taxis require far less total parking space than cars and their higher utilization also provides a good argument for priorities for taxis in congested city centres. Already in Rome several shopping streets near the Corso have been reserved for pedestrians and taxis.

It would seem reasonable for bus operators to diversify their fleets to include other vehicles besides the traditional standard bus. If bus drivers were employed to drive taxis between the peak periods the split shift that many drivers are now forced to work might be eliminated.

Another type of vehicle is the mini-bus, which recently has been used in a new fashion, commonly called 'dial-a-ride'. The intending passenger telephones a dispatching office giving his name and address, time to be picked up and destination. The dispatcher, in radio telephone contact with all the mini-buses of the fleet, then schedules vehicles to provide passengers with door-to-door service and minimal detours to service other customers en route. Dial-a-ride is a cross between a taxi and a standard bus. It provides better service than a bus at lower cost than a taxi.

In some small towns dial-a-ride services have completely replaced conventional bus services. This is the case in Batavia a town of 18 000 people in upstate New York where bus patronage rose by 30 per cent when a 60-cent high-performance dial-a-ride service replaced a 25-cent a ride conventional bus service. In larger cities, such as Regina in the Canadian province of Saskatchewan with a population of 140 000, a 'telebus' service exists in conjunction with the conventional bus service. The dial-a-ride service acts as a feeder for the conventional fixed-route services on high-volume routes along main roads. A similar system operates through a rural area servicing the city of Peterborough in England.

Dial-a-ride services should prove to be successful in linking residential areas in the suburbs with railway stations and express bus services and also for providing a convenient means of making random off-peak journeys within the suburbs. In some cases it may be more efficient to use shared-ride taxis for dial-a-ride service rather than using mini-buses for dial-a-bus service.

All of these developments have been with public transportation systems that share the network of the random-route system and suffer from congestion problems caused by the car. Recently a surge of interest has occurred in the construction of underground railways – typically underground at the city centre and fanning out above ground into the suburbs. Virtually all of the one hundred or so largest cities of the world, with populations exceeding one million, are either constructing new railed rapid transit systems or extending existing ones.

Fixed-route transportation systems operating on their own right-of-way have some considerable advantages. The capacity to move huge numbers of people is the prime advantage. Up to 64 000 people per hour in a single direction have been moved, although the average 24 000 people per hour of London's Victoria Line may well be more typical. Even so to move this volume of people by car at average occupancy levels would require a freeway twenty lanes wide. Railed systems can also maintain higher average speeds because they do not share their track with other vehicles not under system control.

But fixed-route systems also have some disadvantages. At the city-centre end of the trip the operation is quite efficient: the high concentration of activity within the central business district means that all potential passengers are within easy walking distances from the station. At the other end of the trip things are quite different. The rail network radiates from the city centre. In the outer suburbs each house is surrounded by its lawn and garden and the resultant suburban sprawl means that only relatively few can live within walking distance of the suburban railway station. It then becomes difficult for the rail system to combat the feeling of the potential passenger that if the car has to be taken out to drive to the station it may as well be driven into town. Radial rail services are also poor for cross-town trips between neighbouring suburbs. Another common criticism of rail transportation is that for any given sum of money more kilometres of busways than rail lines can be provided.

A more significant criticism is that underground railways change the character of the urban areas surrounding the central stations. Increased real estate values near the underground force up rents and drive out small businesses and residences. This phenomenon has undoubtedly contributed to the startling change occuring in the 'top end' of Collins Street in Melbourne which will be handily located to the new Parliament station of the underground loop.

It is difficult to be categorically for or against underground railway systems. Each system should be evaluated in terms of particular characteristics of the city concerned. Recent experience in the United States cannot be seen as particularly encouraging. The most publicized is San Francisco's new 120-kilometre long B.A.R.T. In order to compete with cars on San Francisco's freeway system B.A.R.T. had to be able to obtain average speeds of 60 to 80 kilometres per hour. To do this, up to 125 kilometres per hour had to be reached between stations which caused stations to be spaced from between 3 to 6 kilometres apart. So the inner city area which was in need of public transportation improvements received few stations. B.A.R.T. spreads over vast suburban areas. It is a system which will service the well-to-do commuters from the more affluent outer suburbs. It will be little used outside the peak periods and will only cater for at most 7 per cent of the travel needs of the area. It is small wonder that performance characteristics like this, set against the estimated

$4000 million cost of the 155-kilometre network in Washington D.C. and the $7000 million estimated cost for the rapid transit system in Los Angeles, generate opponents to such systems.

Several cities have recognized the need to adapt an existing radial rail network to permit intersuburban movement and to provide wide access to suburban retail centres. Toronto has a well-established radial underground system. To complement this system semicircular elevated 'railways' are planned for vehicles supported by magnetic fields rather than wheels. Linear motors will provide the power. This lightweight system will not have the capacity of a traditional subway, but that capacity is not required for cross-town trips. Neither will the system cost as much as a conventional subway. The 90-kilometre system is estimated to cost $8.5 million per kilometre as against the subway cost of from $15 million to $19 million per kilometre. Development has been encouraged at the points at which the radial system crosses the ring system.

In Boston the Master Highway Plan of 1948 recommended three circumferential freeways to be connected to the radial roads emanating from Boston. The outer freeway was planned to be 30 kilometres from the city centre, with the middle freeway at 20 kilometres and the inner freeway 3 kilometres. The first two of these have been built but only one link of the Inner Belt was completed before the plan was scrapped. A restudy of Boston's transportation needs in 1972 proposed building a circumferential rail transit line along the route planned for the Inner Belt. Nine rail lines are planned to extend radially from the city centre to the middle freeway (Route 128) 20 kilometres out. Here large parking lots are planned.

From this examination it seems that some railed transportation systems have far greater potential to serve the transportation needs of most urban residents than do other systems. The systems in Boston and Toronto may well work: those in San Francisco and Washington D.C. may well not.

Just before Christmas 1976 a tent was set up at the city end of the nearly completed Eastern Freeway in Melbourne (usually referred to in typical planning terms as the F19). The Collingwood Residents' Association erected the tent in an attempt to stop the freeway from pushing through the last few blocks from Alexandra Parade, its present ending point, to Nicholson Street the terminal point shown in the plans. Two aspects of this campaign are of particular interest. The first is that the Collingwood Residents' Association's fight on this freeway has been lost* as the bulk of the freeway has already been built and so even if construction of the remaining small portion had been halted the area will receive a large increase in traffic on its residential streets from the F19 terminating in the middle of Collingwood rather than further on. The second point of interest about this protest is that the Collingwood City Council provided toilets and electricity for the squatters. Things have changed over recent years and, as John Bayley who was Director of the Melbourne Transportation Study of the sixties says, 'now freeways are a dirty word'.

But this attitude in Australia has not long been predominant. All capital cities and most major provincial cities (such as Geelong, Townsville, Launceston, Ballarat, Toowoomba, Rockhampton and Bendigo) have completed transportation studies over the past decade and a half. The most recent major study, the Sydney Area Transportation Study, was completed in 1974. Without exception the transportation plans for the capital cities propose freeway systems in combination with minor variations to existing public transportation systems. Concerted opposition, particularly to freeways in inner urban areas, has resulted in very hesitant (if at all) political acceptance of these plans.

A plan for the County of Cumberland (including north to the Hawkesbury River, west to the Nepean River and south to the northern reaches of Greater Wollongong) was drawn up in 1947 and proposed a system of radial freeways linked by a ring road and with a circular green belt around the built-up area to limit further expansion. Figure 2.1 is the freeway plan for Sydney which was issued by the New South Wales Department of Main Roads in 1974 – it is a much pruned down version of the freeway maze in the Sydney Area Transportation Study plan. The option of a circumferential system shown in Figure 2.1 is also currently under consideration.

Planning for urban transportation in Melbourne will be dealt with in detail later in this chapter. But, in brief, the Melbourne Transpor-

---

*The final section of the F19 was completed and open to traffic on 21 December 1977.

Figure 2.1 Planned freeways for Sydney —
the radial and circumferential systems

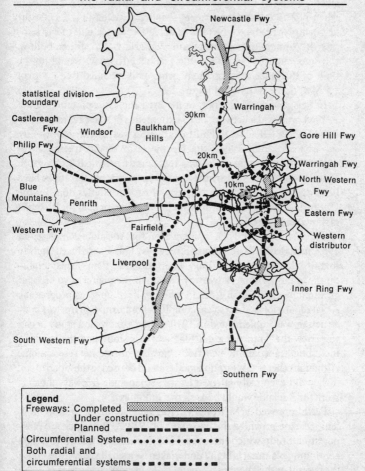

Sources Commonwealth Bureau of Roads *Assessment of Freeway Plans, State Capital Cities,* Melbourne, 1974, p.41 and *Report on Roads in Australia, 1975, Appendixes,* Melbourne, 1975, p.54

tation Study, which was completed in 1969, included a network of 490 kilometres of freeways to be completed by 1985. Only a very small portion of this system had been constructed by March 1973 when the Victorian Government (having accepted in principle the original plan) reduced the total planned freeway length to 240 kilometres. A more limited inter-connected grid would still be built in the outer suburbs but as a matter of policy freeways would not be built in the inner areas of Melbourne. This modified freeway plan for Melbourne is shown in Figure 2.2.

In Brisbane the final report of the Brisbane Transportation Study in 1965 proposed a network of 154 kilometres of freeways to be completed by 1981. The central business district was to be served by inner suburban ring-routes and radial freeways with further freeways providing the basis for inter-regional routes and a principal north–south route by-passing the city on the eastern side. Some modifications have been made to this plan on the basis of further studies done by the Queensland Main Roads Department. The current plan for Brisbane is shown in Figure 2.3.

The Metropolitan Development Plan for Adelaide, completed in 1962, included 157 kilometres of freeways. This was reduced slightly to 140 kilometres by the 1968 Transportation Plan. Considerable public opposition to the freeway section of the plan was voiced and as might be expected in Adelaide the city lived up to its progressive social reputation and a 10-year complete moratorium on freeway construction was implemented in 1970. In the same year a study began to review the Transportation Plan and this study had the result of including 'transportation corridors' instead of freeway reservations. Although other transportation modes could be used in these corridors, if they did eventually (after at least 1980) include freeways the network for Adelaide would be as shown in Figure 2.4.

Perth approved its Metropolitan Region Planning Scheme in 1963. This scheme provided the basis for the 1970 Perth Regional Transportation Study which included 134 kilometres of freeways. While continuing planning is being undertaken by a small study team under the control of the Director-General of Transport the current freeway system for Perth is shown in Figure 2.5. It can be seen from this map that bridge crossings over the Swan River provide a major constraint to any system of roads. Only three road crossings exist between

Figure 2.2   Planned freeways for Melbourne

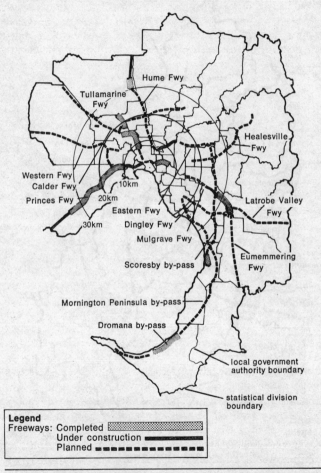

Legend
Freeways: Completed
Under construction
Planned

Source Commonwealth Bureau of Roads, *Assessment of Freeway Plans, State Capital Cities,* Commonwealth Bureau of Roads, Melbourne, 1974, p.49

Figure 2.3   Planned freeways for Brisbane

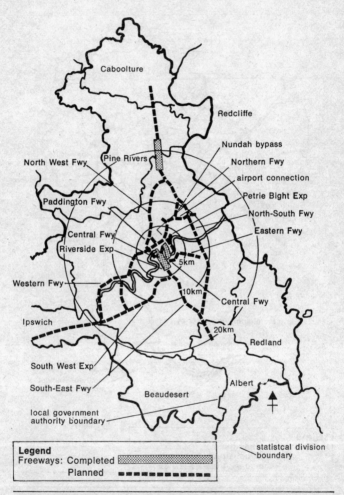

Source Commonwealth Bureau of Roads, *Assessment of Freeway Plans, State Capital Cities,* Commonwealth Bureau of Roads, Melbourne, 1974, p.57

Figure 2.4 Planned freeways for Adelaide

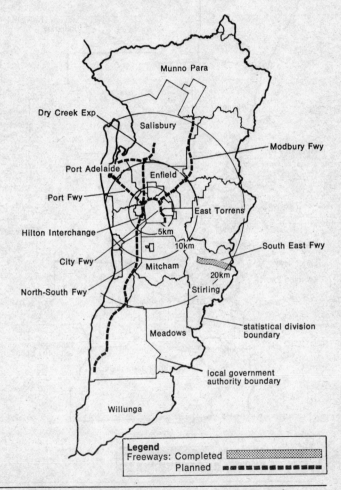

Source Commonwealth Bureau of Roads, *Assessment of Freeway Plans, State Capital Cities,* Commonwealth Bureau of Roads, Melbourne, 1974, p.67

Figure 2.5   Planned freeways for Perth

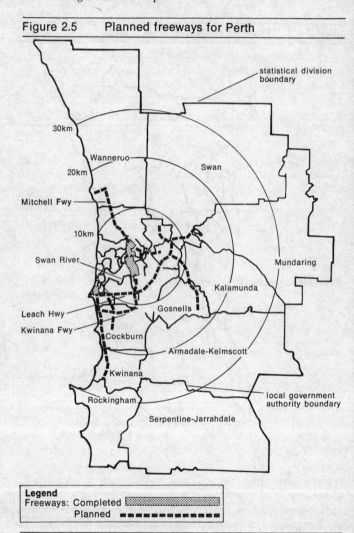

Source Commonwealth Bureau of Roads, *Assessment of Freeway Plans, State Capital Cities,* Commonwealth Bureau of Roads, Melbourne, 1974, p.74

Fremantle and 16 kilometres upstream from the Perth city centre.

Figure 2.6 shows the freeway system currently proposed for Hobart. This system has as its basis the 1965 Hobart Area Transportation Study and the 1970 Hobart Transportation Revision. Any freeway network proposed for Hobart will be constrained by Mt Wellington and the Derwent River.

During the Whitlam Labor government Tom Uren was Minister for Urban and Regional Development. He was instrumental in an Australia-wide re-evaluation of these proposed freeway systems. He viewed freeways as being 'designed to serve the C.B.D. (central business district) . . . while it is the inhabitants of the inner suburbs who see their environment destroyed, they benefit little from the expressways'.[4] '. . . Whatever the merits of freeways – and the issues are different for inner city freeways and other freeways – it is quite startling how little assessment had been made of the social and environmental impact of freeway development. The Commonwealth has been pouring out huge sums of money to the States for the development of these systems without proper regard to environmental factors . . .'[5]

This influence contributed to the decision of the Commonwealth Bureau of Roads (whose reason for existence is to co-ordinate and direct the efforts of all organizations concerned with roads in Australia with the objective of 'minimizing total real transport costs' within the limitations of finance and 'consumer preferences'[6]) to recommend to the government in 1973 that a new strategy should be followed with regard to urban freeways. As this recommendation represented quite a change from the general direction followed by the capital city transportation studies, it is reproduced here in full.

In outer suburbs. The general pattern should follow a grid form but the emphasis should be to move traffic around the built-up area of the existing city. In these areas, as population increases and spreads, there is a need for freeways, particularly for the higher speed links between sub-regional city centres or system cities. There should be no difficulty in locating freeways in these areas so that they add to the attributes of the community and so that there is relatively little disruption of settled areas and community facilities.

In middle and outer suburbs. The general approach should be for encircling or by-pass freeways which can play an important role in separating inter-suburban traffic from local traffic and in the provision of fast routes for goods and

Figure 2.6   Planned freeways for Hobart

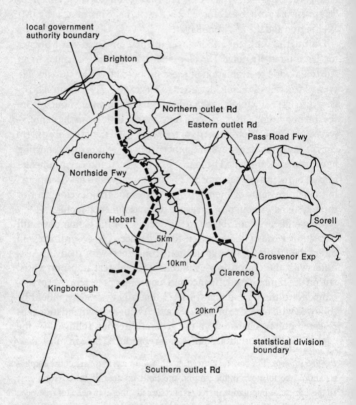

Source Commonwealth Bureau of Roads, *Assessment of Freeway Plans, State Capital Cities,* Commonwealth Bureau of Roads, Melbourne, 1974, p.41

passenger transport to by-pass the inner suburbs and the C.B.D. In these areas dwelling and work places are dispersed at low densities and the movement of goods and people is both cross-town and radial. Only some of the radial movement can be served by rail, and of the balance, both radial and cross-town, only a limited amount can be served by buses. With careful planning and the choice of suitable locations and appropriate design, it is practicable to minimize the adverse impacts on the community.

In inner suburbs. Radial freeways should not be provided, particularly if the journey to work in the C.B.D. is their principal justification. However, where large volumes of traffic, particularly heavy commercial traffic, is forced to travel unnecessarily through the C.B.D. or its adjacent suburbs there could be justifications for the construction of a by-pass road to freeway standard in or around the inner suburbs. In these areas, the impact of freeways on the community is greater than in less developed areas. These impacts together with the high cost of property acquisition and construction are generally such that the majority of proposed freeways cannot be warranted.[7]

In order to assist in the implementation of such a strategy the Bureau prepared, in its 1974 *Assessment of Freeway Plans for State Capital Cities*, maps of the current freeway plans which have been reproduced in this book (Figures 2.1 to 2.6) plus transparent overlays to these maps showing the effect of eliminating planned freeways within 8 kilometres of the city centre of Sydney and Melbourne and within 5 kilometres of the centre of the other capital cities. Although they did not assess in detail the effects of such truncation the Bureau did encourage continuing transportation studies to evaluate such changes, as well as placing freeways and even sections of planned freeways into an approximate priority ordering. These in turn could then be evaluated for social and economic impact. If the decision is made to proceed with any section of freeway the traffic and social implications of that section in relation to the existing road network should have been examined.

While the implications of this change in planning philosophy will be examined later, the Bureau of Roads' new emphasis on the social impact of their roads deserves further attention.

Australian planners have developed a propensity for locating freeways in park land and along river banks. Brisbane has its Riverside Expressway and the South Eastern Freeway in Melbourne veers into park land after following the Yarra River out from the city centre.

Nor is this tendency restricted to the capital cities. The Victorian Country Roads Board, as part of the process of upgrading the Hume Highway between Sydney and Melbourne, plans a freeway by-pass for the towns of Benalla and Wangaratta. This by-pass will run for 5 kilometres through the new 2000 hectare Reef Hills regional park and then slice through the Glenrowan reserve.

Of course in a metropolitan area the choice is between building on land reserved for recreational purposes or demolishing houses. While using park land and river banks is usually politically easier, this land is not always available. Demolishing houses in inner city areas presents a number of quite complex problems. In Melbourne 40 per cent of the planned freeway network will pass through areas with lower-than-average housing values but of all the houses to be demolished 60 per cent are below average value. Individuals and families from low-cost or low-rental housing in the inner suburbs who are displaced by freeway construction will find it very difficult to replace this standard of accommodation. In the immediate vicinity many displaced families will be searching for the few available places, an activity which in itself will force up the purchase price or rent. Low-cost or low-rent accommodation is not readily available in suburbs further out from the city centre and even if it were higher transportation costs would result if the bread-winner could not change job location. State Housing Authorities, the prime source of low-rental housing, typically have long waiting lists: in 1971 26 500 applications were waiting for housing in Sydney and 11 350 in Melbourne.

Compounding this problem is the fact that the inner suburbs are often used as the initial residential area for newly arrived immigrants. Disruption to such relatively small communities who are already experiencing difficulties in adjusting to a new language and a new culture can be devastating.

Participation of women in the work-force is significantly higher in the inner suburbs than elsewhere. This is undoubtedly facilitated by the ready availability of public transportation. Any forced move to the outer suburbs will result in these women having diminished access to employment as a result of reduced public transportation services.

Besides forcing those whose houses have been demolished to sever their relationship with their community, freeways can also have the effect of splitting what used to be a single community into two segments. The path of a freeway can easily make a child's trip to school, to the park or to the cub troop much more difficult and much longer. In the extreme it might mean moving to a new school further away as the crow flies but on the same side of the freeway. It may mean shopping at a different shopping centre, attending a different church.

A rather different consideration, but one that is also very important, when planning inner metropolitan freeway routing is preservation of the national estate. Although with the aid of such bodies as the National Trust it seems today to be rather clear in general terms what should and should not be preserved, this has not always been the case, and quite probably in retrospect will not have been so at the present time. Tastes change. In the 1940s the Victorian terrace houses with their cast-iron lacework were not regarded as worthy of preservation and were demolished at the slightest pretext. Today these same terrace houses are much sought after by upper-middle class families to provide, after renovation, elegant housing with easy access to the city centre. In fact the Victorian terrace house, particularly in Melbourne and Sydney, has provided the means in Australian cities for reversing the process of urban decay which has left the centre of many American cities surrounded by a ring of slums and squalor. As a result inner suburbs such as Paddington, Carlton or South Melbourne are much more politically aware and able to form resident action groups to lobby for their point of view.

In the outer suburban areas freeways can have a more favourable impact. Displacement still occurs but to a lesser extent because of lower residential densities, and relocation in the same community is easier for the same reason. The social make-up of a community can still be split but the effect on the car-based mobility of outer suburban families will be less drastic than on those in the inner suburbs who predominantly walk or take public transportation. Circumferential freeways can link large residential areas with the modern suburban shopping complexes. Freeways in outer areas can provide easy access to recreational areas: access to the National Parks north of Sydney is provided by the Newcastle freeway; access from Melbourne to the beaches of the Mornington Peninsula by the planned F6 freeway and to the Dandenong Ranges by the planned Healesville Freeway (F9).

These considerations led the Commonwealth Bureau of Roads to develop their strategy on freeway construction. But a policy of not building freeways in the inner suburbs, by itself, will not remove all the objections of the resident action groups. In Melbourne the first freeway to be built was the South Eastern Freeway which sweeps out along the banks of the Yarra River then down the Gardiner Creek bed until it suddenly stops on the western edge of the local municipality of Malvern. On the eastern edge of Malvern the Mulgrave Freeway coming in from the outer suburbs ends equally abruptly. Residents of Malvern, led by Jack Hammond, have successfully forced the postponement of construction of the linking freeway section through their area. Final success seemed to have been achieved when in March 1973 the Hamer government announced the massive reduction in planned freeway construction – the freeway section linking the South Eastern and Mulgrave Freeways had been axed. But despite the fact that Jack Hammond has now been elected to the Malvern City Council, another strong faction developed which raised a strongly supported petition to complete the freeway link and so keep the through traffic off residential streets in Malvern. As a result the freeway link has been restored to the Country Roads Board's priority list of planned freeways.

The planned use of residential streets for feeder routes to and from freeways has also been severely criticized in South Melbourne. Pat Brown, chairman of the Perimeter Roads Action Group, held a protest meeting in the middle of Kerferd Road, South Melbourne in December 1976 to protest the plan of a commmittee appointed by the Victorian government to use sixteen residential streets to move traffic from the West Gate bridge over the lower Yarra when it opened in 1978. The Country Roads Board plans a freeway (part of the F9) to carry West Gate bridge traffic and also traffic from the planned Johnson Street bridge (located just below the existing Spencer Street bridge) through South Melbourne, but it is expected that the bridges will be completed about five years before the freeway. In this case the residents also have the support of the local council – the South Melbourne City Council's request to the Victorian government to keep West Gate bridge closed until the freeway is ready has been refused. Pat Brown expressed a feeling shared by many when she said that freeways were planned on the basis of economics and that the planners 'didn't consider people'.

Freeways are little or no use to those who do not own or have access to a car. The Australian Road Research Board estimated in 1970 that about 40 per cent of adults over the age of 18 who are eligible for a driver's licence do not possess one. This percentage had declined slightly from 1964 when the Melbourne Transportation Study was conducted and so it is likely that the present percentage is slightly below the 1970 estimate. In any case this segment of the community is surprisingly large. It is not surprising, however, that this group of non-drivers made fewer non-work (i.e. recreational and social) trips. This difference was most significant for the age group 25 to 39 years and more significant for males than females. As also expected the non-drivers used public transportation extensively to get to work: the 40 per cent non-drivers used 75 per cent of the public transportation trips to work.

Using the 1964 Melbourne Transportation Study data the Australian Road Research Board found that certain characteristics distinguished unlicensed adults from licensed adults and car-owning households from non car-owning households. Most unlicensed adults were female (85 per cent) and of those most (60 per cent) were housewives. The vast majority of car-owning households (84 per cent) had an employed male as the principal income earner of whom just over half held blue-collar jobs. Just under half of the non car-owning households had an employed male as the principal income earner and almost 80 per cent of these men held blue-collar jobs. Of the other half of the non car-owning households most were headed by a pensioner and the remainder by a female below pensionable age. Two-thirds of all non car-owning families had a weekly income of below $50 per week.

These data, despite their age, are the most recent available. But even if the figures have moved by 10 per cent in a more favourable direction over the past decade (probably an optimistic estimate) the situation is still grim. Groups in the community who are less well off in general terms are also disadvantaged in terms of the degree of mobility available to them.

The relationship between family income, car ownership and

Table 2.1   Expenditure on Transportation* as Related to Household
Income, 1974-5

Average weekly income	Average yearly income†	Percentage expenditure on transportation	Yearly transportation expenditure†
less than $80	less than $4 200	12.5%	less than $520
$ 80-140	$ 4 200- 7 300	15.9%	$ 660-1160
$140-200	$ 7 300-10 400	16.3%	$1190-1700
$200-260	$10 400-13 500	17.7%	$1840-2390
$260-340	$13 500-17 700	17.9%	$2420-3170
over $340	over $17 700	16.8%	over $2970

*The Australian Bureau of Statistics classification 'Transport and Communication'.
†Rounded.
Source: Adapted from Australian Bureau of Statistics, *Household Expenditure Survey 1974-75, Preliminary Results,* Canberra, July 1976.

mobility can also be examined from a different direction. Table 2.1
shows household expenditure on transportation according to the average income of the household. A study by the Australian Road Research Board of the fixed costs of operating a motor vehicle between
1965 and 1967 established that these costs would be just over three
cents per kilometre if the car was driven 16 000 kilometres in the
year. On the assumption that some of these costs could be avoided
by the owner repairing his own second-hand car and under insuring
and that these savings would cancel out the inflation in other costs
since 1967 then the fixed costs at three cents would total $500. Fuel
to operate the car over the 16 000 kilometres would be approximately
$200. From Table 2.1 it can be seen that households with an average
yearly income less than $4200 spend less than $520 on transportation
each year. So these families must find it very difficult to own and
operate a car – in 1974 over 40 per cent of Australian families had
a yearly income under $4000. Even many of the next group of families,
earning between $4200 and $7300 per year, would experience severe
difficulty in owning a motor car.* From a social point of view it

*The Bureau of Transport Economics estimated that in 1975 20 per cent of families
in Melbourne did not own a car.

is clear that the mammoth expenditures to provide and maintain an extensive road network primarily for the private motor car are most inequitable.

Comprehensive planning of urban transportation systems is difficult. Transportation and land use are two closely intertwined aspects of city living and because they are so interrelated planning for either must by necessity involve a large number of government and quasi-governmental bodies. Even when plans have been drawn up and accepted by the government implementation is a problem. Changes to transportation systems take a long time and a lot of money and during this time governments can change or public opinion can change which in turn can alter the thinking of governments. Taking Melbourne as an example, transportation planning is done by the Melbourne and Metropolitan Board of Works, the Town and Country Planning Board, the Country Roads Board, metropolitan Councils, the Victorian Railways, the Melbourne and Metropolitan Tramways Board, the Transport Regulation Board in addition to special bodies such as the Metropolitan Transportation Committee. All of this activity is co-ordinated to some degree by the Victorian Ministry of Transport with additional suggestions and advice coming from the federal Department of Transport and such bodies as the Commonwealth Bureau of Roads, the Bureau of Transport Economics, the Institute of Urban Affairs and the Australian Road Research Board.

In 1954 the Melbourne and Metropolitan Board of Works prepared a planning scheme for Melbourne, the first comprehensive proposal since the 1929 Metropolitan Planning Commission. This scheme concentrates on the central business district as the prime focus of Melbourne with considerable redevelopment of inner areas. Five residential districts concentrating on further expansion to the east and south-east of the city would be established and would be serviced by express buses from the city. Future expansion of either the rail or tram systems was seen as unlikely and the report placed emphasis on the expansion of bus services and on better co-ordination of bus services with existing fixed-route transportation.

Both the Melbourne and Metropolitan Board of Works and the Town and Country Planning Board issued reports in 1967 on the long-term development of Melbourne. Both agreed that further

Figure 2.7   The Development Plan for Melbourne

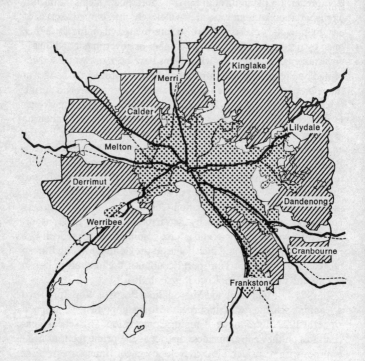

Legend
Existing urban areas
Corridors
Non-urban areas

Source Melbourne and Metropolitan Board of Works, *Planning Policies for the Melbourne Metropolitan Region,* Melbourne and Metropolitan Board of Works, Melbourne, November 1971, p.53

expansion past the present perimeter of the city was inevitable and the Board of Works proposed a series of corridors radiating from the existing urban area with wedges of open country between them. This plan suggested that an effort should be made to redirect growth from the eastern and south-eastern sides of Melbourne to the northern and western sides. The addition of satellite towns at Whittlesea to the north, Sunbury to the north-west and Werribee to the west was proposed as a way of achieving this redirection of growth. In 1968 the Victorian Government adopted the corridor concept as policy and Melton was mentioned as a possible satellite city to the west of Melbourne.

This concept was refined by the Board of Works 1971 Planning Policies Report. Instead of two or three satellite towns, development in each corridor was proposed (see Figure 2.7). The central business district of Melbourne was still to be the urban focal point. If funding for development in each corridor was unavailable or access to the city centre became 'unduly restricted' then a second alternative was to develop a major growth centre to the south-east, presumably at Dandenong.

Following the 1971 Board of Works Report the Victorian Parliament passed legislation (the *Development Areas Act 1973*) which required the Town and Country Planning Board to prepare reports on thirteen areas within the corridors to establish if accelerated development should occur. Consideration of these reports is currently taking place – Sunbury and Melton have already been declared 'designated areas' for accelerated growth. One corridor that the Town and Country Planning Board was not asked to investigate was the Merri corridor running directly north of Melbourne along the Hume Highway. So it came as rather a surprise when in December 1976 the Victorian State Cabinet decided to give approval to the T & G Society to develop a new city on the Hume Highway 27 kilometres from Melbourne. The new city, to be called Mt Ridley, is planned for 120 000 people. It will be built over fifteen to twenty years on 2600 hectares owned by the T and G Society at a cost of $450 million. The company is to donate 140 hectares of land worth $4 million for public facilities such as schools, police and fire stations as well as paying $45 million for water supply, sewerage and drainage which are normally provided by the Melbourne and Metropolitan Board of Works. Planners, such

Figure 2.8   The Transportation Plan for Melbourne

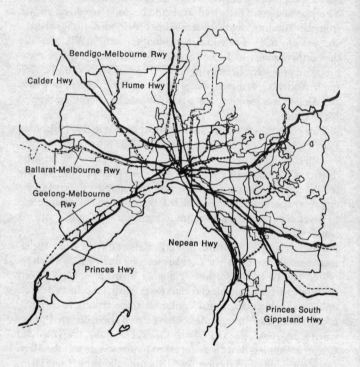

Legend
Freeways ━━━━━━━━
Rail extensions ∙∙∙∙∙∙∙∙∙∙∙∙
Existing rail network ─ ─ ─ ─ ─

Source Melbourne and Metropolitan Board of Works, *Planning Policies for the Melbourne Metropolitan Region,* Melbourne and Metropolitan Board of Works, Melbourne, November 1971, p.31

as the State president of the Australian Planning Institute James Earle, applauded the idea of a completely planned city for Australia but deplored the break-down in the overall planning process developed by the government. Even with the assistance of the T and G Society if Mt Ridley is to develop as planned, government resources such as school buildings, teachers, transportation and power must be reallocated at least in the short term from other areas such as Melton and Sunbury which have already been designated as accelerated growth areas.

Within these broad and rather variable plans for the overall future development of Melbourne the transportation plans must fit. The Metropolitan Transportation Committee* was established in 1963 and a transportation study of metropolitan Melbourne was commenced the following year. In 1969 the results of the Melbourne Transportation Plan were made public. The plan was drawn up on the basis that Melbourne would have 3.7 million residents in 1985 and that a free travel choice would exist although use of public transportation would be encouraged. A massive freeway network of over 490 kilometres in length was the main feature of the plan. In addition improvements were planned for existing arterial roads (for example Victoria Parade and Wellington Parade into the city), and four railway extensions were proposed: the city underground loop; the City-East Doncaster line connecting with the loop; the Huntingdale-Ferntree Gully line; the Frankston-Dandenong line. These developments are shown in Figure 2.8. The Victorian Government approved the plan in principle, but since that time the Transport Plan has had a stormy history. In March 1973 Mr Hamer (who as Minister for Local Government was Deputy Chairman of the Metropolitan Transportation Committee in 1969 when the Transportation Plan was released) bowed to public pressure prior to an election and axed half of the freeway network. Little of the remaining freeway network has been built. The planned rail links between Huntingdale and Ferntree

*Comprising the Minister for Transport, the Minister for Local Government, the chairmen of the Melbourne and Metropolitan Board of Works, the Country Roads Board, the Victorian Railways, the Melbourne and Metropolitan Tramways Board, the Transport Regulation Board, the Victorian Traffic Commission, the Director of State Finance and the Chief Planner of the Melbourne and Metropolitan Board of Works.

Figure 2.9   The Melbourne Underground Loop

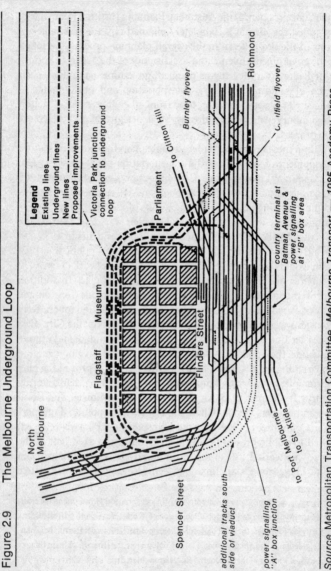

Source Metropolitan Transportation Committee, *Melbourne Transport* — 1985, Academy Press, West Melbourne (not dated)

Gully and between Frankston and Dandenong have been discarded. (Anyone who has ever been to the football at V.F.L. Park at Waverley is well aware of the effects of the non-existence of the Hunting-dale–Ferntree Gully line.) Controversy continues to rage over the effectiveness and the escalating costs of the underground loop and the West Gate bridge over the lower Yarra – two aspects of the plan which have managed to reach the construction stage.

Many trains from the populous eastern and south-eastern suburbs of Melbourne arrive at Flinders Street station then are reversed for another shuttle out to the east or south-east. A similar situation exists at Spencer Street station for many trains from the northern and western suburbs. This has been viewed as a problem by planners for a number of years – the 1954 Melbourne and Metropolitan Board of Works Planning Scheme comments in a section dealing with future needs for public transportation:

As far as the central area is concerned, the most pressing need is for means to be provided to relieve the concentration of passengers at Flinders Street station and to permit travellers to be discharged nearer to their central area destinations.[8]

A solution to this problem was proposed by the Melbourne Transportation Committee. The solution took the form of an underground loop which together with the existing above-ground track linking Flinders Street and Spencer Street stations would encircle the city centre. Two pairs of parallel tunnels running one above the other will service three new underground stations – trains on all four tracks are planned to run in an anti-clockwise direction during the morning peak period and in a clockwise direction during the evening rush. The route to be taken by the loop is shown in Figure 2.9. It is expected that when the loop is completed in 1982 (four years later than the estimate made two years ago) the current frequency of 100 trains per hour into Flinders Street station should be doubled.

A great deal of criticism has been directed at the loop. Planning for the loop was made on the basis of Melbourne's population being 3.7 million in 1985 but the 1974 Report of the National Population Inquiry estimates a population of less than 3 million with a reasonable possibility of it being as low as 2.75 million. In addition, the number of passengers using rail services has been declining. The Metropolitan

Transportation Committee predicted that the number of rail trips per day would increase from 382 000 in 1964 to 663 000 in 1985. So far this increase has not occurred; in fact the number of daily rail trips has decreased by almost 20 per cent since 1964. The Melbourne Underground Rail Loop Authority justifies the project on the basis of being able to stem the tide of the 1000 new vehicles on metropolitan Melbourne's streets each week: 'Each morning a race starts in which everyone is the loser.' These sentiments are admirable but only time will tell whether the underground loop can stem the tide of the private car. Mr Barry Jones the former State Opposition spokesman on transport is sceptical. Besides being critical of the cost escalation from $80 million when the project began in 1970 to the latest estimate of $300 million he feels the radial rail system serves adequately only a relatively small proportion of Melbourne's population. Construction of the loop is 'like providing gold taps to put on water pipes when the pipes are not attached to any water supply'.

On 15 October 1971 piers 10 and 11 of the West Gate bridge crashed to the ground killing thirty-five men. This disaster occurred after the time the bridge was originally planned for completion and characterizes the difficulties being faced in linking the existing F9 freeway on the western side of the Yarra with its planned continuation on the eastern side. On the eastern side of the river the residents of South Melbourne are faced with the common freeway dilemma that is present in many other municipalities, such as Malvern: which is the better of two evils – a freeway or freeway-volume traffic on residential streets? South Melbourne seems to have opted for the freeway. But the eastern section of the F9 freeway, which would link West Gate and the new Johnson Street bridge (crossing the Yarra 750 metres south of Spencer Street and planned for completion by the end of 1977) with Kingsway and St Kilda Road, has not been started by the Country Roads Board because of a shortage of the estimated $80 million needed for it. Once started, construction of this freeway link is expected to take at least six years and strong pressure is being applied by the residents of South Melbourne not to open West Gate until the F9 is completed. As a South Melbourne city councillor told the *Age* Insight reporters: 'No doubt resident groups in our area will be calling on the construction unions for support if they don't get satisfaction. I believe the bridge won't open until the F9 is finished.'

But the problems of West Gate do not end there. Construction of the bridge was organized under the Lower Yarra Crossing Authority Act of 1965 which stipulated that the entire cost, including interest on loans, must be repaid within forty years. When construction began in 1968 the bridge was expected to be completed in 1971 at a cost of $42 million. In the 1975-6 annual report of the West Gate Bridge Authority the final cost of the bridge is estimated at not less than $145 million excluding interest (which was $32 million at the end of the 1975-6 financial year and anticipated to be $9 million per year after that). If this cost estimate can be met (the Authority does not have a very good record on this - for example the cost estimate for the bridge increased by $10 million during September-October 1976) and the bridge is finished by the latest target date of mid-1978 then the bridge will have cost approximately $200 million.* Repayment of this money, together with an estimated $3 million per year operating cost, means that a toll of around 90 cents each way on the bridge would have to be charged. But at this relatively high toll a large proportion of the anticipated 45 000 cars a day will not use the bridge. In fact it appears to be most likely that the amount of money now tied up in the bridge is so great that it can never be repaid by the users of the bridge. But despite the fact that the Victorian taxpayer will most likely have to bail the Authority out, its chairman Oscar Meyer told the *Age*: 'Look old boy, you can do all the calculations you like. I'm not going to give you . . . data. This is our own business. It will be dealt with in our own time.'

West Gate and the underground loop are typical of the magnitude of problems which must be overcome to extend the physical facilities required by either a fixed-route or a random-route transportation system in an urban area.

What can be done in the urban areas of Australia to make the transportation systems work better? Work better in terms of providing greater access to mobility for disadvantaged sections of the community but also work better in terms of not subsidizing advantaged groups.

---

*In partial defence of the management of the West Gate Bridge Authority and other similar projects, these projects do tend to generate more than their fair share of industrial disputes which cause delays and escalating costs.

Again taking Melbourne as an example, consider the following plan. As mentioned earlier it is probably unrealistic to expect that any radical change will occur in the transportation infrastructure in the foreseeable future. The question is what can be done with the existing physical network to make it operate more effectively.

An important point is that the transportation network in Melbourne was developed on a radial basis with the city centre as the hub. There may be strong arguments as to why this is not the best layout for the 1970s but it *is* there, and the massive funding needed to change it is not available nor warranted. So strong encouragement should be given to ensure that a much larger (than the present 30 per cent in the city centre and St Kilda Road) proportion of jobs are located in the city centre. This could take the form of a restructuring of the rates levied by the City of Melbourne and a state tax on organizations with administrative offices in the metropolitan area but not in the city proper. The next step is to ensure that all these additional trips to work are not made by car.

Many studies have shown that given the current cost, convenience and congestion relationships between cars and public transportation, incentives to use public transportation (even in the extreme case where it is provided free) will not work. But if the cost of using a car on the trip to work was increased by a very large amount then at least a reasonable proportion of car commuters would move to public transportation. This increased patronage would help the public transportation system to reduce its mammoth operating deficit. But in addition the extra charges levied on the car traveller could be provided as a subsidy to the public transportation operation.

The city council should ban all on-street parking in the city centre and should buy or close all commercially operated parking lots. Parking in the centre of Melbourne would still be possible, but a tax of say $1000 per car would be charged for parking in a lot and companies with under-building parking would be obliged to pay the $1000 for each parking space.

Within a wider zone of the city centre, about 6 or 7 kilometres in radius, maximum parking of one hour would be allowed except for residents.

Two sets of large parking areas together with bus terminals would be built around the outskirts of this larger zone as well as on the outskirts of the city proper. Parking at the outer terminals would be free as would parking at the inner terminals for residents of the inner suburbs. Others would pay to park at the inner terminals. An express bus service would operate to the city centre from each of the terminals leaving every 2–5 minutes during the peak and every 10 minutes during the rest of the day. These buses would operate on bus-only lanes on freeways which, within a certain distance of the city, would be free for buses, but toll roads for cars. Such freeways are the South Eastern Freeway when connected through Malvern, the Tullamarine Freeway when extended through to the western edge of the city and the Eastern Freeway.

In addition to passengers reaching the bus terminals and train stations by private car, dial-a-ride services could be set up using mini-buses, taxis and private cars plying for hire.

Several minor changes could easily be made to improve the trip speed of trams: at no time should on-street parking be permitted in a street carrying tram tracks, and all vehicles making a right-hand turn from a street with trams must turn from the left-hand side of the intersection and not from the centre.

In the event that the city centre does not have the capacity to cope with this type of expansion, satellite cities could be established at Melton and Dandenong. Express rail and bus (on restricted freeways) could easily link these satellites with Melbourne and in time similar zones and traffic control measures could be established.

The pervasive nature of the car is indicated by the fact that most companies and government departments in Australia provide most levels of management with the use of a company or government car which often extends to unlimited private use. A large tax should be imposed on company cars (the revenue from which could subsidize the public transportation system) while government departments and agencies must show more restraint and responsibility in this direction.

Losses incurred on public transportation (for example, the $243 million loss, of which the Sydney urban service lost $83 million, for the rail operations of the Public Transport Commission of New South Wales in 1975–6; the $139 million loss for the Victorian Railways during the same period) are met out of public revenue. Could this money be better spent on schools, housing or social welfare? In total the urban transportation system should pay its way. The affluent who want to enjoy the relative luxury and convenience of using their own car for the trip to work could subsidize those who are willing to use public transportation. Further subsidization could be carried out by the Australian Taxation Office issuing free travel coupons to those whose family income does not reach some specified minimum.

Of course many places of work will not or cannot locate in the city centre. Circumferential freeways (such as the Outer Ring Road currently under consideration by the Victorian Ministry of Transport) when constructed will help to alleviate this problem. Standard-route buses can operate in the outer suburban areas with such aids as priority lanes and controlled car entry to freeways during rush periods. Companies located in these areas should be given a financial incentive to operate mini-bus services to pick up and deliver employees to their homes.

But a quite strange paradox still exists. For the trip to work, it is desirable to penalize those who want to travel by car. The trip with a recreational or cultural purpose is often difficult or impossible to make without a car. For this type of trip, car (or any other future but more efficient random-route vehicle) ownership should be encouraged to provide equal access. Current government policies to build freeways spanning out through the outer suburbs will make recreational trips by car more pleasurable. This paradox brings forward two main points. The first is the need to develop a more efficient (in terms of space utilization, safety, pollution and fuel consumption) and less costly random-route vehicle than the car. Second, schemes to raise revenue for such purposes as public transportation subsidization or road safety, which are based on fuel tax, are inequitable – the trip to work and not the recreational or cultural trip should be taxed.

The random-route vehicle will always play an important part in the urban transportation network of Australian cities. For quite a long time now the car has held this position unchallenged. In the immediate future the car must have much more severe restrictions placed upon it. Beyond the immediate future hope exists for the replacement of the car with something better.

Notes

1. Melbourne and Metropolitan Board of Works, *Melbourne Metropolitan Planning Scheme 1954*, Melbourne and Metropolitan Board of Works, Melbourne, 1954, p. 167.

2. Bendixson, T., *Without Wheels*, Indiana University Press, Bloomington, 1975, p. 9.

3. Litchfield N., and Associates, *Stevenage Public Transport*, Stevenage Development Corporation, Stevenage, U.K., 1969.

4. Uren, The Hon. T., Minister for Urban and Regional Development, letter to Commonwealth Bureau of Roads, 19 March 1973 quoted in Commonwealth Bureau of Roads, *Report on the Need for Freeway Systems in Australian Capital Cities*, Commonwealth Bureau of Roads, Melbourne, August 1973.

5. Uren, The Hon. T., Minister for Urban and Regional Development, Speech to the Institute of Engineers, Australian Conference on 'Engineering and the Environment', Canberra, 21 June 1973, p. 9.

6. The Commonwealth Bureau of Roads, *Its Origin and Its Work*, no date.

7. Commonwealth Bureau of Roads, *Report on Roads in Australia 1973*, Commonwealth Bureau of Roads, Melbourne, 1973. pp. 147-8

8. Melbourne and Metropolitan Board of Works, *Melbourne Metropolitan Planning Scheme 1954*, Melbourne and Metropolitan Board of Works, Melbourne, 1954, p. 192.

Chapter 3
From Melbourne to Sydney

Queenscliff in 1888 was a 'favourite watering-place and seaside resort' for the well-to-do from Melbourne and the graziers from the Western District of Victoria. 'Queenscliff is the terminus of the Geelong and Queenscliff railway line, the communication with Melbourne, 70 miles north-east, being the train via Geelong . . . As well as by rail there is communication with Melbourne by steamers, which ply from the Queen's wharf and the Queenscliff pier daily during the season.'[1] Five kilometres around the beach is Pt Lonsdale at the entrance to Port Phillip Bay. Pride of Pt Lonsdale in those days were 'three 9 inch muzzle-loading rifled guns of 12½ tons weight' and 'four 80 pounder muzzle-loading rifled guns of 4 tons weight' which, protected by a 4-metre high brick structure, provided 'the most formidable and complete defence works in Australia'.[2]

Today Queenscliff is no longer important as the first contact point for foreign ships reaching Australia nor does it provide a last chance for mail to catch the ship to Europe. Today the Geelong to Queenscliff railway line is not used; ferries from Melbourne no longer arrive at the pier. Queenscliff has been replaced by Pt Lonsdale as the popular summer resort. On a summer holiday, vacationers now drive their cars to Pt Lonsdale; travelling by bus is the only alternative – McHarry's silver and red buses (the Geelong Associated Busline) leave Geelong station at 9.30 a.m. and again seven hours later – so if you miss the bus you may as well stay on the train and go back to Melbourne again.

Recreation, tourism, holidays – several terms to describe one reason why people make trips from Melbourne to Pt Lonsdale, Melbourne to Sydney, as well as from a myriad of other origins to a host of other destinations. Although the mixture seems rather strange, the Australian Bureau of Statistics found for the combined items, recreation and education, the average Australian family earning less than $80 per week in 1975 spent less than 6 per cent of it on these two items, while the family earning over $340 per week spent over 11 per cent – or less than $5 per week against $37 per week. Given that in 1975 15 per cent of families had an income of less than $80 per week, this is an area where considerable inequality between community groups exists. Gough Whitlam, possibly overstating the case to some extent, said in his 1972 policy speech:

... there is no greater social problem facing Australia than the good use of leisure. It is the problem of all modern and wealthy communities. It is, above all, the problem of urban societies and thus, in Australia, the most urbanized nation on earth, a problem more pressing for us than for any other nation on earth.[3]

It is interesting that the total number of trips (where a trip is formally defined as a journey taking more than one day and covering more than 40 kilometres) are relatively evenly spread between community income groups (although more people are in the lower groups) but that the type of trip made is quite different. This is shown in Table 3.1 which contains data obtained from a survey of Australian travel in 1973-4 by the Australian Travel Research Conference. Families with lower incomes make more private visits to family and friends where the accommodation is either subsidized or provided free by the host. Middle-income groups make more trips for their main holiday as well as making more trips for special interest purposes such as sporting activities. The high-income earners take many more business and combined business and holiday trips. This is not surprising but it does enable this group to further their advantage by either having their employer to some extent subsidize their recreational activities or, if they are self-employed, to have a portion of their recreational costs become tax deductible.

This survey also revealed some interesting aspects of the transportation used for recreational travel. Of the total expenditure, transportation comprised one third (private car 18 per cent; air 10 per cent; rail and bus 2 per cent each; and sea travel less than 1 per cent), accommodation and meals just over one-fifth each and the remaining 25 per cent split between excursion fees, social activities, personal purchases and gifts.

These figures do not adequately bring out the dominance of the private motor car. Overall 86 per cent of recreational trips are made

Table 3.1   Reason for Travel Related to the Income of the Head of the Household

Annual income	Total trips		Reason for trip						
			Main holiday	Sub holiday	Conference or convention	Private visit	Combined business and holiday	Business	Special interest
Less than $3999	5 452 000	25%	23%	23%	13%	34%	17%	12%	26%
$4000-$4999	4 222 000	20%	26%	21%	13%	19%	6%	11%	17%
$5000-6999	5 895 000	28%	30%	26%	22%	26%	35%	33%	30%
Over $7000	5 727 000	27%	21%	30%	52%	21%	42%	44%	27%
Total*	21 296 000	100%	100%	100%	100%	100%	100%	100%	100%

*19 per cent of respondents did not give their income.

Source: Survey of Australian Tourism 1973/74, Australian Travel Research Conference, Canberra, no date, p. 34.

by car; plane trips are next with 5 per cent. The expenditure figures for these two modes are much closer because a single plane trip is much more costly than a single car trip. Table 3.2 gives more details of the transportation modes used in relation to the major reasons for the trip. As expected cars, although still dominant, are used less for business trips and trips to conferences and conventions. Most use is made of the car to visit friends or to take a weekend or short holiday.

Reliance on the car for recreational travel is not surprising. Australians have developed, in a somewhat similar fashion to the exodus from Paris in August, the habit of mass holidaying in January. The prime reason for this is that the summer school holidays are from just prior to Christmas to early February. So recreational facilities such as hotels, motels, camping grounds, houses-to-rent at the beach, airline seats and caravans-to-rent are in short supply in January and again, but to a lesser extent, in May and September when the other school holidays occur. For the remainder of the year many of these resources are grossly underutilized. To provide efficient public transportation to these recreational areas where high utilization would occur for only such a short period of the year is obviously not a feasible proposition, so the car only has to compete with a low-frequency bus service.

Breaking this tradition of holiday congestion in January would have several advantages. If the January peak was spread over four or five months the large capital investment of the tourist industry in Australia could be more efficiently used – with maybe even fewer facilities than exist today but with much higher utilization rates and, as a result, more competitive tariffs. More competitive tariffs would enable a large proportion of Australians to take this kind of holiday as well as being more attractive to overseas visitors (the cost of travel and recreation in Australia over recent years has become among the most expensive in the world). A more even flow of travellers to recreational and resort areas would make the provision of high-service public transportation a much more attractive proposition. The staggering of school holidays might well achieve this. Such a proposition would certainly meet much opposition from teachers and school administrators and would be difficult to co-ordinate if set up. But it would provide better utilization of school buildings and equipment and could at least for part of the year provide smaller classes.

Table 3.2   Mode of Transportation Related to the Reason for Travel

Means of transportation	Total trips		Reason for trip						
			Main holiday	Sub holiday	Conference or convention	Private visit	Combined business and holiday	Business	Special interest
Car	22 555 000	86%	86%	92%	64%	92%	83%	69%	75%
Train	965 000	4%	3%	2%	3%	4%	7%	4%	8%
Airline	1 172 000	5%	5%	2%	24%	2%	8%	22%	2%
Bus/coach	617 000	2%	2%	1%	7%	1%	*	1%	12%
Other	897 000	3%	3%	3%	2%	1%	2%	4%	3%
Total	26 206 000	100%	100%	100%	100%	100%	100%	100%	100%

*Less than 1 per cent.

Source: Survey of Australian Tourism 1973/74, Australian Travel Research Conference, Canberra, no date, p. 40.

Travel within Australia exposes us to a diversity of Australian culture. This works both ways: it is important for rural Australians to have access to the main cities and to the cultural activities that the larger market can justify; it is also important for urban Australians to be exposed to Australian rural life around which the myth of the Australian character has been built. An additional factor is at work in Australia. For both the city dweller and the grazier or town dweller of the pastoral plains many of the major Australian attractions are equally remote. Ayers Rock and the centre of Australia, the outback in general, the Great Barrier Reef, the Pilbara and Kimberley regions of Western Australia are all well known but are all vast distances from where the majority of Australians live. Only the more affluent see these parts of the country (most overseas visitors to Australia do not see them either) although recently introduced camping bus tours have inceased the accessibility of remote areas if the traveller can spare the time needed for this type of trip.

Thirty years ago a Vauxhall Wyvern loaded with three children in the back seat took thirteen hours to get from Melbourne to Red Cliffs, a small irrigation town in the Mallee district of Victoria next to Mildura on the Murray River. The road was narrow all the way and only sealed to Ouyen; beyond Ouyen the dirt road twisted around sand dunes and clumps of mallee trees. During the late 1940s the train left Melbourne at eight in the evening, arriving at Red Cliffs at seven the next morning – a trip of eleven hours. In those days a trip to Melbourne, with all its social and cultural benefits, for the people of the Mallee was a rare event indeed. In general, access to the large cities for many inhabitants of rural areas of Australia was very poor. Today the trip from Melbourne to Red Cliffs by car can take half the time; the trip on the Victorian Railways' Vinelander still takes over ten hours. Improved access of the country to the city has been provided by the car and better roads.

Living in the country does have its favourable aspects – clearer air, slower pace, friendlier people – but there are also disadvantages. Just over one-fifth of rural children manage to complete their last year of secondary schooling while over one-third of city children do. Twice as many city students continue on to university. Jobs in the country are always much more difficult to get than in the city. Disadvantage still occurs in terms of mobility. The Australian Travel

Research Conference survey of Australian travel showed that people from non-metropolitan areas made fewer trips for their main holidays or weekend and short-term holidays than did city people. But they made almost twice the proportion of private trips to visit relatives and friends. Those from small country towns and rural areas made twice the proportion of business trips that people from the large provincial towns or the people from the cities made. These differences are due in some part to the difficulty in leaving the farm (especially a dairy farm) or small business for the time needed to take a holiday, and also in recent years to falling rural incomes.

Just as the car has provided the country person with better access to the city so has it provided the city dweller with better access to rural areas. Recently the Australian National Travel Association launched a campaign 'Go See Australia' to try to encourage Australians to see more of their own country. As part of this campaign the Association carried out a series of regional evaluations of travel and tourism. It is interesting to examine several of these appraisals to see what kind of people are already getting out to see Australia.

The Barossa Valley, just to the north-east of Adelaide, is a major Australian grape-growing area in which are located several major wineries. Further to the north-east is a region through which the Murray River flows, at first meandering through a wide flood plain and later in a deep gorge. Of the visitors who came to the area in 1971 90 per cent came by car with another 7 per cent arriving by bus. Almost all visitors came with either their family or friends for a holiday. A heavily disproportionate number of these holiday makers had occupations in the professions and disproportionately few unskilled workers visited the area.

Port Macquarie on the central coast of New South Wales was established as a penal settlement in 1821. Although, apart from the Clarence Street museum and the Church of St Thomas, few historic buildings have been preserved in Port Macquarie the colonial history of the area is of prime tourist interest. Half the visitors to the area in 1970 came from Sydney and almost another 40 per cent from other parts of New South Wales. As with the Barossa Valley visitors with professional and technical occupations were more heavily represented than they are in the total Australian population and unskilled visitors less represented. More than 90 per cent came by car and most were on their holidays.

Marble Bar in the Pilbara region of Western Australia from October to March has an average daily maximum temperature of over 40°C. Despite the intense summer heat the Pilbara does have several major rivers along which are a number of spectacular gorges. These gorges together with examples of aboriginal rock paintings and carvings and some early buildings from the white settlement of the area are of interest to tourists. So too are the recent massive mineral developments such as Mt Newman Mining's iron-ore operation at Mt Whaleback. Of all the visitors to the Pilbara in 1971 less than one-third were tourists, the remainder were visiting the area on business or looking for employment. Three-quarters of the visitors came by air and well over half came from Perth. Present road travel to the area is probably greater than in 1971 when the survey was done because of the sealing of the North West Coastal Highway. Although occupation and income data were not collected in this survey it is reasonable to expect that for the tourists the biases shown in the other two surveys also exist.

These three Australian National Travel Association appraisals indicate that people living in large Australian cities (at least Adelaide, Sydney and Perth) were taking holidays in rural areas. In 1970 almost 200 000 people visited the Barossa Valley region, almost half a million visited Port Macquarie and over 32 000 visited the Pilbara. These figures, it has been predicted, will increase quite considerably over the next few years. The point of concern is that this type of mobility is concentrated among the higher socio-economic groups.

Of all the trips surveyed by the Australian Travel Research Conference only 8 per cent were for business with an additional 3 per cent combining business and holiday. Almost half of the total trips were for holidays (18 per cent for a major holiday and 29 per cent for a shorter holiday) and 31 per cent of all trips were social visits to family and friends. These figures match the Bureau of Transport Economics estimates for 1975 of 74 per cent 'discretionary non-business travel' (increasing to 79 per cent in 1985), 15 per cent 'mandatory non-business travel' (down to 12 per cent in 1985) and 11 per cent 'business travel' (9 per cent in 1985). This decline in business travel during the 1980s is not unexpected, indeed the decline might well be greater, as suggested below.

Peter Link of the Nylex Corporation used a means of forecasting technological change called the Delphi method to establish the future communication needs of his company. He established two independent panels of experts: one of Nylex managers and the other of members of the Fundamental Planning Branch of Telecom (at the time it was the Australian Post Office). After a list of possible innovations had been developed it was given to these two panels who were asked separately to predict the year in which the innovation would be in use. Summaries of the predictions of each panel were distributed and the panels then given the opportunity to review their estimates. This process was repeated several times before arriving at the final consensus prediction.

During the 1980 decade Nylex will introduce video-telephones and advances in computer usage will enable group problem-solving by managers located at different plants throughout Australia. The last decade of the century will see pen and paper replaced by a computer-driven cathode ray tube with keyboard input and a special light-pen. Decisions made by management each day will be recorded on a central computer file. By this stage company attitudes will have modified to the extent that certain employees will have the option to work at home.

If these changes predicted for Nylex are widespread in Australia (there should be no technological difficulties and the cost of such systems should also be reasonable) then the number of business trips should decline by a substantial amount before the end of the century.

In 1974 the *National Roads Act* declared a National Highways System for Australia. The objectives of such a network as stated by the Commonwealth Bureau of Roads were to:

(a) encourage and contribute, to a major extent, to trade and commerce, overseas and among the states;

(b) assist industry located in major centres of population to be complementary to industry located in neighbouring major centres;

(c) reduce, significantly, transport costs of the products of rural and/or secondary industry, between points of production and points of export or consumption;

(d) provide for long distance movement associated with recreation and tourism;

(e) improve movement between defence production centres, defence supply and storage locations, and defence establishments generally.[4]

Although the movement of people is mentioned as an objective for the National Highways System it is a rather poor fourth behind three economically based objectives. Despite this fact and suitable lamentations by the Australian Department of Tourism and Recreation at the time, the system when developed will greatly facilitate travel within Australia.

Any national road network would have to link up the capital cities of each state for economic reasons as well as the fact that the states were helping to pay for it. In addition towns with populations exceeding 25 000 together with any other centres of significant economic activity should be linked into the network. The highway should also traverse through as many as possible of the major primary producing areas. Finally chosen was the 16 000 kilometre network shown in Figure 3.1. It can be seen from the figure that in several areas, such as from Port Augusta to the South Australia–Northern Territory border and from Broome in Western Australia to Katherine in the Northern Territory, the exact route was not detailed but a 'corridor' was specified. Further detailed studies will be undertaken to determine the exact routing of these sections.

Many existing roads forming part of the national system are narrow, unsealed, winding and showing signs of age.* In preparing for the Act the National Highways Study Team set as a 'guideline' the expenditure of up to $3000 million over the next seven years. Expenditure of this order of magnitude was predicted to provide a 'benchmark' standard of a divided highway between Melbourne, Sydney and Brisbane and 8-metre 2-lane carriageway for the rest of the network.

Politically the timing of such a development was good. During 1973 Alan Hughes conducted a study of community attitudes to roads for the Commonwealth Bureau of Roads. He separated out from his respondents what he called a 'key group': those who had completed

---

*At the time the Act was passed 650 kilometres were four-lane divided carriageway, 11 600 kilometres were sealed two-lane road and the remaining 3800 kilometres were not sealed.

Figure 3.1   The National Highways System

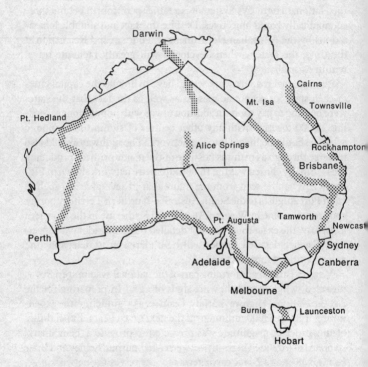

Legend

Corridors for initial designation

Corridors requiring further
investigation before designation

Source   Commonwealth Bureau of Roads, *Report on Roads in Australia 1975*, Commonwealth Bureau of Roads, Melbourne, 1975. p. 158

secondary school, who had described their own socio-economic class as 'upper' or 'middle' and who were qualified to hold a driver's licence. This group was separated because it was presumed they would be more interested in issues concerning roads and also they would be more able to make their views known. For all roads 40 per cent of the key group and half of the remaining respondents wanted to 'greatly increase spending', but for inter-capital roads the situation was reversed: over half of the key group but slightly less than half of the remaining group wanted greatly increased expenditure. Inter-capital and other non-metropolitan roads were viewed by all as not being safe enough.

While most travel throughout Australia is by car and large sums of general revenue are being allocated to road-building programmes, few people travel by train (4 per cent of trips over 40 kilometres) and the railway systems are losing huge amounts each year – $243 million in New South Wales during 1975-6, $139 million in Victoria, $88 million in Queensland, $42 million in South Australia, $15 million in Tasmania and the Western Australia Government Railways doing the best job to lose only $3 million.

Passenger services outside the main metropolitan areas have often been blamed as a primary cause of these financial woes. While country and branch lines are very expensive to service (the Public Transport Commission of New South Wales made $63 million of its $243 million total loss in 1975-6 on country and interstate passenger services) the full financial benefit will not be felt just by discontinuing passenger services. In order to reap the total benefit the whole line must be closed down, passengers and freight, then the fixed costs such as station upkeep and track maintenance can be saved. Even so Sir Henry Bland in his examination of the land transport system in Victoria in 1971 recommended that a large number of passenger services could be withdrawn resulting in considerable savings to the Victorian Railways even if freight services were continued. In one case he found that the Victorian Railways were losing $75 for each passenger carried on a particular line, and other cases were almost as bad. In submissions to the Bland Inquiry there was general agreement, from both road interests and the Victorian Railways, that the railways should give up all passenger services within the state except for certain trunk lines serving major provincial centres. This was the recommendation of the Bland Report but country political pressure based on expected lost jobs has caused the implementation of this segment of the Report to be a very slow process. Generally all rail systems in Australia are trying to follow this strategy with some, such as the Western Australia Government Railways, being more successful in its implementation than the Victorian Railways.

Passenger travel by sea around the coast of Australia is virtually a thing of the past. The Australian National Line is the trading entity of the Australian Shipping Commission which was set up by the Australian Government by Act of Parliament in 1956 and which is required to function as a commercial enterprise paying taxes and endeavouring to return a dividend to its owners, the Australian Government. The Australian National Line is the only operator of interstate sea passenger services. These services are provided by one ship – the 2736 deadweight tonnes *Empress of Australia* which carries cars on its deck, passengers and some freight beneath from Melbourne to Devonport and back. During 1975-6, 131 000 passengers made the trip. Also during that year the only other passenger vessel the *Australian Trader*, operating from Sydney to Tasmania, was withdrawn from service and put up for sale. After a considerable period during which the seamen would neither sail the ship nor leave it the Australian National Line sold the Australian Trader to the navy for $8 million. It is planned to be used by the navy as a training ship.

But even this solitary remaining passenger sea service is anything but secure. In an assessment of Tasmania's interstate transport problems made in 1973 the Bureau of Transport Economics estimated that if the 20 per cent of passengers crossing Bass Strait who go by sea were to travel by air the Australian National Line would save $1 million. As a result of this study the Line received a subsidy of $1 million from the federal government in 1975-6 for the operation of the *Empress of Australia*. For the next two years the subsidy is $2 million per year.

It is not entirely clear why the government wishes to retain the sea passenger service to Tasmania. A strong argument exists for not discriminating against Tasmanians solely on the basis of the geographical obstacle provided by Bass Strait. But even if all passengers crossed Bass Strait by air, tourists' cars could still be carried as freight on freight-only vessels. The existing 50 per cent rate subsidy of cars over general freight could still be retained. Some co-ordination difficulties in shuffling passengers between airports and shipping berths might be experienced at both ends, but these problems should not be insurmountable.

The fare structure is also working towards the eventual demise of interstate sea passenger services. Table 3.3 shows that as of January 1977 the normal fares charged by sea and air from Melbourne to Northern Tasmania were comparable. In addition air concessions are available for certain group bookings. Interstate sea passenger services are not important for any social or other non-economist purposes—if they cannot pay their way they should go.

Australia has developed a unique system of domestic airline operation which, because of its political origin and continued governmental control, goes under the title 'Australia's two-airline policy'.

While in many other countries major battles were waged over nationalization of the railways, in Australia private enterprise rail systems were not a consideration. (Until very recently few existed in Australia, but now private bulk trains move minerals from the mine to the port, particularly in Western Australia and Queensland.) The major battle was waged over nationalization of the airline industry.

In Australia before the Second World War the airline industry was operated by private interests. This situation may have remained if British shipping interests had not provided capital for the rapid expansion of one of the airlines, Australian National Airways, to a position of industry dominance. But this and the possibility of American airlines setting up in Australia in opposition to Australian National Airways led the Labor Government to include nationalization of the airline industry as an important part of their post-war reconstruction programme. In 1942 and again in 1944 referendums to give the Commonwealth, among other powers, complete control over transport, including air transport were defeated. In 1945 the Chifley Labor Government tried a different path to gain the twin goals of nationalization and freedom (at least for part of the industry) from foreign control and passed the *Australian National Airlines Act*.

Table 3.3   Fares for Different Modes of Interstate Travel in Australia*

	Air		Sea				Bus	Rail		
	Economy	1st Class	Sleeping lounge chair	4-berth cabin	Single cabin		One fare only	2nd Class	1st Class	Sleeper
Melbourne–Sydney	$ 48.50	$ 60.60	–	–	–		$ 27.00	$ 25.00	$ 38.00	$46.00
Melbourne–Tasmania†	$ 35.30	$ 44.10	$24.90	$29.80	$40.00		–	–	–	–
Melbourne–Perth	$163.10	$203.90	–	–	–		$103.00	$124.50	$179.50	Included in both fares
Sydney–Brisbane	$ 50.80	$ 63.50	–	–	–		$ 29.00	$ 25.00	$ 38.00	$46.00

*As at 13 January 1977.

† Air fare is to Launceston. Sea fare is to Devonport.

Source: Information supplied by Ansett Airlines, Australian National Line, Pioneer Coaches and Victorian Railways.

This Act set up the Australian National Airlines Commission and its later-named operator Trans-Australia Airlines. This was the birth of the two-airlines policy.

T.A.A. after three years of losses made a profit in 1949. A.N.A. however was feeling the pinch of competition and needed £5 million for new equipment. As it was felt this money could not be raised in the share market if T.A.A. continued to provide lively competition, the options for A.N.A. were for some kind of merger. An ingenious merger scheme, biased strongly in their favour, was proposed by A.N.A. but rejected by the Menzies Liberal–Country Party Coalition government which had come to power in 1949. Menzies, undoubtedly recalling the results of the March 1946 Gallup Poll on the question, reversed previous opposition to T.A.A. and advocated the continuance of both airlines on the basis that 'competition should continue'. Formalization of this policy occurred in 1952 when the *Australian National Airlines Act* of 1945 was amended to remove T.A.A.'s exemption from income tax and sales tax and the *Civil Aviation Agreement Act* was passed. This latter Act ensured the existence of A.N.A. and as a result of this A.N.A. was able to convince the government to guarantee all loans. This took care of the re-equipment problem. The *Agreement Act* also established a procedure whereby the two operators would rationalize air routes, timetables, fares and freight through an independent arbitrator if needed.

It is probable that the government at the time assumed the two airlines would operate similar planes under the spirit of the *Agreement Act*. But this was not the case: T.A.A. ordered Vickers Viscounts as expected, but Ivan Holyman ordered DC6s for A.N.A. Viscounts proved to be far more popular with the flying public and T.A.A. started to gain an upper hand.

Poor selection of equipment was not A.N.A.s only problem. Ansett Airways and Butler Air Transport, two much smaller operators based in Melbourne and Sydney respectively, could force the federal government to allow them to become the second operator on any interstate rationalized route by using section 92 of the Constitution which prohibits restrictions to interstate trade. In practice the two-airline policy was not working.

This changed when, in 1957, after several years of large operating losses, A.N.A. could not meet the payments due under its loan agreements. A.N.A. again made an unrealistic proposal for an industry merger. It was rejected by the government which offered financial concessions to try to keep A.N.A. in business, but these in turn were rejected by A.N.A. Ansett in talks with the government agreed to expand operations either alone, in competition with an A.N.A.-T.A.A. merger, or merged with A.N.A. against T.A.A. After considerable difficulties in negotiation Ansett, with the help of the Shell and Vacuum oil companies, successfully completed the A.N.A. takeover in August 1957. By February of the next year Ansett, after another extended battle, had absorbed Butler Air Transport. Now the two-airline policy existed in fact as well as theory.

In order to attempt to prevent either of these airlines (Ansett-A.N.A. and T.A.A.) from effectively wrecking the two-airline policy by providing excess capacity, the *Airlines Equipment Act* was passed in 1958. Under this Act each airline could not provide more than 50 per cent of industry capacity, as established by the government, although it was possible for either carrier to attract more than 50 per cent of the passengers. In 1961 the *Airlines Agreement Act* extended the time period (to 1977) and also the coverage of the previous rationalization provisions – now similarity of equipment would be enforced. This led to the ridiculous situation experienced by Ansett when a newly acquired DC9 was grounded for a period because T.A.A. had not yet received theirs. The Act also provides for a government guarantee of the interest and principal repayment on loans for Ansett to acquire comparable equipment to that used by T.A.A. The *Australian National Airlines Act* was also amended in this year. As a result of agitation by Ansett, T.A.A. was required to meet a dividend target which was to be set each year by the Minister (6 per cent in the first year 1962–3 and most recently 15 per cent for 1976–7).

By this stage the two-airline policy was firmly established. In 1972 the *Airlines Agreement Act* was amended again to extend the life of the two-airline policy beyond the end of 1977. The policy will continue indefinitely but with either party, Ansett Transport Industries or the Australian government, having the option to terminate it after giving five years' notice.

Because section 92 of the Australian Constitution bars restrictions to free trade across state borders the federal government cannot prevent other carriers operating on interstate air routes. But no suitable aircraft are presently in Australia; Qantas, Ansett or T.A.A. will not sell aircraft to a buyer who intends to threaten the two-airline policy and the government itself will not grant import licences for aircraft except to Qantas, Ansett and T.A.A. There is no doubt that the continuation of the two-airline policy depends upon the federal government violating the spirit if not the letter of section 92.

I.P.E.C., a road-based parcel express operator, managed in 1963 to charter sufficient aircraft to begin an air service across Bass Strait. The success of this operation motivated I.P.E.C. to seek an import licence for five DC4s in order to begin freight services on the mainland. The Director General of Civil Aviation, more than a year after receiving I.P.E.C.'s application, refused both the import licence and the air freight licence. On appeal to the High Court I.P.E.C. won the right to operate freight aircraft in Australia but lost the right to import the aircraft. It was not until 1977 that I.P.E.C. gained government approval for an import licence.

Several other important criticisms have been levelled at the two-airline policy. Probably the most basic criticism is that the two-airline policy was born from a crisis situation which was very strongly influenced by political rhetoric and expediency. A long-term governmental policy should be based on more than this; it should have the backing of a detailed and thorough economic investigation.

The government subsidization of Ansett Transport Industries' non-air activities is also frequently criticized. Even if it seems reasonable to support Ansett Airlines, should the taxpayers support the Ford dealers at Hamilton and Bendigo in Victoria, a grazing property near Narrandera in New South Wales, an insurance company, a road construction company, a pen manufacturer, T.V. Channels O in Melbourne and Brisbane, a chain of hotels, Wridgways furniture removals, Pioneer coaches, Ansett Freight Express (road freight) and others? In general terms the subsidization works this way. With the government guarantee of loan funds Ansett Transport Industries is able to raise capital that it otherwise could not. Some of this capital is then used, for example, to start Channel O in Melbourne which initially incurred heavy losses. These losses reduce the profit made by the company which in turn reduces the tax contribution paid, but in the meantime Ansett Transport Industries is rapidly expanding its assets. The federal government is supporting the growth of a massive industrial empire because it wants to maintain one small portion of it. As Stanley Brogden said, 'The whole problem of the two-airline policy as it exists today is, in fact, to protect the Ansett Transport Industry annual 10 per cent dividend.'[5]

Another question to be asked about the two-airline policy is: Does it provide the kind of passenger air service that the Australian people want? It is easy to become intoxicated by the glamour of the bright and shiny aviation industry. There is a natural tendency to clamour for the latest, most sophisticated, fastest aircraft. The current process of Ansett and T.A.A. choosing between the DC10, the Lockheed TriStar and the A300 Airbus as the wide-body replacement for the current Boeing 727-200s (now anticipated to occur in 1981) certainly contains a sizeable element of this phenomenon. Gordon Barton told the story of the farmer who was considered a fool when he bought a Bentley instead of the tractor he really needed. He was considered completely irrational when he bought another Bentley for his second vehicle. The point of the story is a warning to the airlines to avoid an analogous situation. Do air passengers want high-class, high-cost service to be unavoidable with air travel? Australian domestic air fares have risen by 45 per cent in the past three years and are now relatively expensive. As Sir Reginald Ansett told the *Bulletin* in January 1977: 'Our fares are very high. It is worrying. We have had a pretty severe adjustment in fares and we have got to the stage where we are expensive by world standards.' A third airline operating a shuttle service where the ticket is bought on board and no swags of stewardesses or cups of tea are provided, which uses smaller aircraft and metropolitan air fields such as Bankstown in Sydney and Moorabbin in Melbourne, could provide a far cheaper commuter service up and down the east coast. The demand for such a service may be large: the first step is to make a concerted effort to find out what the customer wants. Great public scepticism may exist about the desirability of less frequent service and far greater congestion with the planned wide-body jets.

It is quite possible that the two-airline policy provides the best structure for airline services in a country with a relatively small population and vast distances to be covered. But in many ways the industry appears as a two-sectioned government monopoly with the 'private enterprise' section enjoying the ride. No room exists for the smaller innovative operator, such as Ansett in his early days, to provide a different type of service for air travellers. But maybe such an operator would cut away just enough of the market to ruin the viability of the two existing airlines. It is certainly time to examine closely the needs of the air traveller and if required restructure the industry accordingly.

Mobility within Australia is required for business purposes and for recreation – recreation in the form of a holiday or vacation and recreation as a tourist possibly with overt cultural objectives.

For the business trip the car and plane are the only realistic options. Inter-capital-city car trips will certainly be facilitated when the National Highways System is completed – but most of these trips are made by air. These roads will only be of peripheral benefit for the bulk of business trips made by car which are intrastate.

Air services for the businessman are relatively poor because of the extended time taken between leaving the city centre and the plane taking off. For most inter-capital-city trips this time exceeds the time of the actual flight. Instead of looking towards the introduction of larger aircraft Ansett and T.A.A. should consider the possible future use of vertical or short take-off and landing (V.T.O.L. or S.T.O.L.) vehicles. These vehicles could use the tops of buildings, roofed-over train marshalling yards (such as Darling Harbour in Sydney and Jolimont in Melbourne) or roofed-over freeway interchanges (integrated with car parking stations) as terminals. The air service would then depart and arrive from close to the concentrations of potential customers. The capacity of these vehicles would be limited to around 100 passengers but the congestion and access difficulties of the major capital-city airports would be avoided.* International and longer interstate trips still using the traditional airports would also benefit from the lessened congestion with the removal of commuter trips. Sir Reginald Ansett has said that the businessman provides the basis of his airline operation. If he is not willing to provide an innovative service which better suits the businessman then maybe a third airline should be allowed to try.

*The Nomad, a successful S.T.O.L. built by the Australian Government Aircraft Factory does not fill this role as even the extended N24 version has only a capacity of sixteen passengers.

Of more concern from an equity point of view is the recreational trip. Most Australians have four weeks annual holiday. Interstate sea travel is virtually no more. Most passenger rail services should be closed but while they are still in existence better use could be made of them. For example, all individuals and families receiving social service benefits could be issued tickets for free intrastate rail travel. Besides making more people accustomed to rail travel again it would provide recreational mobility (even on day trips) to those who may not otherwise have it. This scheme would also provide initial access to some jobs (such as seasonal fruit and berry picking) for the unemployed. The third type of travel, air travel, is still relatively expensive and basically a mode used by the privileged. Road travel provides, and will continue to provide, the basic means by which the bulk of Australians enjoy their four weeks holiday. While use of the private car should be discouraged for commuter trips it should be encouraged for recreational trips. One way to provide such encouragement is to allow the car expenses (fuel, oil and depreciation) associated with one holiday trip per year to be tax deductible. A worthwhile refinement of this scheme would be to allow the full amount of these expenses to be deducted for low-income earners with a declining percentage allowable as income increases to a cut-off point at an income of around $10 000-$12 000 per year.*

Camping has provided Europeans with low-cost holidays for many years. Their willingness to camp is now providing many Australians with relatively inexpensive driving holidays. This type of holiday may not suit everyone's style, but A.A.T. (jointly owned by Trans-Australia Airlines and Mayne Nickless Ltd and established as a tour operating company in 1973) offer bus-camping holidays to Central Australia, Western Australia, Queensland and Tasmania. These range from an eleven-day trip costing around $300 up to the mammoth thirty-seven-day venture to the Centre costing around $650. Substituting hotel accommodation for camping adds around $100 for a short trip and around $200 for a longer trip. Ansett offers similar trips in conjunction with Australian Pacific and Centralian.

Mobility within Australia for recreational and cultural purposes

---

*This scheme does not assist those without cars or without incomes. Other means would need to be employed first to minimize the size of these two groups.

is important but not when compared with urban mobility requirements for work and day-to-day life style. Regional mobility can be provided relatively cheaply by road (car or bus) and the only public assistance that might be justified is the suggested tax concession for the annual holiday and rail tokens for the needy. Australia is moderately well provided with the means of regional mobility.

Notes

1. Ellery, R. L. J., Kernot, W. C., von Mueller, F., Neild, J. E., Le Souef, A. A. C. and Turner, H. G., *Victoria and its Metropolis, Past and Present*, Vol. II, McCarron, Bird and Co., Melbourne, 1888, p. 157.
2. *Ibid.*
3. Whitlam, G., *Australian Labor Party Policy Speech*, 1972.
4. Commonwealth Bureau of Roads, *Report on Roads in Australia, 1973*, Commonwealth Bureau of Roads, Melbourne, 1973, p. 154.
5. Brogden, S., *Australia's Two-Airline Policy*, Melbourne University Press, Melbourne, 1968.

Chapter 4
The International Traveller

Hudson Fysh and his First World War flying mate 'Ginty' McGinness together with two graziers and a man from the Queensland Primary Producers

sat at that now historic glass-topped round table with pencils and paper poised. The outcome was the registration on 16th November 1920 of The Queensland and Northern Territory Aerial Services Ltd. With all our optimism little did we founders dream that Qantas would enjoy the success it has, nor air transport be where it is today, bridging land and sea and conquering the oceans, connecting the whole world by a network of fast air communications.[1]

Today Qantas carries over half of all passengers who travel by air to Australia. During the financial year 1964-5, 95 per cent of the 830 000 people who left Australia for overseas trips went by air. Qantas has come a long way since 1920; instead of two Avro 504ks Qantas now operates a fleet of eleven Boeing 747s as well as ten Boeing 707s. But there are some who would discount this success and claim that false national pride ensures the existence of Qantas by government-set artificially high fares and in recent times by the federal government meeting Qantas losses on operations.

In the year 1973-4, over 700 000 Australians travelled overseas and spent almost $800 million in the process – over half of this amount was spent on the actual transportation. On average the total cost of this travel was about $1100 per person. In that year the average wage was $115 per week, or just under $6000 per year. For the 'average' Australian an 'average' overseas trip would cost more than one-sixth of his before-tax income. It is unlikely, then, that the average Australian will spend this proportion of his annual income (particularly for a family with one income earner) on international travel for purely recreational sight-seeing reasons. Who then does travel overseas?

Many more Australians are now travelling overseas; three times as many people left Australia for overseas trips in the mid-seventies as did at the beginning of the decade. Travel in 1973–4, according to a study done by the Australian Tourist Commission, was concentrated in the middle age groups with men travelling slightly more in their thirties and forties (business trips) and women slightly more in their fifties and sixties (widows on world tours such as those organized by the Women's Weekly). This is as expected. Not expected was that people with incomes slightly lower than the Australian average made more than their share of overseas trips. An explanation is that a considerable proportion of these trips are taken by migrants from the United Kingdom or Western Europe either returning to their homelands because of unfilled expectations of Australian life or returning to visit friends and relatives. One third of all international trips from Australia in 1973–4 were to visit friends and relatives with over half of the trips to the United Kingdom and three-quarters of the trips to Western Europe being for this reason.

Visiting friends and relatives is one of the three main reasons for taking trips overseas. A more common reason is purely for a holiday (half of all trips) and a less common reason is business (just over one-tenth of all trips). As mentioned most trips to the United Kingdom and Western Europe were to visit friends; most trips to the Americas (north, central and south) were for business reasons.

A market the industry has developed is full-time students. Students took over one-fifth of all overseas trips in 1973–4, particularly to the United Kingdom, Western Europe and New Zealand. Organizations such as the Australian Union of Students can provide a wide range and relatively frequent service of group travel during the summer to all parts of the world. Fares for these group trips are generally half the normal economy fare.

For those taking overseas trips for non-business reasons the size of the fare has always been a major deterrent. In 1946 a return air ticket to London cost the average Australian wage-earner two years pay. With the introduction of the special advance-purchase fare in April 1977 a return trip to London cost five weeks wages. But it can be seen from Table 4.1 that in the past most people have not travelled on a reduced fare scheme but have used the normal economy fare. An interesting aspect of Table 4.1 is the high proportion of first class air travel for business trips. Although this proportion tends to fluctuate slightly depending upon the general economic conditions at the

Table 4.1 Analysis of Overseas Travel by Australians, 1973-4

	All trips	Mainly holiday	Visit relatives and friends	Business
First class air	7%	4%	2%	32%
Economy class air	55%	51%	66%	54%
Reduced air fare:				
Inclusive tour	4%	7%	0%	1%
Special round trip	9%	10%	8%	2%
Special family fare	4%	3%	6%	1%
Airline or travel agent employee	7%	5%	11%	6%
Other reduction	3%	2%	3%	2%
Sea	11%	18%	4%	2%
	100%	100%	100%	100%

Source: Overseas Travel by Australians 1973/74, Australian Tourist Commission, Melbourne, February 1976, p.23.

time, it is probably only human nature to consider comfort and luxury service more important when someone else is paying (the consumer of the product or the taxpayer). Table 4.2 shows the relative price of economy air and sea travel from Sydney to London and from Sydney to San Francisco over the past twelve or so years. It is interesting to notice from these figures that the relative cost of overseas travel appears to have bottomed out on its downward trend: air fares over the past few years have remained at much the same cost relative to average earning power while sea fares have risen slightly. With the development in air travel being towards higher-price options and stricter control over cut-price travel while sea travel is suffering from its high labour component, overseas travel is unlikely to become relatively cheaper in the near future, at least for those people not travelling on reduced fare schemes.

The course of development in the international airline industry is of interest when considered in terms of its general contribution to mobility. As already seen during the late 1960s and early 1970s when the wide-bodied Boeing 747s and DC10s were replacing the Boeing

Table 4.2a Relative Cost of Overseas Travel from Sydney to San Francisco

	Air fare	No. of weeks' work to earn fare	Sea fare	No. of weeks' work to earn fare
1965	$472	8.6	n.a.	n.a.
1970	$472	6.2	n.a.	n.a.
1975	$597	4.0	$ 639	4.3
1976	$685	4.1	$ 800	4.7
1977	$748	3.9*	$1026	5.4*

*Estimated

Source: Qantas Airways Ltd and P. & O. Australia Ltd.

707s and DC9s the relative cost of international air travel was decreasing. Airlines saw the vast pool of people who had never travelled by air (estimated at nine out of every ten people) as being relatively easily attracted by the glamour and relative economy of the 'jumbo'. But these additional passengers did not eventuate due to an economic downturn coupled with high inflation. Airlines were left with the twin problems of excess capacity provided by the wide-bodied jets and a declining rate of passenger growth. In an attempt to get over this problem many airlines and travel agents issued tickets at below the fare recommended by the International Air Transport Association (I.A.T.A.) and made legal by the many governments concerned. This

Table 4.2b Relative Cost of Overseas Travel from Sydney to London

	Air fare	No. of weeks' work to earn fare	Sea fare	No. of weeks' work to earn fare
1965	$620	11.4	n.a.	n.a.
1970	$620	8.1	n.a.	n.a.
1975	$775	5.2	$1000	6.8
1976	$854	5.0	$1264	7.5
1977	$940	5.0*	$1591	8.4*

*Estimated

Source: Qantas Airways Ltd and P. & O. Australia Ltd.

situation led Sir Lenox Hewitt, Chairman of Qantas, to complain in the 1975-6 Annual Report that:

The most serious factor in the airlines operations during the year was the loss of revenue which the Company suffered from the growth throughout the world of illegal and unethical marketing practices and the spread to the Australian market-place.[2]

'Malpractice', as this type of activity is called, was seen by Qantas as the major cause of the $14 million loss for the year. Neither was Qantas alone in achieving mixed results with the jumbos – several domestic U.S. airlines simply parked them idle in rows at an airfield in Arizona.

Although the project was commenced in 1956 the British/French commercial supersonic aircraft, Concorde, was seen by many as providing a highly profitable segment of the international airlines operation.

... demand for seats will exceed the available SST capacity for a long time to come, and a very high average load-factor will go a long way towards bridging the cost gap. So, assuming a surcharge of, say, 15 per cent to 20 per cent to be placed on the SST fares by the airlines, the Concorde could turn out to be highly profitable to them.[3]

And more recently:

No vehicle-maker in the history of public transport has failed to sell a product that cuts travel time in half ... Concorde deserves the right to rise or fall on its operational record, not on ... hysterical keenings.[4]

But even this as we will see may have changed.

Concorde will carry fewer than 100 passengers (compared with four times that number carried in a Boeing 747 – 674 people were carried out of Darwin on a Qantas B747 after Cyclone Tracy hit in December 1974) and cost in excess of $50 million. Concorde passengers will pay a fare that is 15 per cent higher than the first class fares on subsonic flights. It is obvious that Concorde will do nothing to increase the general level of mobility. Those who will use Concorde will be a subset of the small minority who now fly first class (7 per cent of all overseas trips in 1974-5 when all public servants travelled on this class). Those who don't fly now on overseas trips certainly will not fly Concorde. By itself this objection to Concorde may be a positive attribute if the high potential revenues from Concorde are used to support normal low-fare flights.

Concorde certainly has generated enthusiastic supporters and detractors. On 28 May 1976, Peter Nixon the Minister for Transport announced that the federal government had given its approval for Concorde to begin regular services to Australia. The planned flight path of Concorde from London when scheduled flights begin in late 1977, enters Australia south of Broome in Western Australia, travels south-east to the Great Australian Bight, then inland again at Mt Gambier, South Australia, and crosses to Tullamarine Airport in Melbourne at subsonic speed. The Victorian Chamber of Manufactures greeted this decision with much enthusiasm. 'Australian businessmen and the Victorian community as a whole will benefit from this decision.' Brian Powell, the Director of the Chamber, said at the time:

'Besides bringing Melbourne hours closer to the heart of Australia's biggest overseas markets, Concorde will dispel the apprehension of overseas businessmen who want to do business here but until now have been unable to afford the extended time travelling and recovering from jet lag.'[5]

Concorde was also expected to turn Melbourne into a popular venue for international conferences and conventions. The Australian Conservation Foundation on the other hand, found little joy in the news and issued a High Court writ on Mr Nixon for breaking the Environment Protection Act.

What are some of the objections to Concorde?

Concorde will probably use at least four times as much fuel per passenger kilometre as does the Boeing 747. Extremely large fuel requirements exist at take-off in order to provide the thrust needed to reach supersonic speeds. In addition fuel requirements increase during hot weather. These voracious fuel needs have created two problems. The first is economic – carrying extra passengers generates revenue but carrying extra fuel does not – and the second is safety – the fuel capacity of the aircraft is not sufficient to allow for extended holding times above airports in all circumstances. It has been estimated that an increase of fifteen minutes holding time at the end of a London–Washington flight will use sufficient fuel to reduce the number of passenger seats from ninety-three to sixty. In order to avoid this problem Concorde must be given landing priority which in addition to upsetting normal commercial schedules will provide unusual turbulence for following planes.

Probably the most widely publicized adverse effect of Concorde is the sonic boom. With a turbulent atmosphere, as often occurs in central Australia as a result of solar heating, distortion and displacement of the sonic boom can occur. A recent study has shown that the boom can cause mild physiological disturbance which tends to increase with the person's age. Another seldom considered effect of the boom is on the Aboriginals. To tribal Aboriginals it is important to maintain, in certain sacred areas, an atmosphere free from man's instrusions – Concorde's sonic boom will be yet another example of white man's lack of feeling for the Aboriginal. A final consideration is the possible effect the boom might have on geomorphic characteristics. Will the sonic boom over time shatter rocks or move sand dunes?

At subsonic speeds the Concorde is also very noisy. Noise reduction can occur to some degree but this involves reducing the payload and making the aircraft even more costly to operate. Noise during take-off is appreciably louder than for existing planes and fuel conservation measures will probably require that Concorde leave at night. Communities near airports will become much more aware of Concorde when the noisy older jets (such as the Boeing 707) are substantially replaced by the quieter wide-bodied jets. These communities tend to be made up, predominantly, of lower-income families who suffer the noise but do not often get the chance to benefit from the overseas air travel.

Meteorologists have established that changes in the composition of the stratosphere have influenced the past changes in world climate. Volcanic eruptions, nuclear explosions and now SSTs inject gases and particles into the stratosphere. This may influence its ozone content which will affect the amount of ultraviolet radiation reaching the earth. The following quotation sums up the problem rather nicely:

Meteorologists . . . cannot now offer reliable forecasts of future regional or global climate . . . but ignorance of consequences should not be taken as a licence to pollute; rather it warns us to minimise human influence on the climate at least until we can become wiser as to what will be the real consequences.[6]

Concorde is designed to cruise at above 20 kilometres altitude. At this height the galactic radiation dose-rate is three times that received at the subsonic cruising altitude of about 12 kilometres. Radiation from solar flares is also of concern and present forecasting methods for solar flares are not very accurate. This problem may cause Concorde aircrew to be classified as radiation workers with no crew aboard being females of child-bearing age.

In June 1974 Concorde flew from Paris to Boston in three hours and nine minutes while an Air France Boeing 747 took seven hours ten minutes for the trip.* When at least an hour is added for the trip from the city centre to the airport and at least another hour for customs and immigration requirements at the airport, and this happens at both ends of the flight, then the travel time by flying Concorde is cut by only a quarter rather than a half. Frequent refuelling on longer trips will also cause the time savings to be of this magnitude.

Set against these costs to the whole community is the saving of a few hours of time for a very few people of upper socio-economic class. Is what they will do with these few hours worth the cost?

Concorde is a regressive development in international air travel. In addition to the wide-ranging problems it will bring, it will not provide excess revenue which could be used to subsidize mass travel: British Airways have asked their government for a subsidy of £25 million per year to keep Concorde operating. Concorde is an extreme example of the aviation industry's obsession with technology to the detriment of economics and ecology.

International airlines are subject to various controls. The basic control comes from the individual countries which the airlines serve. Any country has absolute control over its air space and so can allow or bar entry to any airline and impose whatever conditions it likes on the use of its air space. Landing rights and frequencies are established by bilateral agreement. But any international air route is going to

*By the beginning of 1977 British Airways was operating a Concorde service London–Washington and London–Bahrain while Air France was operating Paris–Washington, Paris–Rio de Janeiro and Paris–Caracas flights. The highest passenger loading was 73 per cent on British Airways' London–Washington flight and the lowest was 33 per cent on the Air France flight Paris–Caracas.

influence a larger number of countries than just the two involved in these agreements. Fiji, for example, has an interest as well as Australia and the United States in the fare structure of the Qantas Sydney to San Francisco flight. It is at this stage that the International Air Transport Association plays an important role.

I.A.T.A. is a trade association just as the Master Builders' Association is, but with additional glamour because its membership represents many nations and its dealings are multi-governmental in nature. I.A.T.A.s most important function is in the setting of air freight rates and passenger fares. I.A.T.A. is structured into seven traffic conferences which are based on geographical regions.* Fares for flights within each conference are established by the unanimous agreement of all member airlines. This action is expressed as a formal resolution which is in turn submitted to the various governments for approval, which is normally given, and then the fare comes into effect.

I.A.T.A. is a voluntary association and has in practice accepted any airline for membership which is also eligible for membership in the International Civil Aviation Organization (I.C.A.O.). (I.C.A.O. is an agency of the United Nations which seeks to standardize communication, air traffic control and navigation requirements as well as the overall technical standards of the industry.) Most airlines belong to I.A.T.A.; those that do not tend to be from smaller nations, such as Nauru, Iceland and Malaysia who strive for viability by cutting the fares offered by the major I.A.T.A. airlines.

Recently I.A.T.A. has come under some criticism, mainly for restraint of free trade and acting as a cartel. As a partial response to this criticism I.A.T.A. on several occasions has reviewed the procedures by which its members agree on air fares and rates.

. . . the subject is inherently a very complex one and unless treated comprehensively and methodically it may give rise to misconceptions. Indeed, it is apparent from some of the comments already made (by critics of I.A.T.A.) that the processes are not fully understood.[7]

---

*Conference No. 1 includes North and South America, Conference No. 2 Europe and Africa and Conference No. 3 Asia and Oceania. In addition four joint conferences exist to deal with matters affecting two or three conferences. (i.e. Joint Conferences 1/2, 1/3, 2/3 and 1/2/3.)

As an appendix to the first of these surveys I.A.T.A. assembled an array of favourable comments on its operations ranging from Clement Attlee when Prime Minister of Great Britain to President Marcos of the Philippines and including Senator Shane Paltridge when he was Minister for Civil Aviation in 1961 at the time of the I.A.T.A. Annual General Meeting in Sydney.

I.A.T.A. certainly plays a valuable role as an apolitical forum where xenophobic demands for use of airspace can be dealt with in a systematic fashion. The key to I.A.T.A.s inefficiency is the low 'passenger load factor' achieved by its 110-odd members – during 1971 just fractionally over one-half of all available seats were filled. Since then seat utilization has increased slightly to around 56 per cent. I.A.T.A. has no control over the capacity offered by its members.

The provision of excess capacity has certainly contributed to their (I.A.T.A. members) difficulties, but I.A.T.A. has no control of capacity either directly or indirectly which, apart from other considerations, must seriously weaken the validity of accusations that the Association is a cartel.[8]

This argument may be valid regarding I.A.T.A.s position as a cartel, but lack of control over capacity means that I.A.T.A. must set fares high enough to cover at least airline operating costs and overheads with planes only half full. If I.A.T.A. did have control over capacity it could ensure that planes were more fully utilized and fares could be lower.

An association performing I.A.T.A.s functions would be much more effective if it could control capacity if not membership. But these facets of international air operations would be difficult to control.

Even the smallest and poorest of banana republics aspires to its own international airline with the latest, largest and fastest equipment. Even in countries where people are actually starving to death, airline and airport facilities are elaborate and, indeed, in many cases, monumental.[9]

I.A.T.A. functions effectively in the particular role it has cast for itself. With the organization of the world into strongly nationalistic states and the prestige associated with a national flag airline maybe it is idealistic to expect any more of I.A.T.A.

In recent years sea cruises through the Pacific have become a popular way for some Australians to spend their annual holidays. But other types of sea travel have been on the decline – sea travel is now more expensive than the equivalent air trip and few travellers can afford to spend the time taken for the sea voyage if the main purpose of the trip is to 'do Europe' or 'do America'. In the past shipping companies such as the Chandris and Sitmar Lines have benefited from the large numbers of sea passengers travelling from Europe to Australia under the federal government's assisted migration scheme. The over-capacities carried on the southern leg of the voyage enabled northbound Australians to benefit from cross-subsidization of fares. Now the assisted migration scheme has been much scaled down and the few passengers arriving in Australia under the scheme come by air. This change has certainly had an influence on the relative cost of sea travel.

A reasonable social long-run aim of an isolated country such as Australia might well be to enable as many people as possible, if not all, to be able to exercise the option of taking overseas trips. The choice of having the cultural and recreational benefits of overseas travel should not be restricted to the affluent. Because sea travel in itself consumes too much time air is the mode to use for such a development. Qantas should leave I.A.T.A. and Australia should alter its regulations on charter flights. At present a group can only charter an aircraft or a portion of an aircraft if they can establish some long-standing reason for association or 'affinity' which is not related to their travel desires. This situation is naturally favourable to students – vast numbers of people with a common 'affinity' who have time during the summer break to take overseas trips. But why should particular groups, who are more often than not privileged sectors of the community, have greater access to reduced-fare overseas travel? Charter regulations should be changed so that any group could organize a charter flight as long as they had sufficient numbers. As Terry Lane in an interview on the A.B.C. radio network suggested travel agents should be allowed to underwrite such charter flights for any types of groups, for example groups of pensioners; even groups who have no common interest at all other than travel. Such a scheme would greatly expand access to overseas travel for all sectors of the Australian community as well as helping Qantas to return to profitable operations by considerably increasing the number of passengers and the level of utilization of aircraft. And if Qantas cannot financially break even it should be closed down and another carrier given the rights to service Australia in its place. It is all too easy to forget that the prime reason for a transportation service is to provide access efficiently not to provide national prestige.

Notes

1. Fysh, H., *Qantas Rising*, Angus and Robertson, Sydney 1965, p. 97.
2. Qantas Airways Limited, *Annual Report 1975-76*. Sydney, p. 2.
3. Watkins, J. L., 'Technological Developments in Air Transport' in *Special Lectures in Transport: National Transport Policy*, Transport Section, Department of Civil Engineering, University of Melbourne, Melbourne, 1968, p. 13.
4. 'Concorde Deserves its Chance', *Australian Transport*, Vol. 18, No. 3, March 1976, p. 31.
5. *News Release*, Victorian Chamber of Manufactures, Melbourne, 28th May, 1976.
6. Landsberg, H. and Machta, L., *Ambio*, Vol. 3, 1974, p. 146.
7. International Air Transport Association, *Agreeing Fares and Rates*, International Air Transport Association, Geneva, First edition, January 1973, p. 2.
8. Ibid, p. 5.
9. Barton, G., 'Some Critical Remarks About the Australian Two Airline Aviation Policy', in *Special Lectures in Transport: National Transport Policy*, Transport Section, Department of Civil Engineering, University of Melbourne, Melbourne, 1968, p. 1.

Chapter 5
Urban Delivery

When Nevile Owen, long-time General Manager of East Coast Transport, was a boy he often went with his father and elder brothers delivering freight around Sydney. In the 1930s much of the talk on these trips was about the poor road conditions, congestion on the roads and the expected customer reactions to the poor customer service which resulted. When participating in a workshop on urban goods movement organized by the Commonwealth Bureau of Roads in 1975 Owen said, 'Looking back over the years, I find that the problems of those days are still with us in the 1970s.'[1]

Narrow streets in most inner city areas force the carrier to use a relatively small truck, even when the load would be more efficiently carried in a larger vehicle. Receiving facilities, even for brand new buildings such as Nauru House in Melbourne, are inadequate often forcing vehicles to unload while parked on adjacent roads. The result is more vehicles and more congestion in inner city areas. Owen and others in the road freight industry believe that adequate receiving facilities for goods should be enforced as part of the building regulations.

During 1970 a carrier could expect to deliver between sixty and eighty parcels per day in Melbourne and charge around 15 cents per parcel. Recently the same carrier could make fewer than twenty parcel deliveries in the day and charges had increased by five times in addition to a minimum delivery charge.

Part of the reason for this rapid increase in cost is due to the generally high level of inflation in Australia and part of the reason for the fewer deliveries is the increased congestion. But other factors are also at work. One of the key factors is the reduction in effective working time per vehicle due to reduced receiving time for deliveries at many premises. When making deliveries a truck driver may find he cannot unload at some places before 9 a.m., or after 3 p.m. at other places; the receiving dock can be closed for an hour for lunch any time during the period 11.30 a.m. to 2.30 p.m. The driver may have to wait for a staff member of the receiving organization to check the load in. At the waterfront long queues can develop. Waiting at a cost of 15 cents per minute can become very expensive. East Coast Transport has experienced the situation where freight has been moved by road from Melbourne to Sydney (a distance of 960 kilometres) at less cost than its subsequent movement from the truck terminal in Sydney to the Sydney wharves. Freight has sat on trucks in ranks at the wharf for up to three days. Long delays can also occur at the rail yards – with the exception of the Kewdale complex in Perth, Australia's terminal facilities for general rail freight are antiquated and inefficient. At the time the Lees committee examined the Mile End rail yard in Adelaide not one fork-lift truck was being used; at the South Brisbane rail terminal access space is not sufficient for a truck to get into the proper position to unload freight from a rail wagon.

Road transport operators are one group who have not been influenced by arguments against inner city freeways.

. . . it must be recognized that a major city that is not serviced by freeways must result in traffic chaos and unnecessary delays.

Freeways radiating from the city are not popular with governments or people living in the inner suburbs. However, it is hoped that fashion will change again, and that the demand for better access to the city and outer suburbs will be so great that governments will be unable to ignore it.[2]

This argument for an inner city freeway network is based on the fact that freeways enable truck operating costs to be reduced: 25 per cent reduction in fuel needed, 25 per cent reduction in maintenance and repairs costs, together with an increase in the distance covered in a day by 15 per cent. In addition the general level of pollution is decreased with trucks spending less time idling at traffic lights and in heavy traffic. A final point put forward is that freeways, contrary to public opinion, do not consume a large portion of inner city land: the city of Los Angeles with its 600 kilometres of freeways has a lower proportion of its total land area paved as roads than does Rome.

These are the views of the transport owner and operator on the urban delivery problem. But a large degree of the difficulty of the problem is because urban freight delivery affects several other community groups, and most of these groups do not hesitate to make their case known.

An attempt to identify these groups has been made by Peter Rimmer of the Australian National University. He classifies eight groups who have close interrelationships with urban freight. These are:

- the shipper of goods
- the receiver of goods
- the vehicle owner
- the highway authority
- the terminal or warehouse operator
- the 'impactee' (the beneficiary or victim of transport's unintended effects on the environment)
- the 'activist' (the lobbyist against the undesirable effect of goods movement)
- government (local, state or federal)

Of course any particular organization may perform several of these functions. For example, Myer department stores own their trucks and warehouses and so would act as the shipper of goods, the receiver of goods, the vehicle owner and the warehouse operator. Also the highway authority in all states is a government instrumentality.

The shipper and receiver both experience urban freight problems similar to those of the vehicle owner to the extent that they are concerned with minimizing the delay in delivering the order to the customer or having their own order delivered into their warehouse. But the shipper has control over his loading dock and so will install an efficient set-up because it will save money in the long run. Unless the delivery contains items needed to keep production going, delays at the receiving dock are not a direct cost to the receiver. So the receiver tends to let facilities at the inbound dock run down. Nevile Owen tells of his recent visit to a modern Sydney warehouse. For despatch, trucks were loaded from both sides with palletized orders. Within ten minutes of arriving the truck was fully loaded, the load secured, the necessary documentation completed and the truck on its way again. On the other side of the building raw materials were being delivered. Here there was a narrow dock and a queue of ten trucks backed up into the street. When a forklift truck was not in use on the outbound dock it was put to work unloading raw materials.

Although this quite widespread neglect of receiving facilities does not represent a direct cost to the receiver the increased delivery cost is eventually passed on. Jim McGrath, the Distribution Manager of Australian Safeway Stores Victorian operation, suggests that improvements in receiving facilities would occur if demurrage was charged after an initial waiting time. If the receiver knew his goods were costing more the longer they waited outside his warehouse then he would improve the receiving facilities. One way of doing this is to provide priority unloading service to trucks which have made an appointment. Trucks arriving without an appointment, or arriving late would have to queue.

The terminal can be government or privately owned. It can take one of two major forms. It can operate as a breakbulk warehouse where consolidated shipments arrive from the factory, are broken down into individual customer orders and shipped out, or it can operate as a transfer facility where goods arriving by sea, rail or air are transferred to road transport for the final delivery. In either case the aim of the terminal operator is to maximize throughput which involves trying to think of ways by which the peaks and valleys of goods movements can be levelled.

The highways authority (such as the Country Roads Board in Victoria and the Department of Main Roads in New South Wales) can influence the urban delivery situation by providing more roads, improving existing roads or altering the traffic control system. It is natural for these authorities to be influenced by the belief that more roads are better although this view may be moderated by political influences.

Impactees and activists are related in the fact that both are affected by the unintended influences of urban road transport; but the activists try to do something about it. In 1976 activists took action to try to stop trucks using residential streets to get to and from the Australian National Line terminal at Balmain in Sydney. In addition to noise and air pollution residential property values can be lowered by developments for urban goods transport. But it is interesting to note that commercial property values can increase for the very same reason.

Government at all three levels (local, state and federal) can exert a considerable influence on urban goods delivery by regulation, taxes, subsidies and the option of public ownership of certain facilities.

A summary of this classification is given in Table 5.1 which shows

Table 5.1 The Process of Urban Goods Movement

	Shipper	Receiver	Vehicle owner	Terminal operator	Highway authority	Impactee	Activist	Government
Variants	Long haul Short haul	Long haul Short haul	Ancillary, Hire and reward, Owner driver	Government Private	Australian State, Local governments			Australian State, Local governments
Objectives	Minimize perceived costs	Minimize perceived costs	Maximize vehicle earnings	Maximize throughput	Maximize net social benefits	Minimize disruption/ maximize benefits	Minimize undesirable proximate activity/ maximize accessibility	Resource allocation at each level Operational norms
Constraints	Labour relations	Labour relations	Spatial/temporal access	Terminal congestion	Capacity	Noise		Urban structure (land use)
	Loading facilities	Unloading facilities	Terminal congestion	Terminal site	Design of infra-structure	Air pollution		Equity (e.g. rural *vs* urban, motor vehicle *vs*

			congestion	cation			erance
	...ability	...ability	Vehicle use				Community disruption
	Access problems	Access problems	Security				Safety
	Handling equipment	Handling equipment	Documentation				
			Regulation				
Options	Improvements *in situ*	Improvements *in situ*	Vehicle scheduling and routing	Scheduling vehicle arrival	Change control signals		Regulation
	Re-location	Re-location	Number and type of fleet	Re-siting or re-location of buildings	Widen roads		Taxes
				New and different sized buildings	Construct new roads		Subsidies
							Public ownership

Source: P. J. Rimmer, 'A Conceptual Framework for Examining Urban Goods Movements', in K. W. Ogden and S. K. Hicks (eds), *Urban Goods Movement*, Commonwealth Bureau of Roads, Melbourne, 1975, p. 20.

the objectives held by each group, the constraints they feel to their participation in the urban freight process and the options they have for action to achieve their goals.

With all these different groups influencing and being influenced by the urban freight process, improvement in the system will only occur with a much greater level of voluntary co-operation and co-ordination or a much firmer hand being shown by government. Indeed an 'improvement' will be difficult to define. In the end government is the group in the strongest position (and also least biased as it theoretically represents the will of all the people) so the government should define the criteria by which the urban freight process should develop. Even if this selection could be relatively easily made a great deal of co-ordination would be needed between the various arms of government to implement it.

Many different criteria exist by which the performance of the urban freight task may be judged. From the individual firm's point of view the objective of urban delivery is most often the minimization of the direct private costs involved. The process of distribution only adds costs to the product, it does not change the product itself in any way. This extra cost should be minimized. Cost minimization can also be the objective of those with a much wider view of the urban delivery process. The costs to be minimized in this case are the social costs involved: the cost of the product to the community as well as the cost of noise and air pollution, the cost of time wasted due to congestion caused by trucks, the adverse and positive effects of urban delivery on living styles and standards.

More enlightened firms see profit maximization rather than cost minimization as their primary criterion for urban delivery. Any particular customer may be located in a geographically inaccessible area, may place a very small order and may demand immediate delivery. Even if the manufacturing or distributing company makes this delivery at the least cost possible it will still make a loss on the sale.

Revenue or sales maximization might be used as the criterion for measuring the performance of urban goods delivery. Marketing departments in firms often operate on this basis and can easily fall into the same trap as attempting to minimize distribution costs: non-profitable customers are retained. Independent warehouse or terminal operators have more justification in using this criterion as fixed costs are allocated more thinly over a larger volume and so the unit charge can be lower and in turn the profit, per unit handled, higher.

A popular basis upon which urban freight movements are judged is the minimization of the amount of inconvenience caused. This criterion can be used both in private operations and in public policy. For the private firm as long as the orders are being filled and the customers are not complaining then the local delivery operation is left alone regardless of how inefficient or costly it might be. Public policy also tends to react to crises. Changes will be made to placate the community group which is complaining the loudest.

Also from a public policy viewpoint it is often thought that the transport of goods in an urban area should take place with minimal cost or delay to passenger transportation. Several other criteria could also be used such as marginal economic efficiency, maximization of utility or satisfaction and the achievement of social goals such as giving assistance to certain industries.

Stuart Hicks, of the Commonwealth Bureau of Roads, has selected from this long array of options the criterion of minimizing the social cost of urban goods movement. He views social cost to be comprised of four parts: transport operation costs, external costs, community costs and urban structure costs. Transport operation costs are the private costs of distributing the goods including the delivery price or cost (vehicle running costs, drivers' wages, overheads) and other distribution costs such as packaging, storing, handling, order processing costs, insurance, pilferage and damage. External costs include delays caused to other vehicles and pedestrians, personal and property damage caused by road accidents, pollution (noise, air and visual), building damage due to vibration and psychosocial disturbances caused by close proximity to trucks. Community costs are those incurred when a government agency is responsible for a freight transportation activity. These costs include the building and administration of roads, the building and operation of transhipment facilities such as railway stations, ports and airports, the operation of government freight services such as garbage removal and mail delivery, and the operation of regulatory and planning bodies. The final set of costs are urban structure costs – with a growing urban area different forms of development are going to result in different total urban goods delivery costs.

This approach does not in fact select one criterion from the list previously discussed and the tag 'social costs' is not broad enough to encompass the wide variety of costs included. In effect the main points from the list are taken and combined into one multi-faceted criterion – social costs. Justice would certainly seem to be done if government control could be exercised over the urban goods transportation process in such a way as to minimize the sum of these social costs. Even if this were an impossibility (and it undoubtedly is) great improvements would be made if decisions were taken with this aim in mind.

In the past two decades most major cities in the developed part of the western world (notably the United States, Canada, Britain, other western European countries and Australia) have carried out urban transportation studies. Most of these studies have been scrapped or only partially implemented. Most have ignored the problem of urban freight movements, with those who have not giving it only passing consideration.

The Sydney Area Transportation Study, completed in 1974, made the most comprehensive attempt of any Australian urban transportation study to examine freight movements. The major objective of the freight section of the study was 'to ascertain the volume of goods carried by each transport mode (road, rail, sea and air) into and out of the Study Area, and the nature of the distribution of goods within the Study Area'.[3] Achievement of this objective would allow the study team to relate distribution patterns to current congestion levels, to determine how goods deliveries were being affected. Also the actual location of major loading, unloading, transit and storage points could be compared with their 'probable optimum locations' and the effect of improving freight handling methods and greater rationalization of freight facilities could be examined.

The primary method used in this study was to select major commodity groupings (general freight, wool, grain, fruit and vegetables, meat and livestock, dairy and other agricultural products, iron and steel, petroleum products, coal and coke and building materials) and then to superimpose the transportation requirements of these commodities on to the existing freight structure. The approach led to the examination of particular freight flows into and out of the study region to the exclusion of freight movements within the region. As an example take the commodity coal and coke. Of the 11 million tonnes of coal exported from New South Wales in 1972-3, 96 per cent went to Japan to be used in iron and steel production. Coking coal from the Burragorang Valley has come under strong competition over recent years from the superior coking coal obtained from the open-cut mines in Queensland. European demand for the steaming coal from the Western District may increase but future demand is difficult to estimate. New South Wales coal leaves for overseas from Sydney, Port Kembla or Newcastle with the volume moving through Newcastle being about twice that of the other two ports. Domestic consumption of coal in the Sydney area has declined over recent years. Coal for the cement and iron and steel industries moves directly from the mine to the point of production. Future increases in iron and steel capacity will occur at Port Kembla and so coal for this industry will not need to pass through Sydney. Cement plants also will tend to be located near sources of limestone and coal rather than in metropolitan Sydney. Competition from natural gas as an industrial power source has also reduced the movement of coal into the Sydney study area. Although a large proportion of Sydney's domestic coal requirements comes by sea from Newcastle and Catherine Hill Bay the total volume of this movement is declining rapidly. The prime transport consideration examined by the freight study was the location of new coal loading facilities. At present the Port of Sydney (at Balmain) can only accept ships up to 44 000 deadweight-tonnes (dwt). Port Kembla is marginally better accepting ships up to 58 000 dwt while Gladstone and Hay Point in Queensland can berth 100 000 dwt and 120 000 dwt vessels respectively. The recommendation of the freight study was, somewhat halfheartedly, to locate coal loading facilities capable of handling 120 000 dwt ships at the new Botany Bay port development. This would enable Sydney and New South Wales generally to supply the new steel plants in Japan and Europe which are located on the coast with unloading facilities for 150 000 dwt coal carriers.

This example points out some of the shortcomings of the Sydney Area Transportation Study's approach to the problem of urban freight. The movement of coal within the metropolitan area of Sydney is not a problem. Instead of ensuring that this continues to be the case by recommending that bulk coal movements leave New South Wales from Port Kembla or Newcastle, the recommendation is to divert large quantities of coal almost through the heart of Sydney. In addition the new port development at Botany Bay has serious access limitations to the west because of the location of Mascot airport. In any case movements in and out of the area are not the major cause of the urban freight problem – movements within the area are and these were ignored to a large extent.

But despite these shortcomings the description of the freight system in itself is of value because it clearly defines the structure of the problem.

Road transport operators are either classified as professional carriers or ancillary carriers. Professional carriers, such as Mayne Nickless, T.N.T. and Brambles, operate vehicles for 'hire and reward', while ancillary carriers operate vehicles as an adjunct to their main business (for example the delivery trucks owned by the bakeries). Within the group of professional carriers are the freight forwarders who under a single consignment note and an inclusive rate move freight 'door-to-door'. Freight forwarders normally provide warehousing and terminal facilities and with access to all transport modes can provide a wide range of services. Working for both the professional carriers and the ancillary carriers is a group of owner drivers. These individuals own one or two trucks and work for the carriers; many are permanently sub-contracted to the major freight forwarders. Terminals are required for road transport operators for storage of product, for the consolidation of goods coming from a number of sources, for break bulk (the opposite to consolidation) and for mixing (for example products from many manufacturers arriving at the Safeway distribution centre at Mulgrave in Victoria to be 'mixed' for shipment out to their retail stores). The main industrial axis of the Sydney region is approximately on a line joining Botany to Blacktown with the main concentration of road freight terminals in the Burrows Road, St Peters and Mascot areas. It is expected that future terminal development will take place on the western end of this line. This will allow interstate and intrastate road freight after being consolidated at the terminal during the afternoon to be quickly free of regional congestion. In addition the outer western suburbs provide adequate amounts of land at reasonable prices and removed from residential areas.

Except for several privately owned single-product lines, railways in Australia are owned and operated by government departments. In New South Wales this government body is the Public Transport Commission. Freight moved by rail can be categorized as bulk, expedited volume freight, general freight in less than carload lots and parcel express. Most urban freight is general freight requiring loading and unloading into general purpose rail wagons from rail terminals. Six major rail terminals exist in the Sydney metropolitan area: Darling Harbour, Alexandria, Cooks River, Clyde, Enfield–Chullora and Rozelle. Darling Harbour goods yard is located close to the southern base of the Sydney Harbour bridge. It is the major freight terminal for intrastate general rail freight but its facilities and equipment are outdated and in need of repair. The terminal is congested but the high value and residential zoning of adjacent land makes expansion impossible. In 1947 the Cooks River goods yard was opened to the north-west of Mascot airport in an attempt to alleviate the congestion at Darling Harbour. Poor road and rail access and a shortage of usable land will reduce the effectiveness of this yard particularly when the Botany Bay port development is completed. The Alexandria goods yard just south of the University of Sydney also suffers from a lack of land for future expansion. Its position close to the central business district together with its accessibility to passenger services provide pressure to redevelop the site for different purposes. The fourth terminal at Rozelle is also close to the city centre but it is ideally located to serve as a marshalling yard for the bulk port facilities at White Bay, Glebe Island and Rozelle Bay. Clyde and Enfield terminals are located in the western suburbs of Sydney. Clyde is well suited to retain the present workshops which are in urgent need of rehabilitation and consolidation. Enfield, of the existing terminals, is best suited for development as a major rail–road freight transfer terminal. This is because there exists a large amount of available and suitable land, the site is on the main Sydney to Melbourne highway and close to the main industrial areas and the terminal is located almost in the middle of Sydney's goods-only rail network (linking all six terminals mentioned and extending down to Botany Bay). Railway land of over

50 hectares at Homebush Bay and of over 90 hectares at Yennora provide additional potential for the development of further terminals in Sydney's western suburbs. In general rail terminal development should follow road terminal development in moving westward. The freight study recommended the sale of most of the land on which the Darling Harbour terminal stands, closure of the Alexandria goods yard and the sale of some of the land at Rozelle. Development should occur at Homebush Bay and Yennora as well as the establishment of a rail freight transfer terminal in the Blacktown–St Mary's area. A practical and considerable barrier to such development is that the revenue generated by the sale of railway land does not return to the Public Transport Commission of New South Wales but goes into consolidated revenue for the state, so the Public Transport Commission has no incentive to sell any assets.

Freight transport by sea and air, considered by the Sydney Area Transportation Study, are not discussed here because these modes are of direct concern to interstate and intrastate transportation, not to intracity transportation. The use of pipelines is a feasible option for urban freight delivery – this mode was not examined in the Sydney freight study but will be examined later in this chapter.

The Sydney Area Transportation Study should be praised because it did consider urban freight movements to be worthy of study in addition to passenger movements. But it asked the wrong questions. It ended up looking at interstate and intrastate freight movement instead of intracity freight movements. The magnitude of this mistake was pointed out by Robert Wood of the Tri-State Regional Planning Commission when he established that for one day in one square mile in Brooklyn, New York, 28 trucks were needed to enter or leave the area with the freight required, while 4200 trucks were needed for internal delivery within the area. Failing to consider internal movements is failing to consider most of the problem. For this reason the study failed to provide adequate descriptive data which is but the first step towards tackling the problem. The study also confined itself to unimaginative recommendations involving relatively minor changes to the existing system.

A net effect of the nature of the Sydney freight study is that an adequate up-to-date description of the urban delivery situation in Australia is not available. Ken Ogden has examined the Melbourne

Transportation Study data and developed a description of the characteristics of urban delivery in Melbourne in 1964. Although these data are rather old they at least provide a lower bound to the problem – the situation now is clearly worse than it was then. In Melbourne in 1964 91 000 commercial vehicles (15 per cent of all vehicles registered) made 530 000 trips per day. This is an average of 6 trips per vehicle per day although almost one-tenth of these vehicles made no trips on any given day. The average load for a trip was 0.66 tonnes with 33 per cent of trips being made empty and 5 per cent of trips carrying a full load. Each trip averaged 6 kilometres in length and seventeen minutes duration. The average time spent travelling per day was less than two hours per truck for ancillary carriers and just over three hours for hired vehicles, all trucks covering just over 35 kilometres.

The overall picture generated for urban freight delivery is that it is a small-scale operation with small, single-unit vehicles picking up or delivering relatively few shipments. It is an unco-ordinated and unplanned transportation function although it may be part of a highly planned corporate marketing or production function. This picture of Melbourne in 1964 has intensified for Melbourne of today but presents essentially the same problem. Observation of freight transportation in Sydney and studies of freight movements in New York and Chicago confirm the situation.

Before trying to outline some strategies by which the process of urban freight delivery can operate more effectively it is useful to examine some additional side effects of urban freight movements.

In most cases the interaction of goods and passenger traffic produces detrimental results. This interaction occurs on the streets and highways where passenger vehicles and trucks compete for road space. Most Australian drivers at one time or another have been stuck behind three articulated trucks travelling abreast grinding through their gears. In addition to blocking passenger traffic in this way delivery trucks often load and unload from the kerb, again creating a barrier to passenger vehicle flows. Goods vehicles because of their large size and slow speed reduce the capacity of the roads to handle passenger vehicles.

But goods movement is essential to the existence of any urban area: food, energy and raw materials must flow in, industrial products and waste must flow out and various commodities must flow within the area. The characteristics and capacities of the process of urban goods movement will have a substantial effect on the form that urban development will take. Development of suburban residential areas and regional shopping centres followed the development of efficient means of distribution to these shopping centres and an increased level of mobility in the surrounding residential areas. Changes in urban form will undoubtedly follow future changes in the method of urban goods delivery. It is interesting to contemplate that developments in methods of urban goods delivery may be used as a future policy tool to influence the nature of subsequent urban growth. Facilities for goods transportation have engulfed large areas of prime real estate close to the city centre: Jolimont and Spencer Street railway yards and Victoria Dock in Melbourne and the wharves and railway terminals and sidings around Darling Harbour, Blackwattle Bay, Rozelle Bay, Johnston's Bay, White Bay and Mort Bay in Sydney. As pointed out in the Sydney Area Transportation Study, many of these facilities are not really needed today with the movement of industry away from the city centre together with the efficiencies brought by containerization. Procedural barriers should be removed so that the operating authorities (for example the Public Transport Commission and Maritime Services Board of New South Wales) can dispose of underutilized real estate and re-invest the funds to better use in other parts of the system.

'No single aspect of road transport arouses more ill-feeling than the pounding of houses and the stinking up of streets by heavy lorries. Everyone is affected and most people feel helpless.'[4] While this may be a general overstatement of the situation in Australia it certainly does not overstate the feelings of the residents of Balmain who suffer trucks from the A.N.L. terminal at Mort Bay and the Seatainer Terminals Ltd container berths at White Bay roaring in low gear through their narrow residential streets. Despite the fact that it takes four times the amount of fuel to move a tonne of goods by road than by rail, virtually all urban goods delivery is currently done by road (over 99 per cent in Melbourne in 1964). Until a radical change occurs in the technology of urban freight delivery this will continue to be the case.

The whole process of urban goods flow interacts with many other

complex aspects of urban life. For example the 17½ per cent devalu-
ation of the Australian dollar in November 1976 had repercussions
in the movement of urban goods. Instead of the same volume of imported products moving from the docks to warehouses and on to consumers, fewer products travelled this path while an increased number
of products moved from domestic manufacturers through the distribution channel to the final consumer. It is likely that the urban transportation system as a whole could cope with this change without a
problem although individual specialist carriers might well have felt
the pinch. Changes in the general lifestyle of the community or sizeable swings in consumer preferences can also require adaptation by
the urban goods movement process.

Industrial organizations do have some leeway with their local delivery frequency and speed. Customers do not always perceive delivery
time or the reliability of delivery to be the most important aspects
of customer service. With care the manufacturer or distributor of
the product can substitute other aspects of customer service for delivery speed and reliability without reducing the level of customer satisfaction. An interesting example of this phenomenon was found in
a Monash University study of the Australian scientific instrument
and supplies industry. Six major suppliers and five groups of customers (scientific laboratories in private industry, government departments, secondary schools, universities and hospitals) exist in this
industry. The customers and the suppliers were asked to rank nine
aspects of customer service in order of importance. Table 5.2 shows
the results of this process.

Comparing the suppliers with all the customers considered together reveals some interesting differences. Both groups consider the
general availability of the product to be the most important factor.
But the suppliers consider telephone operations to be next important,
while the customers rank after sales service as second in importance.
Some difference in opinion between the two groups also occurs with
the ranking of technical representatives – ranked third by suppliers
and fifth by customers. Delivery time, delivery reliability, ordering
convenience, equipment demonstrations and the availability of published material all are ranked about the same by both groups.

Further differences occur when the five customer groups are examined separately. Private companies view delivery time and telephone

Table 5.2 Ranked Aspects of Customer Service

Customer Service Element	Suppliers	All customers	Private companies	Government instrumentalities	Secondary schools	Universities and C.A.E.s	Hospitals
Availability of item	1	1	1	5	1	1	1
After sales service and backup	5	2	5	1	7	2	2
Efficient telephone handling of orders and queries	2	6	4	6	4	7	7
Ordering convenience	7	7	8	9	2	6	8
Competent technical representatives	3	5	5	2	8	5	3
Delivery time	5	4	2	6	5	3	5
Reliability of delivery	4	3	3	4	3	4	4
Demonstrations of equipment	8	7	7	3	9	7	5
Availability of published material	9	9	9	8	6	9	8

Source: Gilmour, P. *et al.*, 'Customer Service: Differentiating by Market Segment', *International Journal of Physical Distribution*, Vol. 7, No. 3, 1977, p. 146.

handling as more important and after sales service as less important than do all the customers as a group. Government departments are the only group that did not consider availability to be the most important factor – after sales service was their first choice. Government departments also considered technical representatives and equipment demonstrations to be more important than the customer norm. Telephone operations as well as availability was considered to be less important by this group. Secondary schools considered ordering convenience to be more important, as well as telephone handling and published material to a lesser degree, while after sales service was considered much less important and technical representatives and equipment demonstrations still less important. Universities and colleges of advanced education ranked the nine factors very closely to the overall customer rankings. Hospitals considered technical representatives and equipment demonstrations to be more important.

Laboratories in private companies often perform relatively standard quality control and analysis tasks. This means that it is important to be able to easily obtain regular orders. So delivery time and the ability of the supplier to handle telephone orders efficiently is important and after sales service becomes less important due to the relative infrequency of new instrument purchases.

Government laboratories on the other hand perform a much higher percentage of experimental and research work requiring highly specialized equipment. This makes after sales service as well as equipment demonstrations and the quality of the technical representative much more important. This situation also exists in a large public research-orientated hospital laboratory.

Secondary schools' laboratories are used exclusively for teaching purposes. Standard equipment and supplies are regularly purchased making ordering convenience and telephone relations with the supplier important service factors. Published material allows the science teacher to keep track of current improvements in equipment and new chemicals and supplies.

Laboratories in universities and colleges of advanced education fall between the extremes of the government laboratory and the laboratory in the secondary school. Split teaching and research requirements make a combination of service factors relating to regular and one-off purchases important.

This study shows quite clearly that there is considerable potential for the manufacturer or distributor to examine the service requirements of his customers and to alleviate the local delivery problem by providing high levels of other aspects of customer service as a trade-off for too frequent or underutilized transportation services.

Although urban freight movements are usually considered to involve only the truck leaving the despatch dock of the manufacturer or distributor, making a series of deliveries and returning, the actual process is more complex. It involves the entire order cycle: the time taken for the customer's order to reach the warehouse, the time the order takes to be picked (assembled from the warehouse shelves or racks) and packed and loaded on to the truck, and finally the transportation time itself. This means that more effective urban goods delivery can occur if the transportation time is reduced, but also if order placement time is reduced or if the warehousing operation is streamlined. David Holdings Pty Ltd, a large grocery wholesaler in Blacktown a western Sydney suburb, has chosen to improve urban goods delivery by concentrating on their warehouse operation. David Holdings have built an automated warehouse, an automated 'order picker', which when built was only the third of its kind in the world. The machinery in the warehouse works like a giant vending machine. Set behind it are racks which are filled with palletized bulk products by fork-lift trucks. Individual cartons are then taken from the racks and fed manually into rows of sloping shelves by warehousemen standing on elevated walkways. Each product handled by the warehouse has its own row with an automatically operated gate at the bottom of it. The customer's order is fed into the computerized system and the appropriate gates automatically open allowing the correct items to move on to a conveyor system. All the items on a particular customer's order are automatically directed to a particular packing station where the items are stacked by hand on a pallet and a plastic film is shrunk, by heating, over the pallet load to form a compact unit load. The system can assemble over 4500 cartons per hour which compares rather favourably with the rate of 125 cartons per hour attained by a manual system. As the customer is interested in the total time taken from when the order is placed until it is delivered into his own warehouse, reducing the order assembly stage of the process is just as effective as reducing the amount of time spent by the truck on the street.

By far the most interest in the urban freight problem has centred on making truck movements through inner city areas more efficient, or substituting other movement systems for truck travel. Looking at the problem from the point of view of an economist rather than a manager or an engineer presents another approach. The whole proces is characterized by the interaction of supply and demand: demand for the transportation of goods and supply of transportation services. Reduced congestion and greater efficiency can theoretically be achieved by reducing demand as well as manipulating supply.

But in practice it is rather difficult to reduce the demand for transportation of goods. One possible way is to replace a transportation movement with a 'movement substitute'. This is most easily done with passenger transportation where a trip may sometimes be replaced by improved methods of communication – a multiple link-up telephone conference may replace several trips for the business organization. Better communications may also reduce freight transportation by reducing the volume of mail carried. Electricity with its own transportation system may be considered as a freight substitute for heating-oil and coal – the more energy needs that are satisfied by electricity, the fewer trucks carrying oil and coal will move on the roads. Another way to reduce the demand for transportation of goods is by restructuring the urban area so that the users of urban freight movements are located optimally so that shorter urban freight trips are made with much higher utilization of the vehicles. But this approach is unrealistic except for the case of planning a new city.

Reducing the demand for freight transportation is difficult, changing the conditions under which the transportation is supplied offers far more potential. Various schemes have been proposed for improving the supply of freight transportation services within urban areas. These schemes fall broadly into two categories: improvements using current facilities and conventional technologies which can be implemented in the short term, and long-term improvements which involve replacement or major modification of existing facilities or the application of technology not currently in use.

Short-term proposals involve either better management of urban goods delivery or else the provision of improved loading and unloading facilities. One attempt to manage the freight operation better is to provide 'temporal separation': urban freight deliveries to be made at a time when other urban activity is at a minimum – at night. Night delivery means that the customer must remain open to receive the goods or else a specially secured receiving container must be provided. 'Operation Moondrop' was a large-scale experiment with night delivery of goods in London in the late 1960s. Six warehouses and ninety-five individual stores participated in the experiment. But it was not successful because the low volume and large travel distances together with overtime payments resulted in night deliveries costing one-third more than deliveries during the day. Max Brown of John Danks and Son, a Melbourne hardware wholesaler, does not expect night deliveries to be a feasible option in Australia for several years. The main problem with implementing night deliveries is that the customer has to pay the overtime to keep his premises open at night or else provide a security cage, but he does not receive any direct financial benefit from the reduced transit time at night for the supplier. Night deliveries will be a long time in coming unless some means of allocating the costs of the scheme more equitably between supplier and customer can be devised.

More efficient scheduling of delivery vehicles is another management-based proposal. In 1970 the Organization for Economic Co-operation and Development (O.E.C.D.) held 'policy assessment' discussions on urban goods movements in Paris. Representatives from the United States, Germany and France all confirmed that the major problem with current urban goods movements is the small size and the dispersed origins and destinations of shipments. Re-scheduling in the current context will achieve little, consolidation must occur first.

Robert Wood of the Tri-State Regional Planning Commission (New York, New Jersey and Connecticut) has developed a model which illustrates the considerable benefits to be achieved by consolidation. The inefficiency of the current urban goods delivery process is illustrated rather clearly by comparing the urban region to a huge industrial organization. If this organization operated in a similar fashion to the urban freight process then each foreman would make his own arrangements for delivery of required raw materials and each regional sales manager would arrange for the pick-up of his requirements of finished product at the plant. This is clearly unacceptable for any single organization – both inflows of raw materials and outflows of finished product are consolidated. Why cannot the same be done for urban freight? The urban area would need to be divided into areas with each area having its own terminal. All freight moving within the area or entering the area would have to go to the terminal for sorting and consolidation. Many small vehicles would still be making trips to the terminal, but these trips would be on average much shorter because the long trip by the small partially-loaded truck would be eliminated. Consolidated movements would occur from other areas into the terminal and also from the terminal outwards to other terminals. Wood estimated an overall cost saving of around 12 per cent from such a system together with reduced social costs of air pollution and congestion. The Ministry of International Trade and Industry in Japan is in the process of implementing a plan to construct five large consolidation warehouses on an outer ring road around Tokyo. It is not clear how much coercion will be applied to industry to use these facilities and to reduce the amount of truck traffic in the central city area.

The other changes proposed for urban freight delivery are much more romantic and gain much greater publicity because they involve radical change – new technology or existing technology used in dashing new ways. Of course the probability of any of these proposals being implemented is much smaller. In fact several schemes have been developed in the past only to end in failure for one reason or another. Robert Wood at the 1973 International Physical Distribution Management Conference in Tokyo recounted several of these ventures. For 100 kilometres under the city streets of Chicago runs a narrow-gauge railway built in 1904. This railway was to provide interchange of less-than-carload freight between the fourteen large railway companies serving Chicago at the time. Also included in the system were twenty large individual shippers. Access to the streets above was provided at thirty-eight points by elevators which transferred coal and ashes as well as general freight. The development of the motor truck killed this scheme and no freight has travelled in these tunnels for many years.

Less-than-carload railway freight was also the reason that the Port Authority of New York and New Jersey built a terminal on Manhattan Island in 1932. At the time several railways terminated on the New Jersey shore opposite Manhattan. Each railway floated its freight wagons across the Hudson River on special barges and unloaded them without removing the wagon from the barge. The freight was then transferred to the particular freight terminal owned by the railway. Extensive congestion at the Manhattan waterfront resulted. The Port Authority terminal was to replace the many smaller terminals and enable consolidated shipments to move from the waterfront so reducing congestion and increasing efficiency. But the railways refused to mix their freight with that of their competitors and so the Port Authority terminal was not the success it had planned to be.

Just because these two projects ended in failure does not mean that every other proposal which is a little out of the ordinary will also end in failure. One relatively simple scheme which has its ardent supporters and detractors is the proposal to use the existing urban passenger transportation system for extensive freight movements. Critics of the scheme say that the diverse origins and destinations of freight movements make the use of existing passenger facilities operationally impractical. In addition the extra investment needed to convert the passenger system to a dual-purpose system would be prohibitive, and in any case the capacity of the passenger system is not sufficient to cope with the anticipated freight flows. Those who support the scheme point out that passenger systems operate at far below capacity for most of the time and the additional revenue generated for the system by freight may ease the current financial woes of passenger transit systems.

Researchers at the Melbourne and Metropolitan Board of Works are currently investigating the possibility of establishing a light railway grid at 2-kilometre intervals over the city of Melbourne. Such a railway would be elevated over existing right-of-ways and architecturally submerged into the surrounding environment. Virtually non-polluting and relatively quiet such a system would also be constructed at a much lower cost per kilometre than would a freeway. Very few houses would need to be demolished to make way for this system. The system would operate automatically in dual mode – passengers during the morning and evening peaks and freight movements in between. Automated warehouses, such as David Holdings, could eventually hook their automated warehousing operations into an automated distribution system. Any freight which was too heavy for this system, possibly all full-wagon-load freight, would move on the existing rail network.

Another proposal, based on the concept of spatial separation of urban freight and passenger movements, is for the construction of a network of underground concrete pipelines of about 2 metres in diameter through which urban freight would move between distribution depots and large individual freight shippers. Two versions of this scheme have been considered in Canada: freight moving in standard containers on powered wheeled conveyors through the pipeline and non-containerized but banded freight moving in the same fashion. It is not yet clear whether such proposals are economically feasible and able to compete with the current method of on-ground distribution of freight.

At the O.E.C.D. seminar on urban goods movement mentioned previously, a proposal was put forward by a team from the Prague Institute of Architectural Design for a completely new goods distribution system for a new town Etarea to be located 15 kilometres south of Prague in Czechoslovakia. The plan for this town is based on thirteen housing districts each of approximately 10 000 people. A rapid rail transit system will link the town centre of Etarea and ten of the residential districts with the centre of Prague. Within each district is to be built two distribution centres, one for foodstuffs and medicine and the other for manufactured items and mail. A network of thirty-eight pneumatic pipelines will connect both of these distribution centres to 100 flats in the district. Goods deliveries of a weight up to 4 kilograms can be made at twenty-second intervals through the pipeline. Users of the system, after consulting a catalogue kept in their flat, place an order by telephone and the required items, out of a range of over 600 different items, are delivered within three to twelve minutes. Linking the distribution centres in each of the thirteen districts with a central distribution facility at the centre of Etarea is a system of automatically controlled electric trolleys running underground in a 2-metre tube. Trucks and conventional surface transportation will also be used to link the district centres.

While plans for developments such as Etarea are still far from implementation, even though all the technology needed is already available, the town of Jarva in Sweden does have a rather sophisticated method of solid waste disposal. The system is similar in nature to a giant vacuum cleaner. Each flat connected to the system has a refuse chute which is linked to the main waste delivery pipe by means of a hydraulically operated valve. Several times a day this valve is opened automatically for twenty seconds and refuse in the chute falls into the main pipe where it is sucked away at a speed of 20 metres per second and stored in a silo. The Swedish system costs approximately one per cent of the cost of the flat to install. This system is also an example of spatial separation of freight and passenger transportation when garbage is broadly considered as 'freight'.

If a broad criterion is accepted by which to judge the urban delivery process (such as minimizing jointly the costs to the manufacturer, distributor and consumer as well as the external costs involved) then governmental motivation and direction is needed to achieve efficiency. In a formalized fashion this is shown in Figure 5.1 where the costs incurred by four different parties to the urban delivery

Figure 5.1   Costs and decision making for urban
                freight delivery

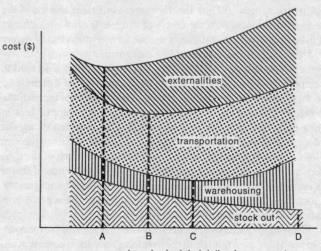

number of scheduled deliveries per week

process are shown. On the horizontal axis or abscissa of the figure
is the number of deliveries made per week, while on the vertical axis
or ordinate is the cost of these deliveries. Goods are sold to the customer f.o.b. destination which means that the delivery charge is hidden in the list price. So the direct cost of delivery to the customer
is the cost to him when he needs the item – to resell or as a raw material
for another product he is making – and he has run out or it has not
yet been delivered. This is the stock-out cost (shown at the bottom
of Figure 5.1) which will decline as the number of deliveries scheduled per week increases. The next party involved is the warehouse
operator. With very few deliveries scheduled per week warehouse
costs will be high due to goods arriving from the factory and remaining in the warehouse for some time until the next delivery. With a
large number of scheduled deliveries a great deal of effort and expense

is spent on picking a larger number of smaller orders. Somewhere in between these extremes is the least costly position for the warehouse operation. The actual transportation operation is next: too few deliveries does not allow for full utilization of the delivery trucks themselves, while many deliveries may require additional trucks and low utilization of truck capacity. Like warehousing the best position for the delivery operation is somewhere between these extremes. Last to be considered is the citizen who suffers from truck congestion, noise and fumes – the costs to him are less with the fewer trucks on the roads and the fewer deliveries being made each week. As shown in Figure 5.1 these costs are accumulated: the stock-out costs are shown at the bottom then to these are added the warehousing costs, then the transportation costs and finally the externalities. The lowest point on the curve which shows all of these costs combined is at A. For the manufacturer who warehouses and delivers his own products the least cost position is at B – somewhat more deliveries would be scheduled each week. If the warehouse operation is considered alone the least cost position is at C – more deliveries – and if only the direct costs to the customer are considered the least cost is at D – even more deliveries. The important point of this illustration is that the customer, the operator, the distributor or the manufacturer left to his own devices will not choose the solution which minimizes the sum of the costs involved by all parties to the urban goods delivery process. In order to achieve this governmental influence must be exerted.

Direct government action cannot achieve this end because such incursions into the decision-making processes of private enterprise would be strongly resisted and in any case the procedures and red tape required for such a scheme would render it impracticable. But more subtle government action can do much to improve urban freight delivery. Trucks moving on arterial roads or freeways should receive priority over passenger cars in a similar manner to buses. But restricted entry to central business districts should operate for trucks. A small number of specified trucks should be allowed to deliver within central business districts and other highly congested industrial areas after consolidation has occurred in one of a ring of special terminals set up for that purpose.

Government action should also occur on other fronts: introducing legislation to ensure that buildings have adequate loading bays;

co-ordinating and encouraging trial projects in night delivery; initiating means of co-ordination between competitive organizations on urban delivery; encouraging research into new technological forms of urban delivery.

Urban freight delivery if inefficiently performed increases the cost of all products. This increase is regressively spread across the community because the lower income earner spends a larger proportion of his income on food and other relatively low-cost essentials which reflect a proportionately high increase in price as a result of increased delivery costs. Congestion, noise and air pollution as a result of urban delivery is also suffered to a greater extent by low-income earners as they cannot afford to move away from the low-cost residential-industrial areas.

Notes

1. Owen, N. J., 'Urban Goods Transport: A Vehicle Operator's Viewpoint', in Ogden, K. W. and Hicks, S. K. (eds), *Urban Goods Movement*, Commonwealth Bureau of Roads, Melbourne, May 1975, p. 75.
2. Ibid, p. 78.
3. Sydney Area Transportation Study, *SATS: Volume 4, Freight Transport Systems*, New South Wales Planning and Environment Commission, Sydney, 1974, p. I-1.
4. Bendixson, T., *Without Wheels*, Indiana University Press, Bloomington, 1974, p. 158.

Chapter 6
Trucks or Trains

The transportation of goods in Australia comprises about 9 per cent of the Gross Domestic Product. Transportation provides place and time utility for goods: goods cannot be consumed or used exactly at the place of manufacture, neither are goods desired by consumers at exactly the same rate as they are made. For an industrialized country with specialized equipment and skills, time and place utility must be provided. But time and place utility in themselves do not add to the basic characteristics of goods or services. A reduction in transportation costs will reduce the cost of providing a product with time and place utility and will reduce the cost of the goods but it will not change its essential nature.

Transportation costs can be reduced most easily by moving large volumes. Loading and unloading can be done much more efficiently if the volume to be moved justifies the use of mechanical materials handling methods and unitized loads. The per unit cost of the main movement (the line-haul) is also much lower if the fixed costs associated with the transportation equipment can be split up among more products. Considerable economies of scale exist in the transportation of goods beyond the city limits.

Australia suffers by comparison with other industrialized western countries from a lack of economies of scale in manufacturing. The same situation also applies with transportation. In order to generate large volumes, the freight forwarders grant considerable discounts in freight rates to the larger shippers. Scheduled door-to-door freight rates per tonne from Sydney to Melbourne are around $70 for normal road service or road–rail container service. One chemical manufacturer with large volumes to ship from Melbourne to Sydney has negotiated freight rates of less than half this amount per tonne. This situation illustrates the considerable disadvantage that the smaller organization operates under in Australia. And most Australian manufacturing organizations are small: 'of the 32 291 "enterprises" engaged in manufacturing in 1968-9, 30 399 of them employed fewer than 100 people (no figures are available later than 1968-9) . . . and collectively they accounted for 32 per cent of employment in manufacturing, and 26 per cent of the value added.'[1]

Further inequities exist between the large organization and the small organization. It is often feasible for the large manufacturer to run his own fleet if he feels he has the management skills required to maintain high utilization of the equipment. The small manufacturer has no such choice, he must use the freight forwarder regardless of the freight rates being charged.

Even among the freight forwarders size brings considerable advantages. Because of its uneven geographical distribution of population Australia has a back-loading problem. This means that the volume of freight generated for movement in one direction exceeds the volume available for the return trip. Even with the most trafficked route between Sydney and Melbourne the amount of road freight generated in Melbourne for shipment to Sydney is 20 per cent greater than the amount generated in Sydney and destined for Melbourne; Melbourne to Brisbane freight exceeds that from Brisbane to Melbourne by 50 per cent; Melbourne to Adelaide is greater than Adelaide to Melbourne by 20 per cent; and the worst situation is to the west – Melbourne to Perth road freight exceeds that coming back from Perth to Melbourne by 85 per cent. This situation often means that small companies (and often large companies also) cannot operate their own trucks as for half of each round trip they would be empty. The four biggest freight forwarders, Mayne Nickless, Thomas Nationwide Transport, Brambles and Ansett Freight Express, with efficient vehicle scheduling and propitious rate-setting, manage to cope with this problem quite adequately. But the smaller freight forwarders and transport companies have been conspicuously unable to cope with the problem. Road operators with one or two trucks typically do not know the true cost of their operation – they compete with the big four on the high-volume leg by offering attractive rates and then find that a return load cannot be found. For the past several years transport companies have been among the first few on the bankruptcy list.

All four of the largest freight forwarders are indigenous companies, but they either started operations before the industry was dominated by a few large operators or else, as with Ansett Freight Express, began as an extension of an already successful transportation-based venture. These companies have been particularly successful – T.N.T. for example controls a huge world-wide operation which includes profitable ventures in the United States. But now the freight forwarding industry is so dominated by these companies that future development is sure to see further consolidation for them and diminished opportunity for any other organizations (particularly if small) to break in.

Rail, like road, has also become the preserve of the large organization. Moving small-volume general freight by rail is a very slow and very costly operation. Economies can be achieved by moving general freight on container unit trains. The goods are loaded or 'stuffed' into the container at the shipper's premises and then delivered by road to the rail terminal where a crane lifts the container from the truck tray and places it directly onto the rail wagon. No time is lost combining the wagons in correct order into a 'train'; when all the rail wagons have a container loaded the train is ready to depart. But of course only the large manufacturing or distributing organizations have at least 20 tonnes of goods (the capacity of a container) to go to one destination at any particular time.

Similar developments have occurred with sea freight. The newer freight shipping methods, such as the roll-on roll-off ship, the container ship, and the L.A.S.H. (lighter aboard ship) all are based on the movement of a large unit load of freight. Air freight has moved more slowly in this direction because of the relatively high cost of transportation. But it is inevitable that an air freight system based on the 20-tonne I.S.O. container will develop.

Methods of line-haul freight movement in Australia have built-in advantages for the large organization and these advantages will continue to increase over time. Is the concentration that will occur in this segment of the transportation system best for Australia?

The magnitude of the long distance freight task can be measured in two ways. Tonnes weight, the first measure, gives an indication of the cargo handling task in terms of quantities which must be loaded, unloaded, stored and delivered. The second measure is obtained by multiplying the weight of the consignment (tonnes) by the distance it travelled (kilometres). Tonne-kilometres, which result, are often preferred as a measure of the transportation task because both the

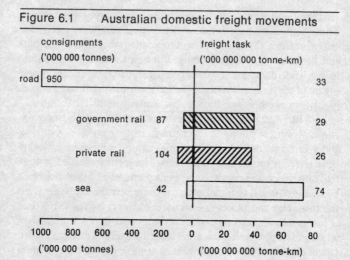

Figure 6.1   Australian domestic freight movements

Source Bureau of Transport Economics, *Transport Outlook Conference, 1975: Papers and Proceedings,* Australian Government Publishing Service, Canberra, 1976, p.38

quantity moved and the length of the haul are reflected. Figure 6.1 shows total domestic freight movements for Australia in 1974–5 measured in both these ways. Road transportation dominates in terms of tonnes carried while sea transportation leads in tonne-kilometres.

There are several interesting characteristics of Australian freight movements that this figure does not bring out. First is the growth in air freight: in terms of tonne-kilometres, air freight has doubled over the past decade, but its total share of the freight transportation task is still less than one-tenth of one per cent. Another interesting feature has been the phenomenal expansion of the private railway sector. Ten years ago private railways carried far less than one-tenth of the freight carried by the public railway system, now private rail carries a quarter more tonnes and has almost equalled the public system in tonne-kilometres performed. This extremely rapid growth is primarily due to the iron-ore railways in Western Australia and South Australia. Details of the growth of all modes are given in Table 6.1.

Table 6.1a Analysis of Freight Transportation in Australia by Mode, 1950-75

Year ending 30 June	Public rail	Private rail*	Road	Sea	Air	Total
	Thousand million tonne-kilometres					
1950	10.9	0.4	8.2	16.1	0.03	35.6
1960	12.9	0.5	13.3	30.3	0.05	57.1
1965	18.0	0.6	17.4	41.5	0.06	77.6
1970	23.6	9.2	24.9	65.0	0.09	122.8
1975†	29.0	26.0	33.0	74.0‡	0.10	162.1
	Percentage of total					
1950	30.6%	1.0%	23.1%	45.2%	0.1%	100.0%
1960	22.6%	0.9%	23.3%	53.1%	0.1%	100.0%
1965	23.1%	0.8%	22.4%	53.6%	0.1%	100.0%
1970	19.2%	7.5%	20.3%	52.9%	0.1%	100.0%
1975†	17.9%	16.0%	20.4%	45.6%‡	0.1%	100.0%

Table 6.1b Analysis of Freight Transportation in Australia by Mode

Year ending 30 June	Public rail	Private rail*	Road	Sea	Air	Total
	Million tonnes					
1965	59.3	4.7	440.0	23.4	0.1	527.5
1970	75.5	37.2	700.0	32.5	0.1	845.2
1975	87.0	104.4	950.0	42.0	0.1	1183.5
	Percentage of total					
1965	11.2%	0.9%	83.4%	4.5%	0.0%	100.0%
1970	8.9%	4.4%	82.8%	3.9%	0.0%	100.0%
1975	7.4%	8.8%	80.2%	3.6%	0.0%	100.0%

*Includes only iron ore railways in South Australia and Western Australia and the Emu Bay Railway in Tasmania.

†Preliminary estimates.

‡New series commencing 1971-2; not strictly comparable with earlier estimates.

Source: P. J. Rimmer, 'The Australian Transport Industry: Its Changing Structure, Content and Performance', in P. Gilmour (ed.), *Proceedings of 1977 Physical Distribution Seminar*, Monash University, Melbourne, February 1977.

Because of the unusual population concentration in the capital cities of Australia freight movements between capital cities take on particular significance. Table 6.2 shows the percentage share of the transportation task for road, rail and sea between each of the five mainland capital cities. (Most freight to Darwin and Hobart is by sea, and Canberra receives twice as much freight by rail as by road.) The table shows that excluding Perth road and rail rather evenly split the inter-capital city movements with the exception of a few routes such as Sydney to Adelaide, Adelaide to Brisbane and Brisbane to Melbourne where road is the dominant mode. Traffic from Perth to the Eastern States was dominated by sea transportation in 1971-2. This situation will have changed quite significantly with the collapse of container services from Fremantle to the Eastern States in 1976 with containerized freight switching to rail.

Control of overseas transportation, of transportation to, from and within the territories and of interstate transportation is given to the federal government by the Australian Constitution. Regulation of transportation within the state boundaries is the responsibility of the individual states. Over the years this situation has allowed railway systems operating on different gauged tracks to develop in adjoining states while regulations for road haulage also differ significantly between the states. Further complications arise because of the difficulties individual states have had in adequately financing transportation requirements when the major revenue generating capacity has rested with the federal government.

While the Australian government has had the Constitutional prerogative to regulate freight it has chosen to do so only for sea and air movements. Trans-Australia Airlines as the Australian government-owned carrier operates over competitive routes with comparable flightline equipment to its sole privately-owned competitor Ansett Airlines of Australia under conditions of the two-airline policy laid down by the *Airlines Agreement Act 1952* and the *Airlines Equipment Act 1958*. Similar controlled competition exists between the Australian government-owned merchant service, the Australian National Line and the private shipping companies under the *Australian Coastal Shipping Agreement Act 1956*.

The Whitlam Labor government when in office from 1972 to 1975 did attempt to extend its right to regulate interstate movements by

Table 6.2   Analysis by Mode of Transportation of General Freight Between
Mainland Capital Cities, 1971-2 (Tonnes, percentage)

From	To: *Melbourne*	*Sydney*	*Adelaide*	*Brisbane*	*Perth*
Melbourne					
Road	–	61%	42%	44%	9%
Rail	–	34%	48%	20%	37%
Sea	–	5%	10%	36%	53%
Sydney					
Road	58%	–	84%	48%	3%
Rail	35%	–	16%	44%	30%
Sea	7%	–	0%	8%	67%
Adelaide					
Road	36%	56%	–	69%	14%
Rail	52%	17%	–	31%	78%
Sea	12%	27%	–	0%	8%
Brisbane					
Road	57%	46%	59%	–	9%
Rail	14%	45%	20%	–	11%
Sea	29%	9%	21%	–	80%
Perth					
Road	7%	6%	10%	0%	–
Rail	3%	5%	24%	3%	–
Sea	90%*	88%	66%	97%	–

*Use of container movements accounts for 42 per cent.

Source: Adapted from *Transport Outlook Conference 1975*, Bureau of Transport Economics, Australian Government Publishing Service, Canberra, 1976, pp. 177-9.

road and rail. During this period the *Australian National Railway Act 1975* was passed which replaced the Commonwealth Railways with the Australian National Railways Commission, which was given the task of consolidating all the various state railway operations into a single system: the railway in Tasmania and the non-metropolitan sections of the South Australian railway took advantage of the federal offer and transferred, while Queensland, New South Wales, Victoria and Western Australia (all under non-Labor governments at the time) chose not to join an Australia-wide system. To facilitate road movements the *National Roads Act 1974* formed the basis of a nine-year

construction programme to build a National Highways System linking all capital cities with each other and with other industrial centres.

But the key to the Whitlam government's plans for firmer control
over interstate road and rail transportation came unstuck in November 1975. When the Governor-General removed the Whitlam government from office a Bill for an Act to re-establish the Inter-State
Commission was under consideration by the Australian Parliament.
Section 101 of the Constitution makes provision for an Inter-State
Commission.

There shall be an Inter-State Commission, with such powers of ad-
judication and administration as the Parliament deems necessary for
the execution and maintenance, within the Commonwealth, of the
provisions of this Constitution relating to trade and commerce, and
of all laws thereunder.[2]

Such a commission was in fact set up, and sat from 1913 to 1920.
The Whitlam government intended the three-man commission to
have wide powers to investigate interstate trade and commerce with
the Act making it unlawful to 'give to any person, state, locality or
class or kind of transport any preference or advantage; subject any
particular person, state, locality, or class or kind of transport to any
discrimination or disadvantage'.

These powers certainly would have made the commission capable
of making significant changes in Australia's transportation system.
Centralized legal and executive capability would have been provided
to add to existing centralized financial power to enable the federal
government to establish and implement an effective National Transport Plan. But this did not happen and the major control over transportation still lies with the individual states.

Preservation of traffic for the railways was the basis for regulation
of road transportation as early as the 1930s although some early
credence was given to the need to prevent monopolistic practices.
All forms of regulation were suspended during a nationwide rail strike
at the beginning of 1949. This provided road transport with a vital
chance to penetrate the rail freight market – many road carriers began
operations during the strike and even when taxes were reimposed
at the end of the strike much of the traffic stayed with road due to
the faster and more reliable service. Given their increased strength

the road haulage industry mounted an attack against restrictive legislation. In the case of Hughes and Vale versus the State of New South Wales in 1954 the Judicial Committee of the Privy Council ruled in favour of the transport company and freed all forms of interstate transportation in Australia from regulation except for a carefully established charge for the use of the roads (0.17 cents per tonne-kilometre based on the tare weight plus 40 per cent of the vehicle's registered carrying capacity). This left the states with only intrastate traffic to regulate. A prominent aim in the legislation has been co-ordination – in general terms this means that regulations should result in transportation services being provided at minimum cost in terms of total resources required.

The exact nature of regulation of road competition against state-owned railway systems varies to some degree between states. It is of interest to look further at this type of regulation in Victoria because it has recently been investigated by the Board of Inquiry into the Victorian Land Transport System (chaired by Sir Henry Bland) and also by Susan Wheeler in a Master of Administration thesis at Monash University. Under the direction of the Victorian Transport Regulation Board, road hauliers are allowed the following licences, permits and rights:

'As of right' licences are granted more or less automatically for primary producers, decentralized industries, and specified items such as bulk petroleum, fruit and vegetables on a state-wide basis. These licences are also granted for the pick-up area of dairy factory vehicles, for an ancillary operator within an 80 kilometre radius of his place of business, for hire and reward operators within a 40 kilometre radius of the G.P.O. in Melbourne and the P.O. in Ballarat, Bendigo, and Geelong and 48 kilometres of their place of business.

Discretionary or 'D' licences permit the carriage of goods by road which are regarded by the T.R.B. as non-competitive or inadequately provided for by rail transport. The main categories permitted on a state-wide basis include marine goods, contractors equipment, cars and refrigerated traffic. Other categories under 'D' licences include regular services from Melbourne and Geelong to non-rail areas.

Permits allow a considerable volume of goods to move between Melbourne and Geelong and the commercial movement of wool within an 80 kilometre radius of Portland including places on the Mt Gambier-Hamilton road and those to the north which are 32 kilometres from a railway station. The permits are also granted without question for some products such as bricks and roofing tiles, glazed doors and timber windows on a state-wide basis, superphosphates within 160 kilometres of Melbourne, Geelong and Portland and drummed petroleum products within 258 kilometres of Melbourne.

Section 92 of the Constitution extends freedoms for road operators. The effect of section 92 was to restrict the area of regulation to within a 160-kilometre radius of Melbourne with the exception of longer hauls to Gippsland, the Western District, and the northwest of the state.

Despite this quite elaborate regulatory structure Susan Wheeler estimated that less than 10 per cent of the freight volume moved by Victorian industry came under its control. Indeed most unusual and irregular means were used to avoid control. One means is by what is called 'border hopping': road carriers delivering from Melbourne to towns near the border either actually or supposedly cross the border into New South Wales or South Australia returning to Victoria to make the delivery – this then becomes an interstate trip not subject to control. An interesting aside of this system is its effect on rail rates. Table 6.3 taken from the Bland Report shows that rail rates per tonne and per tonne-kilometre (per bale and per bale-kilometre in the example used for wool shipments) decline markedly towards the state border. Ron 'Spot' Hutton for the past ten years has applied to the Transport Regulation Board for a permit to deliver groceries from Melbourne to Lakes Entrance. Each time the T.R.B. has disallowed his application, but despite this he has made the trips anyway. His

Table 6.3   Freight Rates by Rail for Wool

Location	Distance from Melbourne	Cost per bale	Cost per bale-km
Seymour	98 km	$1.20	$0.0122
Benalla	195 km	$1.60	$0.0082
Wangaratta	235 km	$1.40	$0.0060
Wodonga	301 km	$1.20	$0.0040

Source: Report of the Board of Inquiry into the Victorian Land Transport System, Government Printer, Melbourne, 1972, p. 105.

justification is time and money: he can deliver the goods for $25 a tonne as against $56 a tonne for rail to Bairnsdale and then road to Lakes Entrance; his service is much faster. 'The rail service to Bairnsdale is shocking. Last year, Lakes Entrance ran out of beer for the first time. I just couldn't let that happen this year.' In future to avoid the wrath of the T.R.B. Spot Hutton intends to set up as an interstate operator with a depot in Bombala, New South Wales. An extra 440 kilometres will be involved travelling from Melbourne to Lakes Entrance via Bombala but 'even with all the extra distance, it'll still be far cheaper and more efficient than using rail'.

South Australia phased out this type of regulation in 1968 and New South Wales followed in 1974. In December 1976 the Victorian Minister for Transport announced that Victoria also will phase out the regulation of rail-road competition within the next five years. The general trend is toward de-regulation in this area and the effects on the railways have proven to be not as catastrophic as expected. After analysing the situation in South Australia four years after de-regulation, Susan Wheeler and Peter Gilmour drew these conclusions:

Firstly, the amount of traffic that is regulated is so small that the costs of enforcing the legislation must come close to the benefits accruing to the railways.

Secondly, the railways should concentrate on interstate and contract movements. These have far more profit potential than short, country hauls. However, as the railways are needed to do much of this low-profit work, they should be subsidized for their community service.

Finally de-regulation seems to be the prod that is necessary to make the railways become cost conscious and more efficient. It is unfortunate that this is so, but too many years of monopoly seem to have left their mark.[3]

Regulation of the competition between road and rail is but one of the five types of regulation of freight described by John Taplin, then Director of the Bureau of Transport Economics, and two of his staff in the book *Physical Distribution Management in Australia*. They classified regulations to perform these functions:

(a) Control of entry to the industry: two airline policy; licensing of road operators.

(b) Achieve and maintain operational safety: licensing of drivers,

pilots and masters; vehicle standards; navigation laws and road rules.
(c) Protect amenity and environment: weight and height limits; restriction on carriage of dangerous goods; operational curfews.
(d) Protect the user: common carrier obligations; legal liability; insurance regulations.
(e) Influence the distribution of traffic: co-ordination taxes; permit systems.

While regulation is aimed at changing certain characteristics of the transportation operation it cannot alleviate many of the problems caused by Australia's demography and geography.

Australia is a country which is characterized by a range of quite different transportation problems in moving goods between regions: high-volume routes between Sydney and Melbourne; cross-water routes between Tasmania and the mainland; long, low-volume routes between the east and west coasts.

Sydney and Melbourne are cities of approximately equal size and with similar industrial characteristics, but despite this there is some imbalance in traffic flows between the two cities. During 1974–5 over 2000 million tonnes of freight moved between Sydney and Melbourne with almost two-thirds of it travelling by road. Given the rather poor condition of the Hume Highway linking the two cities, particularly in southern New South Wales, and the fact that the cost of moving freight by road is at least as great as the cost of moving it by rail, it is interesting to examine what does influence the choice of mode for freight between Sydney and Melbourne.

In 1974 the Commonwealth Bureau of Roads carried out an extensive investigation of the possibility of re-routing a portion of the Hume Highway so that it passed closer to Canberra. Any development of the road link between Sydney and Melbourne is of course dependent upon the expected future split of freight and passenger traffic between road and rail. Part of the Bureau of Roads investigation was a study done by Peter Gilmour of the modal choice decision for freight – why road or rail is chosen for movements of freight between Sydney and Melbourne. Until recently the freight rate charged by the professional carrier or the cost to the company of providing its own transportation has been considered to be the prime criterion for freight modal choice. But as already pointed out road traffic has dominated Sydney to Melbourne freight movements (64 per cent of the total in 1974-5 as against 23 per cent for rail) despite the fact that the cost of going by road is at least as much as by rail. So some other factors must play an important part in the decision. To investigate this a representative sample of forty large organizations were asked to participate in the study. Decisions on many matters in large organizations are made on the basis of factors which are perceived by the decision maker to be important. In order to generate these factors for the method of choice for freight, the participants in the study were asked, without any prompting, to list all the factors they normally considered before making a decision to send Melbourne-Sydney freight by their own road transport, by normal road service with a freight forwarder, by express 'overnight' road service with a freight forwarder, by containerized unit train, by normal rail freight, by sea or by air. Many factors were given with the ten most frequently mentioned being in order: cost; delivery time; product characteristics; size of shipment; services provided by the carrier; availability of particular equipment; packaging requirements; product damage; urgency; and, regularity of service. Although cost was mentioned by all respondents, not all placed it within the top five most important factors. Freight can move between Melbourne and Sydney in the seven ways listed above. As the next step in the study participants were asked to rank each of the possible pairs of ways (forty-two in number) on the basis of how similar they were to each other. Methods of analysis called non-metric multidimensional scaling and cluster analysis were used on these data resulting in groupings of modes by similarity and groupings of decision-making factors by importance. The result of the study was that the direct cost of the transportation service is not among the most important determinants of the modal choice for freight shipped Melbourne-Sydney. Important determinants are the ability to control the shipment, availability of specialized equipment and reliability. These characteristics of freight movements do favour road over rail, air or sea and the result of the study is consistent with the actual split of freight traffic.

Roughly mid-way between Melbourne and Sydney and reaching westwards from the Hume Highway is the Riverina, a rich agricultural area growing a variety of grain crops (importantly wheat, rice, barley and oats), soft fruits for canning and livestock. The choice of method of transportation to move these products out of the region and to move general goods, petroleum products, fertilizer and building materials in, is somewhat different from that for Melbourne–Sydney freight.

The Riverina is in New South Wales although the nearest port is Melbourne. While restrictions on intrastate trade imposed under the N.S.W. State Transport (Co-ordination) Act were in operation (these restrictions were removed in 1974) road transport developed a series of interstate transportation options. Freight into the Riverina is only about one-third of that out of the region; however, considerable quantities of fertilizer are shipped in from Sydney and Port Kembla by road. Road hauliers operate what is called the 'Wagga triangle': Wagga Wagga (or the Riverina more generally) to Melbourne with grain, livestock and canned fruit; Melbourne to Sydney with a variety of freight, taking advantage of the favourable imbalance in road freight volume in this direction; and finally Sydney or Port Kembla back to the Riverina with fertilizer. Operating in this manner the road carriers were able to keep the freight rate on the Riverina–Melbourne leg below the rate by rail. Other road operations included the 'Griffith/Leeton Ricochet' – grain from the area around Griffith and Leeton delivered to Geelong with the return trip to Dubbo – and the 'Portland Drop' – products from the western portion of the Riverina delivered to the port at Portland.

Rail movements south involve an intersystem arrangement between the Public Transport Commission of N.S.W. and the Victorian Railways; freight is carried subject to the rates and conditions of the Railways of Australia. Railways of Australia Intersystem Distance Rates are less than the sum of the rates applied by the individual state rail systems to their segments of the journey. But these rates do not apply to the wool, coarse grains and fresh fruit shipped out of the Riverina – these products when carried by rail mostly go to N.S.W. ports on an intrastate movement.

For coarse grains, wool and fertilizer, price was the important factor as these products move by road. Wheat is marketed by the Australian Wheat Board which has firmly established arrangements with the railways. Contract rates with the railways have also been negotiated for rice, fruit and vegetables; shippers of these products also like the express train service to Sydney to meet the Sydney markets. Livestock shippers preferred rail because of speed, reliability and less damage. From this examination of freight movements into and out of the Riverina it is apparent that price plays an important part in the modal choice for the freight movements to port for export products. But even so this is product dependent – for some products other characteristics of the trip are more important than a slightly higher price.

A completely different transportation situation exists for Tasmania. With no land links to any other states, Tasmania suffers particular hardships: sea transport for general freight is slower and more expensive than shipment by road or rail, although this is not the case for bulk movements. But the Tasmanian economy is small and small shipments of freight are typically generated (Hobart generates only about 3 per cent of the total freight moving between Australian capital cities). For low-density cargoes the Bureau of Transport Economics, in their assessment of Tasmania's transportation problems, estimated that the disadvantage of sending the goods by sea instead of by road or rail could be as high as $25 per tonne. Most classes of goods suffered a $1 to $5 per tonne disadvantage but bulk cargo shipments suffered no financial disadvantage. However, not all this disadvantage is due to the sea line-haul, as the portion of the freight rate due to the line-haul movement is just over half, terminal costs and wharfage charges paid to the ports each contributing about a quarter. So some potential for reducing costs lies in each of these three directions.

In order to evaluate the efficiency of existing line-haul sea operations between Tasmania and the mainland for non-bulk freight, the Bureau of Transport Economics established a model of a hypothetical 5000 dwt roll-on roll-off vessel (similar to that under consideration by the Australian National Line and the Union Steamship Company and viewed as close to the best for the Tasmanian trade). If this vessel were in use on 150 round voyages between Melbourne and Northern Tasmania per year carrying 700 000 tonnes (70 per cent of capacity) the cost per tonne for the shipping companies could be reduced by between $1 and $2. In addition to inadequate vessels the cross-subsidization of passenger traffic by freight rates is also contributing to A.N.L.s financial problems on the Tasmanian trade.

Terminal costs are high because of over-investment and under-utilization of non-bulk cargo facilities. Too many ports operate in Tasmania (for example the Bureau of Transport Economics determined that the cargo moving through the five roll-on roll-off ports in northern Tasmania could adequately be handled by only two) and freight forwarders feel obliged to maintain depots at them all despite the small volume, and this pushes up the freight rates.

Wharfage or port charges are also high because of under-utilization. Also no incentive exists to reduce these charges: shipping lines set a uniform inclusive freight rate to the northern ports which includes the highest charges levied by any port. This means that the only way open for any port to attract larger volumes is to invest more heavily in facilities. The result is a circular process pushing up the freight rates.

Tasmania does have a transportation problem, but Bass Strait is only one of a number of causes. More efficiency could be obtained by reducing the number of ports, reducing the frequency of service, (a larger vessel carrying 10 000 tonnes could cope with the northern Tasmania trade with two round trips per week), introducing newer more efficient vessels and removing the financial burden of subsidized passenger travel. Then the argument that Tasmania suffers unfairly because its interstate freight does not travel by government subsidized (in terms of meeting operating losses) rail or government subsidized (in terms of the carrier not meeting the full cost of road wear and tear) road has some validity. Although it must be remembered that the government covers any operating deficits generated by A.N.L.

A situation similar in many respects to that in Tasmania exists with the movement of general freight between the eastern states and Western Australia. While the one effective mode for Tasmania is sea, for Western Australia it is rail - interstate container services from Fremantle were cancelled in 1976 and freight rates by road are not competitive. The considerable length of the trip together with the severe imbalance of shipments have made for difficulties in the industrial development of Western Australia. Many manufacturers treat the West as a 'special case'. This means that if there was not some sense of importance attached to having national distribution of a company's products, if profit alone was the deciding factor, then Western Australia would be cut off. In line with the current movement to centralize distribution activities a manufacturer may distribute to all parts of the country from a single warehouse in Sydney - with the exception of Western Australia. Separate warehousing facilities will be set up in Perth because the volumes are low and freight rates are less if full wagon loads move. This requires consolidation in Perth.

Another strategy tried occasionally is to locate a manufacturing plant in Perth. This works quite well if the local demand is sufficient to absorb the productive capacity of the plant as is the case with Brisbane and Wunderlich, producers of metal, clay, porcelain and plastic products for the building trade. But the strategy is not so successful if a prime reason for locating in the West is to take advantage of the back-loading problem out of Western Australia and achieve low freight rates back to the eastern states – freight rates may be lower in this situation but the total transportation cost certainly is not.

Characteristics of freight flows between Sydney and Melbourne, across Bass Strait and to the West underscore some of the transportation difficulties which must be faced daily for the country to operate its economy. These difficulties are unique in degree to Australia – no other country has the vast areas together with few densely concentrated population centres. But the problems do not end with the line-haul movement.

Because Australian centres of population are widely spread, difficulties occur in line-haul transportation and because these population centres themselves (particularly Sydney and Melbourne) are so large difficulties of access arise. The problems involved with transportation access to the freight demands of large urban areas turned out to be the prime consideration of the freight investigation by the Sydney Area Transportation Study. Of the forty recommendations (seven for road operations, eighteen for rail operations, eleven for sea and four for air freight) only five of the recommendations concerning road freight operations were directly related to the problem of urban freight delivery, the remaining thirty-five recommendations were primarily concerned with improving access of transportation vehicles which were moving goods in and out of the investigation areas.

Gaining adequate access to the cities for long distance freight can easily raise politically sensitive issues. One example of such a situation is the planned development by the Melbourne Harbor Trust of Webb Dock located in Hobson's Bay at the mouth of the Yarra River. At the present coastal trade, particularly roll-on roll-off shipping but also containerized freight, is concentrated at Webb Dock. This traffic is planned to remain but in addition overseas container movements are expected to increase. Swanson Dock further upstream with four berths for cellular container ships and two additional berths currently being dredged is the main overseas container handling facility for the Port of Melbourne. But by 1985 it is expected that Swanson Dock will have reached capacity and that Webb Dock will have taken over as the Port's major facility. Webb Dock currently has four berths, three for coastal cargoes and one for overseas cargoes; a fifth berth is under construction, and further reclamation of land into Hobson's Bay is taking place to enable additional expansion.

L.C.L. containers (less-than-full container load) are moved from the dock to depots by road. The depots are typically along Footscray Road on the other side of the Yarra, a trip up Williamstown Road in Port Melbourne, across the Yarra at the Spencer Street Bridge and then back down the Footscray Road. Containers which are to go to Adelaide (Adelaide does not have container facilities and is serviced from Melbourne) or to country areas of Victoria must be delivered by truck to the Montague rail yards in Port Melbourne or to Freightbases, the container terminal operation, at East Swanson Dock. Any full containers (F.C.L.) destined for the metropolitan area are delivered direct by road. Three-quarters of the container movements from Webb Dock are made by road with Australian Motor Industries in Port Melbourne generating heavy traffic on Williamstown Road and Motor Producers in Clayton generating heavy traffic around the adjoining seafront on the Boulevard and Beach Road – both these organizations import Japanese cars through Webb Dock.

All traffic to and from Webb Dock must pass through a suburb called Garden City which is part of the municipality of Port Melbourne. (See Figure 6.2.) Port Melbourne, because of the port facilities and other industrial sites, and because of its relative isolation between Port Phillip Bay and the Yarra River, has developed as a closely knit community regarded by outsiders with a relatively negative image. Garden City is a more recently settled residential area of Port Melbourne originally named Fishermen's Bend.

It is a pleasant bay-side area planned and developed during the 1930s and 1940s by the State Savings Bank and, more recently, the Housing Commission. The street lay-out and subdivision design which retains extensive open space

Figure 6.2 Map of the Port Melbourne area

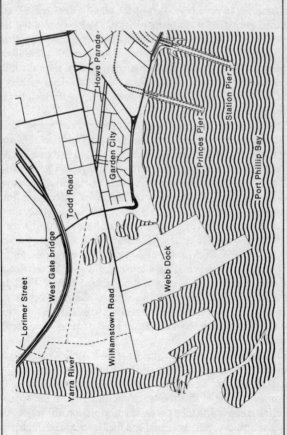

Source *Melway Street Directory of Greater Melbourne*, Melway Publishing Pty. Ltd. Malvern 1977. Map 56

reflects the use of advanced and thoughtful design concepts in a residential area.[4]

The impact of Webb Dock traffic through this area is already considerable and with the anticipated expansion of activity at the dock it is expected to get worse. Part of the plan for the area, issued and modified periodically since the early 1950s, has been a rail link to Webb Dock. A rail link already exists to the neighbouring Princess and Station Piers and one alternative is to extend this line along the seafront to Webb Dock. Another alternative is to have the rail link travel a more direct route down Howe Parade, the main street of Garden City. Finally the line could follow the Yarra through land with current heavy industrial use.

Several alternatives also exist to improve the efficiency and environmental impact of road traffic to and from Webb Dock. Currently most of the road traffic uses Williamstown Road to the railheads and container depots and one alternative is to upgrade the condition of Williamstown Road. All other alternatives effectively remove the Dock traffic from Williamstown Road: two alternatives involve minor road extensions and alterations (extending Lorimer Street to the lower part of Williamstown Road and constructing a curve in Todd Road where it enters Williamstown Road); two additional alternatives feed Dock traffic eastward onto the approaches to the West Gate bridge. For all four alternatives Williamstown Road will be closed to traffic just east of Webb Dock, so forcing Dock traffic to use existing roads much to the north of Garden City or to use the freeway connections to the West Gate bridge. In all cases relatively easy access to the new Johnson Street bridge (when completed) and the western suburbs is provided.

The Centre for Environmental Studies at Melbourne University examined the problem and evaluated all alternatives including several options of submerging underground the proposed rail link along the seafront. First the evaluation was done in terms of the economics of each alternative and then the noise and vibration impact, the visual impact and landscaping potential and finally the social impact to the community were added to the analysis. The Centre concluded that a direct road link to the approaches of the West Gate bridge together with a surface rail link along the Boulevard were the best alternatives. Some hesitation was expressed about the willingness of the West Gate

Bridge Authority and the Country Roads Board to agree to the road proposal and the rail recommendation was hedged with the comment that 'the surface rail proposal is worth public consideration'.[5] According to the study careful landscaping could enable the rail link to be built and at the same time even increase public utilization of the beach front. Acceptance of the alternatives proposed would remove the major burden of freight movements to and from Webb Dock from the residential area of Garden City and yet would not involve major relocation problems.

Access to Webb Dock does not present the problems that exist at Balmain in Sydney but still almost thirty years have passed without direct action being taken to improve the situation. The history of Webb Dock merely points out how difficult it has become to arrive at a solution to the problem of handling urban freight which affects so many individuals and organizations with such diverse interests.

Road has one great advantage over other modes of freight transportation – flexibility of movement. It is relatively easy for a truck to provide door-to-door service. If heavy inner-city congestion forces the use of regional consolidation and distribution centres on the road operator this advantage will be lost, but such a change does not appear likely to happen in Australia in the near future. Of course it is possible for the other modes to provide door-to-door service. Unilever (Australia) Pty Ltd, for example, has established a network of distribution warehouses which are leased from the railways and are located on railway land. Rail provides a door-to-door service. But such a situation is unusual; more common is the situation of H. J. Heinz Co. Australia Ltd where a main railway line runs right behind their Dandenong property but all shipments are made by road. A partial cause for this is that the individual company has to outlay the entire cost of building a siding, no contribution is made by the railway. Door-to-door delivery is virtually impossible with a single sea or air movement – some form of road transportation is needed at each end of the line-haul.

Virtually all rail, sea and air movements require transfer from road transportation at the beginning and transfer to road again at the end of the trip. Also with many long-distance road movements the goods have to be transferred from the large articulated truck to a smaller vehicle for pick-up and delivery. Unless this transfer between modes can be made efficiently with minimum lost time the cost advantage from volume line-haul movement can easily be lost. Efficient intermodal freight transfer has become a prime concern of the transportation industry.

One way to perform this intermodal transfer efficiently is to use containers. Containers most commonly come in two sizes which were laid down at the June 1967 International Standards Organization (I.S.O.) Agreement on Containers: 8 ft x 8 ft x 20 ft (2.4 m x 2.4 m x 6 m) and 8 ft x 8 ft x 40 ft (2.4 m x 2.4 m x 12 m). But in a number of ways these standard sizes do not suit the domestic freight situation in Australia. Coastal shipping services had already developed container sizes to suit their own particular purposes and operations: Australian National Line, Bulkships Ltd, Union Steamship Co. of New Zealand Ltd and William Holyman and Sons Pty Ltd all use special-sized containers as well as I.S.O. ones. The I.S.O. container proved to be even more of a problem with the Australian road transport industry. Australia has been in the fortunate position in the past of having one standard pallet size 46 in x 46 in (1165 mm x 1165 mm). One considerable disadvantage was that two Australian standard pallets side by side would not fit into an I.S.O. container. With metrication this has led to the adoption of another standard pallet size, the 1120 mm x 1120 mm which will enable two pallets to fit inside an I.S.O. container. The hope is that in time the metric equivalent of the old 46 in x 46 in pallet will be completely replaced by the 1120 mm x 1120 mm. But this hope probably will not be fulfilled. Two 46 in x 46 in pallets fit nicely within the 2.5-metre maximum road vehicle width allowed in all states and the Northern Territory. Also the new R.A.C.E. (Railways of Australia Container Express) service originated by the Public Transport Commission of N.S.W. operates with 2.5-metre wide containers instead of the I.S.O. dimension of 2.4 m. There is the obvious advantage of using I.S.O. containers – products imported in I.S.O. containers in cellular container ships can move straight through to the receiver's premises without rehandling. But replacing the 46 in x 46 in pallet is not an easy task. Most companies in Australia have developed costly and extensive warehousing systems based on the old 46 in x 46 in pallet. From an individual company point of view the vast expense needed to replace or modify this system is not worth the slight benefit obtained from not having to unload imported I.S.O. containers at the container depot.

Containerization does offer the potential of economies of scale, but there are some traps to its use in Australia. A 12-metre I.S.O. container imported from Europe into Australia full but returned empty (as is most often the case in Australia) incurs handling charges of over $600 or an addition to the cost of the imported cargo of about $20 per tonne.

Transportation costs for an operation which is containerized will be lower than for a non-containerized system. Packaging requirements will also be less costly. But balanced against these savings will be the additional inventory cost of dealing in large volumes as well as the capital required for the materials handling equipment needed for containers. For most companies in Australia volumes are not large enough to justify containerization. Freight forwarders may have continued success in generating smaller shipments which are then consolidated into containers for the line-haul movement, but it is extremely unlikely that the projection by the National Materials Handling Bureau of a considerable increase in the use of 12-metre containers and of 80 per cent of non-bulk goods travelling between Australian capital cities in containers by 1984 will eventuate.

Neither are containers free from union problems. The Transport Workers Union and the Waterside Workers Federation in Sydney are in dispute over who has the right to load containers onto trucks in the port area. A member of the Federated Clerks Union must be present at the direct delivery of a container from the port unless the receiver's own staff unload it. Freightbases operate the container terminal right behind Swanson Dock East in the Port of Melbourne. But separating the dock and the terminal is a road. The Transport Workers Union insist that they transport the containers across the road although the Waterside Workers Federation carry out the rest of its trip to the depot.

Containerization is certainly one way to cope with the intermodal freight transfer problem in Australia but it is not the universal panacea once thought. The decision to containerize is difficult, one that involves a large commitment to high volumes and large capital costs, and a decision once taken is costly to reverse.

How have some of the other modes handled the intermodal freight transfer problem?

Railways in Australia have a long history of trying to encourage freight forwarders to place a sizeable portion of their business on rail. The unit train idea evolved with the movement of bulk products: if all the wagons of a train contained the same product then much faster turn-around times could be achieved because no shunting was required. The same principle could easily be applied to containers – trains made up of nothing but containers sitting on rail wagons could also achieve a fast turn-around. Thomas Nationwide Transport developed the flexi-van in the 1950s – a truck carrying a container or van backed up to the train, the van then was pushed over the rail wagon rotated through 90 degrees and locked in position. Although this system required no cranes it was superseded in the late 1960s by a gantry crane removing containers from trucks and putting them on rail wagons in what has become the conventional manner. Mayne Nickless (operating as M.E.T.S. – Maynerail Equipment Transfer System) and T.N.T. now operate twice-daily container trains between Melbourne and Sydney as well as similar services between Sydney and Brisbane and Melbourne and Adelaide. As yet these trains have been rather small to obtain maximum economies and also their reliability has been seriously impaired by labour problems. As already mentioned the railways themselves have also entered this market with their R.A.C.E. system.

Railways have also suffered from the legal inability to operate their own road vehicles. This situation has been eased recently and now most state rail systems are setting up regional freight centres. The Victorian Railways have set up the first of a series at Horsham with sub-centres at Nhill and Warracknabeal. Rail freight movements are consolidated to Horsham and then L.T.L. deliveries and pick-ups are made by road over a considerable region. This concept allows the railways to avoid extremely costly branch-line freight operations and the efficiency of the whole scheme rests squarely on their own shoulders and not on some-one else's.

Containerization has certainly had its most spectacular success with sea transportation. Problems with stevedores had reached such proportions that any move towards reducing the high labour content in loading and unloading ships was bound to be a success. Another success at sea has been the development of the roll-on roll-off vessel – the trailer as well as its contents are carried on the ship. For relatively short voyages, such as the trans-Bass trade, the cost of transporting the trailer does not become excessive, while avoiding expensive lifting equipment is a major benefit. Although Australia has reason to be proud of the fact that Associated Steamships Pty Ltd commissioned the first cellular container ship in the world for the Fremantle–eastern states trade in 1964, the great success of containerization at sea has been on the international routes: in 1976 container services between Fremantle and the eastern states were discontinued due to an inability to compete with rail services.

Domestic air freight services have failed to fulfil their early promise because they could not cope with the intermodal freight transfer problem. 'Overnight' road freight leaves Melbourne in the early evening hours and arrives in Sydney the next morning taking about twelve hours. Air freight is also ready to leave for Sydney by early evening reaching Sydney in a little over an hour flying time. But then nothing happens to it until the next morning when it is delivered only an hour or two faster than road freight but costing considerably more. Most air freight is not ready for shipment before late afternoon or early evening and most high-volume routes are only of an hour or two flying time. Vertical take-off and landing equipment may eventually solve this problem by reducing the distance and time taken by the road trips connecting the air line-haul with the customer. If the customer is willing to receive the goods slightly after normal closing hours the service will easily better that of road. Moving freight in the belly lockers of the wide-bodied planes planned for the 1980s will have no effect on the ability of air freight to compete with road.

One transportation system which does not suffer intermodal problems is the pipeline. When the Whitlam Labor government was in office it established the Pipeline Authority (*Pipeline Authority Act 1973*) which had as one of its major functions the establishment of a national pipeline network for moving petroleum. Under the Fraser government this aim has lapsed although a major study of natural gas resources and demands to the year 2000 was completed, together with options for a national pipeline system for natural gas. An important component of any such network, the Moomba–Sydney natural gas line, was completed in December 1976. In the press release accompanying publication of the study it was announced that: 'The Pipeline Authority would be promoting as wide a discussion as possible throughout Australia. This would enable it to be as fully informed as possible of all the views available before advising the Government on appropriate action concerning the role of natural gas in energy planning in Australia for the remainder of this century.'[6] This suggests that pipelines will not play an important part in the transportation of goods in the near future although petroleum pipelines are being planned from Altona (the location of the refinery) to a new multi-company depot at Somerton, north of Melbourne, and from Sydney to Newcastle.

Intermodal freight transfer problems will always be an important component of domestic freight transportation because there will always be the small shipment and the small customer, some amount of packing, repacking, storing, sorting and trans-shipping will always be required.

Road building in Australia has always been a popular political activity. It

takes an unusually enterprising and risk-accepting government to engage in novel manufacturing activities instead of going on with its port and highway projects. Highways never fail, and, as they are usually not maintained, they can be built over and over again, thus turning out to be ideal outlets for government funds, involving no risk and a bare minimum of mental effort in general.[7]

This criticism could well be levelled at the beef roads programme which was firmly established in northern Australia in the early 1960s with the passage of the *Queensland Grant (Beef Cattle Roads) Act, 1961* and the *Western Australia Grant (Beef Cattle Roads) Act, 1961*. Funding for road construction was provided by the Australian government under these Acts outside the normal road funding channels.

Until 1923 road construction was entirely a state and municipal funded activity. With the *Main Roads Development Act, 1923* the Commonwealth financed developmental, trunk and arterial roads by four year grants, three-fifths of which was allocated according to the population of each state and the remainder according to the state's area. In 1959 a new rule-of-thumb for allocating federal money to road building was adopted with the *Commonwealth Aid Roads Act, 1959*. After Tasmania received 5 per cent of this money the remainder was allocated to the other states one-third by area, one-third by population, and one-third by number of motor vehicle registrations. Within states this money was also allocated on a similar basis which meant that a disproportionate amount was spent on rural roads. Funds provided by the *Commonwealth Aid Roads Act, 1969* were allocated to states on the basis of a 'mix of economic merit and past allocations' with specific provisions made for rural and urban arterial roads and for planning and research. In 1974 road funding for the next three years was formally split into three segments with the passage of three acts: the *National Roads Act, 1974* providing funds for the construction and maintenance of the national highway system, export roads and major commercial roads; the *Roads Grants Act, 1974* funding rural, arterial and local roads, beef roads in Queensland ($24 million) and minor traffic engineering and road safety improvements; and, the *Transport (Planning and Research) Act, 1974* providing $26 million, plus $13 million from the states in matching grants, for planning and research. Total road expenditure for 1976 was estimated by the Commonwealth Bureau of Roads to be just under $900 million with the federal government providing 35 per cent of this from sales tax on new motor vehicles and from fuel taxes, the state governments providing 34 per cent from motor vehicle registration, drivers' licences and road maintenance charges and local government providing the remaining 31 per cent from rates, loan funds and state government grants.

Initially the beef roads programme was financed above the normal process of road financing and was implemented as a method of trying to solve the marketing problems of beef producers in northern Australia. At the time, meat exports had expanded with demand from the United States for poor quality cattle. This demand was strong enough to cover the cost of road transportation to the port and, in addition, these exports helped to alleviate balance of payment problems. It was felt that full advantage could not be taken of the export potential of the beef industry without federal aid for road construction. Formally the objective of the beef roads programme was stated to be to:

provide pastoralists with improved access to outlets for cattle and to enable cattle to reach their destination in better condition and at an earlier age than previously. The increased return to producers following the construction of the new roads (was) expected to result in more improvements being made to properties and stock, and these (would), in turn, result in the production of more and better cattle.[8]

But instead of increasing the already existing geographical differentiation in road expenditure, could the aim of stimulating Australian beef production have been achieved in another manner? Could the $30 million spent on road construction in the Northern Territory have been used with better effect for the beef industry? More effective use of the money could have been made, according to J. K. Johnson who examined the situation, if engineering standards had not been so high: instead of 1590 kilometres of sealed road 2350 kilometres of completely adequate all-weather gravel road could have been built. Export abattoirs established in the Northern Territory, or subsidization of the use of hovercraft instead of trucks to transport stock, might have been more beneficial to the industry than beef roads. But Johnson questions the wisdom of trying to promote the beef industry in the north in the first place. Beef operations are effective and profitable when three characteristics are achieved: intensive stocking, low mortality and quick turnover. These characteristics are more easily achieved in areas closer to population centres which have sown pasture rather than on the widely scattered pockets of natural grassland in the Northern Territory. In fact the beef industry has expanded most rapidly since the Second World War in south-east Australia.

Another area in Australia for which transportation plays a vital role is the Pilbara in Western Australia. This region developed as a marginal pastoral area with some limited mining activities. Transportation services to the Pilbara and the Kimberley region to the north of it were an unattractive economic proposition to private operators, which led to the establishment of the Western Australian State Shipping Service which operates small multi-purpose vessels up the coast to Darwin. Over the past decade large-scale mining operations have commenced in the Pilbara, resulting in a sealed highway link with Perth and improved air services to the area. Naturally the Western Australian State Shipping Service has lost general cargo and passengers to this improved land transportation service and in an attempt to reverse its poor financial fortunes considered the possibility of acquiring L.A.S.H. (lighter aboard ship) vessels. These ships carry barges in which general cargo is stored. Instead of having the mother ship wait at vast expense while unloading takes place, these barges can be quickly lowered over the side of the ship (without the ship needing to berth), waiting barges loaded and the ship sent on its way again. Much higher utilization is made of the ship although additional capital costs are incurred in the fleet of barges required, and stevedores again unload the barges. In any case the Western Australian State Shipping Service did not purchase L.A.S.H. vessels because of the $12 million price tag (in 1971) but instead imported two ex-Cunard cargo ships and two unit-load ships.

The Western Australian government has big plans for the Pilbara. Key to their plans is the natural gas production on the North West Shelf which will provide the impetus for the Pilbara Industrial Complex including an aluminium smelter, steel plant, caustic soda processing plant, ethylene dichloride production, an iron-ore pelletizing plant and possibly a uranium enrichment facility together with new towns and a wide variety of service industries.

The Bureau of Transport Economics examined the transportation needs of the Pilbara and Kimberley regions on the basis that the proposed Pilbara Industrial Complex did not get off the ground, and then re-examined the effect on their results if the Complex did eventuate. The Bureau found that linking the present terminal point of the Western Australian Government railway system at Meekatharra with the Newman to Port Hedland iron-ore railway of the Mt Newman Mining Company was 'as cheap a way of meeting the transport needs of the Pilbara as either shipping or lower levels of railway development'.[9] A stronger case for this option exists if the Pilbara Industrial Complex gets off the ground. Of interest, but not included in the study, would be the Mt Newman Mining Company's view of having this extra traffic on their private standard gauge track. Also somewhat curiously the alternative of road transportation was glossed over:

Some road construction and upgrading are already planned for the region. It was established in this study that, for the freight transport task alone, major construction and upgrading beyond current plans was not economically justified. The evaluation therefore concentrated on a range of ship and rail alternatives.[10]

In any case in this important area of development for Australia once again is seen the synergistic relationship of transportation and economic activity: the Pilbara will develop its potential only with efficient transportation, which in turn can only be justified by large freight volumes generated by a thriving Pilbara.

Economies of scale do significantly aid the larger organization in Australia with the line-haul transportation of goods. Large companies can bargain with the freight forwarders for advantageous freight rates or generate sufficient freight volumes to efficiently run their own truck fleet. Small companies can do neither of these. The large carriers and freight forwarders can schedule their vehicles and their loads efficiently using owner-drivers to fill in the peaks. Smaller carriers typically cannot do this and go broke. But size of infrastructure and number of vehicles is not the only criterion for success: rail is hampered by its common carrier obligation and out-dated freight wagons; air freight has not met its potential; coastal sea freight is on the skids.

Union action is currently the key problem to domestic containerized sea freight services and to containerized unit train operations. If this problem could be overcome, most efficient freight transportation would be achieved by linking Brisbane, Sydney, Melbourne, Adelaide and Perth with containerized unit train service. Cellular container ship service should be re-introduced from Fremantle to Melbourne and Sydney with roll-on roll-off vessels crossing Bass Strait from Melbourne and Sydney to one northern Tasmanian port and to Hobart. The remaining transportation task could be handled by road, with road and air transportation competing for products with high value in relation to weight. Road, rail and sea have shown a willingness to innovate over the past decade in the movement of freight, air must do the same in order to compete for their share of the freight.

Smaller manufacturers, distributors and carriers do suffer a transportation disadvantage. But options are open to them. Voluntary co-operatives of these shippers would provide sufficient volumes for transportation economies of scale to be achieved. These co-operatives would have to be formed from manufacturers and distributors who are in different, non-competing fields in order to avoid contravening the *Trade Practices Act 1974*, whereas a similar joint effort between a group of small carriers might not be possible. Care in forming these co-operatives would enable a handful of organizations to get together, whose joint transportation requirements would provide a degree of balance and so avoid the back-loading problem. Maybe a manufacturer in Western Australia could join with three or four in the eastern states to provide such balance. In addition to combining transportation operations combined warehousing might be feasible. The small organization does suffer, but a little ingenuity could remove much of the burden.

Transportation costs add a sizeable percentage to the cost of Australian products. More efficient and less costly transportation should mean cheaper goods. Basic commodities are typically relatively low-price items and so the transportation component in the price is high. The advantage of better transportation will be most strongly felt in the price of basic commodities which themselves form a higher proportion of the weekly earnings of disadvantaged community groups. The final result is that the benefits of more efficient and cheaper transportation will be felt more by the disadvantaged – it will have a progressive rather than a regressive influence. Two main barriers exist to achieving better line-haul transportation in Australia: a lack of creative management and a lack of constructive union leadership.

Notes

1. *Policies for Development of Manufacturing Industry*, A Green Paper, (The Jackson Report), Volume 1, Australian Government Publishing Service, Canberra, October 1975, p. 93.
2. Constitution of the Commonwealth of Australia, section 101.
3. Wheeler, S. J. and Gilmour, P., 'Road Transport Regulation in Australia: Protection of the Railway?' *International Journal of Transport Economics*, Vol. 1, No. 3, December 1974, pp. 321-2.
4. Atkins, A. S., Kuczera, G. A. and O'Brien, W. T., *Assessment of Land Transport Alternatives for Webb Dock*, Port of Melbourne Environmental Study, Centre for Environmental Studies, University of Melbourne, Melbourne, December 1976, p. 20.
5. Ibid., p. xi.

6. Acting Minister for Natural Resources, Press Release, Canberra, 7 November 1976.

7. Hirschman, A. O., *The Strategy of Economic Development*, Yale University Press, New Haven, 1958, p. 166.

8. *Report Relating to the Proposed Construction of Beef Roads, Western Barkly Tablelands, Northern Territory*, Government Printing Service, Canberra, 1967.

9. Bureau of Transport Economics, *Freight Transport to North West Australia 1975 to 1990*, 1973 – Parliamentary Paper No. 100, The Parliament of the Commonwealth of Australia, The Government Printer of Australia, Canberra, 1975, p. 1.

10. Ibid.

Chapter 7
An Isolated World Market

Australia's relatively small size as an economic entity coupled with its isolation from Western Europe has been a considerable problem ever since first settlement. As Geoffrey Blainey says in the preface of his book *The Tyranny of Distance*, 'Distance is as characteristic of Australia as mountains are of Switzerland. By sealanes or airlanes most parts of Australia are at least 12 000 miles from western Europe, the source of most of their people, equipment, institutions and ideas.'[1]

During the first years of Governor Phillip's colony at Botany Bay one ship from England could bring provisions to last a year or more. Early sailings were therefore irregular in leaving England and even more irregular in arriving in Australia: sailing from the Cape of Good Hope across the Indian Ocean to Australia was aided by taking a southerly route through the Southern Ocean and riding with the Roaring Forties. The rough seas, high speed, hidden icebergs and extremely cold water made this part of the voyage particularly hazardous. Once the cargo of convicts and provisions had been landed in Australia these ships sailed north to China or India under charter to the East India Company. Many months usually elapsed waiting for and loading a cargo of tea and heading back through an unfavourable monsoon to the Indian Ocean, around the Cape of Good Hope again and home to England. Blainey estimates that it was often as long as two years between the time the governor at Sydney issued a request for provisions to the master of a returning ship and the time the requested cargo arrived at the colony.

During the nineteenth century, as Australia developed economically, great reliance was placed on the ability to sell wool and wheat in Europe. Distance from the market placed Australia at a considerable disadvantage with rival producers located in Europe and in the Americas, but a favourable climate and the high-quality Merino sheep kept Australia competitive. Essentially 'Australia rode on the sheep's back' until the mid-twentieth century. By the 1970s wool was still

Australia's main export but exports of meat (beef and lamb), wheat and iron ore had increased rapidly; sugar and other ore exports had also experienced a sizeable increase. Another interesting change had taken place: the United Kingdom had always been Australia's dominant trading partner, but by the late 1960s both Japan and the United States had surpassed the United Kingdom. In the early 1950s the United Kingdom had purchased over 40 per cent of the value of Australia's exports, with Japan taking under 10 per cent and the United States just over 6 per cent. By the early 1970s Japan's percentage had jumped to over 30, the United States share had doubled to 12 per cent while Britain's had plummeted to under 10 per cent.

When the United Kingdom entered the European Economic Community the general feeling in Australia was of uncertainty and despair for the export trade. But concentration of overseas trade with nations within the Pacific region (particularly Japan and the United States) does make sense as the lower transportation cost burden carried by exported products makes them more competitive on the world market, and the lower transportation cost component in the price of imported products makes them less expensive on the home market.

Goods moving by sea are classified as either bulk cargo or general cargo. Bulk liquid cargoes are carried by tanker while bulk dry cargoes now move in bulk carriers. Before the advent of the bulk carrier a couple of decades ago, dry bulk cargoes were carried by general purpose tramp: the vessel was contracted for a particular trip or a period of time to carry cargoes such as grain and ore. Bulk carriers still operate on this charter basis with a time-charter vessel being more likely to concentrate on carrying a single commodity over the period of its contract. Because of the long lead time between ordering a vessel to be built and having it operational, the supply of tramp shipping at any one time is relatively fixed. So any change in the demand for transportation of bulk commodities is magnified in the change in the freight rate charged. In addition Australian exports of iron ore, black coal, bulk wheat and sugar greatly exceed bulk imports of rock phosphate, sulphur, potassium fertilizers and asbestos. This means that many bulk carriers have to make the voyage out to Australia in ballast.

In contrast to bulk cargoes, general cargo is carried by cargo liners which are scheduled to call regularly at ports along a particular trade route. Vessels in this trade also are experiencing change with the conventional cargo liner being replaced by unit-load ships and cellular container vessels. Instead of loading an odd assortment of boxes, bundles and bags into the hold using shore cranes or ships' gear, products are unitized into pallet or container lots which are much more rapidly and less expensively loaded and unloaded. The liner trade to and from Australia is organized into shipping conferences. These conferences are associations of ship-owners, operating particular trade routes, which determine freight rates for their members and often establish a set share of the cargo for each member. On occasion conferences have operated revenue-pooling schemes. Shipping conferences are either closed or open. Open conferences have no restrictions on membership as long as the entering member is willing to abide by the published conference rates and observe the conference rules – members are free to carry whatever tonnage they wish as long as it is carried at the specified rates. The United States government insists that all trade links with the United States operate under the open conference system. All other Australian trade routes operate closed conferences where additional members can only join the conference with the unanimous consent of the existing members. With the introduction of container services in the late 1960s the shipping conferences have collaborated to an even greater extent than in the past forming container consortia to ease the financial burden to individual members imposed by the high capital costs associated with containerization.

Before the introduction of the overseas container service its potential benefits were probably oversold. The greatest advantage of containerization was that it kept the stevedores away from the product: it is easy to break a cardboard carton or a wooden box, it is not easy to break a metal container or even a properly assembled pallet load; it is easy to rationalize taking home individual damaged products, it is a major crime to steal a container – and difficult to achieve; a large amount of labour is needed to operate traditional shore cranes and ships gear, relatively little labour is required to operate a container crane. This benefit alone has certainly justified the introduction of cellular container ships but speed of handling and a reduction in transportation costs were also pushed as major benefits. Many container terminals experienced organizational problems in the early days, which did not enable them to live up to promises made about delivery speed. Often containers were stacked five high in the terminal yards only to have a truck arrive to collect the one at the bottom. Although these sorts of problems are now under control a poor initial impression was given. Containerization was introduced during a period of rapid inflation and so transportation costs rose instead of falling. Container operations were then, and still are now, subject to major disruption by labour disputes. But despite these initial difficulties containerization has been the most significant advent in transportation since the second world war.

Another advance in the sea transportation of goods has been the L.A.S.H. vessel. This vessel carries cargo barges which are quickly unloaded at the end of the line-haul portion of the trip and waiting, fully-loaded barges taken aboard. This process can be done at sea, without berthing, by a shipboard crane. The ideal application of this concept is for the trans-Atlantic trip from the mouth of the Rhine River in Europe to the mouth of the Mississippi River in the Gulf of Mexico. At both ends of this journey the lighters or barges, once unloaded, can move for extended distances up these large river networks. The large investment in the ship itself is almost fully utilized, loading and unloading time is at a minimum. During 1974 the Pacific Far East Line introduced two L.A.S.H. ships into the Australian trade. These vessels carry 49 lighters each of 376 tonnes capacity, but they are also built to carry 356 standard I.S.O. containers. Carrying containers immediately removes a basic advantage of the L.A.S.H. concept as the vessel has to berth to unload the containers. While it is berthed the lighters are also dropped but they then have to be unloaded by stevedores which means the main advantage of containerization is lost. In the Port of Melbourne union pressure has resulted in Pacific Far East Line being unable to drop lighters in Port Phillip Bay. The vessels tie up at Station pier and drop the lighters there, they are then taken in tow and moved up the Yarra River to Victoria Dock where they are unloaded. The L.A.S.H. concept is an example of a good idea applied in a poor manner – Australia does not have the inland waterway system to make it work.

Yet another idea for future development is that of tug-barge systems. The essential feature of these systems is that the propulsion unit (the tug) is physically separated from the load carrying unit (the barge). This type of ocean transportation system has four main advantages over self-propelled vessels. First, the crew required to man the operation is only slightly over one-quarter of the manpower required on a self-propelled vessel – the prime economic advantage. Second, as with the L.A.S.H. vessel, utilization of crew and vessel is much higher because the propulsion unit does not have to wait for unloading and loading. Third, as access to the barges for unloading and loading is relatively unrestricted – the barges have to wait for the return of a tug – expensive and fast cargo-handling equipment is not needed. In addition, the barges can serve as temporary storage space, so reducing warehousing requirements at the dock. The final major advantage of this type of system is that the capacity and type of cargo carried can easily be changed by varying the number and type of barges in the flotilla. A current disadvantage of the tug–barge system is its low speed, between 13 and 17 knots for a deadweight of between 10 000 and 13 000 tonnes. The Matson Research Corporation studied the potential of such systems under a research contract to the Maritime Commission of the U.S. Department of Commerce. Tugs pushing the barges as well as tugs pulling barges were investigated over a range of barge size, annual volume carried, distance and number of port calls. Freight in the barges was considered in three forms: bulk, unitized and break-bulk. The study concluded that the tug-pushing-barges system was already cost competitive with conventional container, bulk, and especially break-bulk, ships and that the capital required was only 40 per cent of that required by an equivalent self-propelled ship. Some improvements in technology were needed to increase tug–barge speeds and to improve the linkages between barges. This concept is interesting but not suitable for the longer distances associated with the Australian sea trades. Longer distances make the marginal savings in loading and unloading time much less important. In addition the over-manning forced by the unions on container shipping will eventually cease, making the differential in crew size also less important. Less mechanized, more labour-intensive barge loading and unloading in the Australian context will be more expensive than container operations.

Overseas shipment of goods by sea requires an intermodal transfer at the ports. In all states the capital city ports are the main terminals for both interstate and overseas general cargo. Of course the largest recent development in general cargo movements has been containerization and the capital city ports, especially Sydney and Brisbane, have insufficient land adjacent to their wharves for efficient container operations – a container handling rate of far less than the rate of 25 an hour achieved at ports like Rotterdam, Tilbury, Oakland and New York is the norm for most Australian ports. Adelaide is not a container port but receives containerized shipments by rail from Melbourne. Some degree of dissatisfaction with this arrangement was expressed by South Australians to the Maritime Industry Commission of Inquiry in 1975. Regional ports handle a wide variety of cargo including both general cargo and some bulk cargo. The major regional ports in Australia include Whyalla (South Australia) primarily servicing B.H.P.s needs, Newcastle and Port Kembla (N.S.W.) servicing the steel industry and Townsville (Queensland), Bunbury (Western Australia) and Portland (Victoria). In general these ports operate satisfactorily, although cargo has been lost to the capital city ports with the concentration required by containerization.

Bulk ports have been developed for large volumes of a single product which are handled in bulk. Port Hedland, Port Walcott and Dampier are mineral ports in the Pilbara region of Western Australia which can handle iron-ore vessels up to 150 000 deadweight-tonnes in size. Coal ports are located at Gladstone and Hay Point in Queensland (large coal loading facilities also exist at Newcastle, Sydney and Port Kembla). A number of sugar ports such as Lucinda and Bunbury exist in Queensland and many ports have the facilities required to handle bulk grain. Plans were considered for the development of a receiving facility for crude oil in Botany Bay capable of receiving 200 000 dwt tankers from the Middle East.

Bulk ports are an interesting aspect of the Australian transportation network. Take Port Hedland in the Pilbara region of Western Australia as an example. Before the late 1960s Port Hedland was a tidal port which could not receive ships larger than 5000 dwt. Port Hedland now handles the largest volume of any port in Australia and is capable of receiving 160 000 dwt ore carriers. This transformation has occurred because of the establishment of an iron ore open-cut mining operation by the Mt Newman Mining Company at Mt Whaleback, together with a 426-kilometre standard-gauge rail link between the mine and Port Hedland. The railway was laid in a record-breaking time of less than six months and now carries ten trains per day each with a payload of 13 500 tonnes. Capacity of the rail link and the port operation has recently been expanded to be able to handle an annual throughput of 40 million tonnes. This scale of development and expansion is not atypical for Australian bulk ports.

Sea transportation and port operations always appear to be fair game for criticism from the Australian primary industries when economic conditions are tight. A recent example is the criticism by the Victorian Fruit Exporters Committee of the excessive costs added to the price of Victorian pears by inefficient handling and transportation. Freight is about 50 per cent of the final overseas selling price of the pears and the Committee estimated that over half of this freight bill occurred within Australia, the ocean voyage and unloading charges overseas being about 40 per cent of the total freight cost. The industry pays 20 cents per carton of pears for loading at Shepparton and transportation 190 kilometres to Melbourne, and then pays 23 cents per carton for stevedores to load the ship. John Pring, Chairman of the Victorian Fruit Exporters Committee, puts the case rather strongly:

agricultural products . . . high volume carries the burden of the Australian balance of payments . . . and high tonnage carries the transport system. Agricultural export industries have been sucked dry by a mass of inefficiencies, feather-bedding, go steadies and lurks that have been building up for years in protected service industries including the transport industry, the seaboard and the shipping lines at Australian ports. No new efficiencies, no production break-throughs, no marketing initiatives, including Marketing Boards, can overcome the appalling waste of money that the wage structure, the transport system, the wharf handling and shipping freight charges rip off the export agricultural industries – costs which cannot be recovered in the market place overseas.[2]

The wool industry has also been critical of overseas shipping methods. A report by the Bureau of Transport Economics on the industry in 1971 suggested that instead of shipping wool in conference liners a bulkship service should be established. As conferences charge what the market will bear, the introduction of bulk services for wool would bring a considerable reduction in freight charges. Earlier in 1971 the Australian Wool Board issued a report which estimated additional sizeable freight savings if the trip from the producer to the port was not subject to state legislation and could be made by the least-cost mode.

Without doubt sea transportation should bear some of this blame. But efficiency on the waterfront and at sea has improved markedly over the past decade and so all the blame should not rest with the handling and transportation of export products.

Besides travelling by sea the only other way goods can leave Australia is by air. International air freight, in terms of tonnes moved, is insignificant when compared with sea movements – less than one-tenth of one per cent of total exports travel by air. In terms of dollar value of exports 3¼ per cent goes by air. Air freight has increased over recent years but the rate of increase has been far short of the rosy expectations of the air industry. Air freight has not been able to make large inroads into the traffic traditionally carried by sea transportation.

Most international air carriers have adopted the 'total cost concept' as the way to sell air freight. Qantas in a booklet called *Total Cost Concept: The Great Paradox* presents the idea in terms of the cost effectiveness in distribution:

If an increase of 10 per cent in the cost of a distribution system results in a 20 per cent increase in profits, then cost effectiveness is increased. Conversely, if distribution costs are cut by 10 per cent and profits reduced 20 per cent cost effectiveness is reduced.[3]

Obviously air freight costs more, but by using it, total distribution costs can be reduced and in turn profits increased, so the argument goes. A faster response to customer orders means that less inventory and even fewer warehouses, holding back-up stock, are needed. With less inventory insurance, damage and pilferage costs will also be less. The capital tied up in the excess inventory will be freed to be put to work in more profitable ways. As goods handling methods are less violent and in-transit vibrations and shocks less severe by air, packaging requirements and costs are less. Finally customers will get faster and better service. Adding all these benefits together easily justifies the additional cost of the air freight, or so the airlines hope. Examples are often given of air freight users for which this has been the case:

Canadair Limited cites the examples of Renault Incorporated air freighting automobile parts from France to New York for a total distribution cost saving of 20 per cent, and of the Raytheon Company which reduced distribution costs by 17 per cent with a domestic United States air distribution system for electronic products.

These arguments make a lot of sense and yet they have not been particularly successful in generating air freight. The essential reason for this is that the cost differential between air freight and surface freight is still too great and only a small proportion of products with a high value compared with weight (such as electronic components) can make the arguments for air freight work. Even with these products care must be taken. Ansett Airlines designed for Philips Industries an air-based distribution system centred on Adelaide. Despite the high value-to-weight ratio of the electronic products the system did not work effectively because it was operated from Adelaide. It probably would have been a success if it had operated from Sydney or Melbourne with a large home-based market.

Some of the problem with air freight rates rests with I.A.T.A. In addition to general commodity freight rates I.A.T.A. issues special commodity rates for certain products over specified routes in an attempt to attract additional trade to air. Unanimous agreement of I.A.T.A. members is a condition of general rate setting and of commodity rate setting. This means that sometimes an airline with wide-bodied aircraft and relatively low operating costs is unable to offer a low, but still profitable, rate to attract volume movement because another I.A.T.A. member is currently carrying a small volume of the same product at premium rates.

Air is the last mode to move into full-scale containerization. Because of the internal shape of the cargo holds on planes prior to the wide-bodied jets, containers used for air had to take odd shapes, looking like igloos. Full efficiencies of containerization were not possible because the odd-shaped containers were not suitable for use on other transportation modes. With the introduction of the Boeing 747 this situation changed. This plane could handle a standard 6-metre I.S.O. container. Seaboard World Airlines is a freight airline situated at Kennedy Airport in New York which is establishing a sizeable freight operation based on movement of 6-metre I.S.O. containers by air. The new Tokyo Airport at Narita has built its cargo terminal on the assumption that in the near future the bulk of air freight will move by 6-metre I.S.O. container.

Containerization presents a chicken-and-egg situation to the air freight industry. Containerization will bring efficiencies of operation which will enable reductions in freight rates and larger volumes, but until a certain minimal level of air freight business is generated containerization will not be justified.

From a general equity point of view efficiencies and low-cost transportation for exports is more important than for imports. The giant multinational consortia exporting minerals and other bulk products from Australia can certainly look after themselves, but the Australian family farmer has shown that he cannot. If an efficient system of transportation and marketing of primary products in overseas markets could be established, then the farmer would have to live up to his own statements about how efficient he is by world standards. Certainly the key to more effective transportation of primary products is to reduce the high cost and inefficiency at the dockside. Imports are almost all non-essential items and so the influence of transportation costs on the price of these items is not of much concern.

Indeed, international mobility of goods is relatively unimportant in social welfare terms. Although the primary producer is at the moment living on record low levels of disposable income, he would not be considered as belonging to a disadvantaged community group. The process of international movement of goods has no grounds for any kind of subsidization.

But overseas transportation of goods could be done more efficiently. Bulk sea movements are efficient because virtually no labour is required. Movement of general cargo by container should also be efficient but to date the system has been too vulnerable to industrial problems. If all overseas general cargo, except over-size loads, was containerized then labour problems would be the only remaining obstacle to obtaining a much more efficient system. Containerization is the best solution for Australian overseas freight movements - L.A.S.H. or tug–barge systems will not prove effective.

Inefficient but expensive handling at the point of exchange between modes is also a key problem for air freight. If all international air freight operations were concentrated at Mascot (or at Tullamarine if there is insufficient space at Mascot) then volume handling would take place at one location. This would, with time, take the form of 6-metre I.S.O. containers moving in Boeing 747s. From Sydney smaller shipments could then move by Ansett Electra or T.A.A. belly lockers or even by overnight road to other destinations within Australia. This would allow a much more efficient international line-haul movement.

But despite any possible efficiencies Australia will always suffer a transportation disadvantage in its relations with the rest of the world.

Notes

1. Blainey, G., *The Tyranny of Distance*, Sun Books, Melbourne 1966, p. viii.
2. Pring, J. G., Chairman, Victorian Fruit Exporters Committee, mimeographed letter, Melbourne, 17 December 1976.
3. *Total Cost Concept: The Great Paradox*, Qantas Airways Limited, Sydney, no date.

Chapter 8
Accidents

On Friday night 19 November 1976, a twenty-year-old youth was riding his motor cycle home. He fell off his bike at the corner of Cotham and Burke Roads in the Melbourne suburb of Camberwell. As he lay on the road he was hit by a car. The driver of the car did not see him and did not realize that the boy had been snagged by his clothing under the car. The boy was dragged 5 kilometres through the streets of Camberwell before the driver heard his screams. During the night of Tuesday 28 December 1976 he died in the intensive care ward of the Box Hill Hospital.

During the year 1976, 3577 Australians died on the roads.* For most, death was not so gory and prolonged as it was for the twenty-year-old, above, but each created a personal tragedy. 'What do you do? . . . He was good, really good' said his father.

In addition to the 3500 people killed on Australian roads in 1976, 100 000 were injured. The number of fatalities and casualties on the roads has steadily increased over the years until the early 1970s when there was a dip in the figures followed by a flattening out period. Generally it is believed that the introduction of seat belt legislation in Australia is responsible for this situation which occurred despite the continuing increase in car ownership and use. Of course some variation occurs in the accident rate depending upon type of vehicle: a motor cycle driver is fourteen times more likely to be injured than is the driver of a car or light commercial vehicle; the car driver in turn is four times more likely to be hurt than is a truck driver; riding in a bus is twice as safe as in a truck. In any competition for the use of road space a bicycle rider or pedestrian is particularly vulnerable.

The first fatal accident for five years on a scheduled air service

---

*This fatality rate is only slightly less than that of the Second World War when 27 073 Australians were killed in action in six years.

in Australia occurred in October 1975 with eleven people killed when a Connair Heron aircraft crashed near Cairns. Eighteen people died in the year 1975–6 in non-airline flying, such as aerial agriculture, private charter and flying training. Figures included in the book *Destination Disaster* (which dealt primarily with the faulty locking device on the freight compartment of the DC-10) showed that there is a considerable difference in the safety performance of the world's airlines. The information is shown in Table 8.1. It is interesting to note that Qantas rates as the second safest airline. Ansett and T.A.A. also rank within the world's 15 safest airlines.*

On Tuesday morning 18 January 1977, the 6.09 a.m. daily commuting train from Mt Victoria in the Blue Mountains to Sydney derailed just west of the Granville station in Sydney's western suburbs. The locomotive and the first two carriages slammed into the supports of the Bold Street bridge and an entire 300-tonne section of the bridge collapsed and flattened the third and fourth carriages, killing 83 passengers. Vivian Gene Steward, a factory hand from Blacktown, was in the front toilet of the third carriage when the accident occurred. 'I opened the door to the toilet and came out . . . I saw a bald-headed man on the left side of the train still sitting in the seat, bent over with his head in his lap and the concrete on his back,' Steward said. 'He was gasping and turning blue in the face.'

The Granville train crash and the subsequent inquiry received wide press coverage and detailed descriptions of the accident similar to that given by Mr Steward. But in the past dozen or so years only 84 people have been killed on the N.S.W. rail system – in 1976 alone 1124 people died on N.S.W. roads. Travelling by rail, sea or air is much safer than travelling by road, but a rail, sea or air accident is a far more spectacular and a far less frequent event and so gets greater publicity than a road accident. In fact a rather odd situation has developed: most people are slightly nervous about taking-off and landing in a plane; many people dislike sea travel; some people are nervous about trains thundering through tunnels and roaring through the night; but very few people feel any threat to their safety when they

---

*Ansett has carried 38 million passengers during the period 1950-74 and has suffered three fatal crashes, killing 34 passengers, while T.A.A. has carried 41 million passengers, killing 25 in its single fatal crash.

Table 8.1a   Airline Safety Statistics for the Years 1950-74
             Better than World Average

Airline	Nationality	Passengers flown (millions)	Passengers killed	Fatal crashes	'Expected' crashes based on world average	Fatal crash record *cf.* world average
Delta	USA	194	99	2	18	9 x better
Qantas*	Australia	10	6	1	6	6 x better
JAL	Japan	66	125	2	10	5 x better
American	USA	288	288	9	35	4 x better
British Caledonian	UK	21	101	1	4	4 x better
Continental*	USA	57	42	2	7	3 x better
United	USA	347	574	15	45	3 x better
Eastern	USA	324	389	9	29	3 x better
Lufthansa	W. Ger.	67	126	3	8	3 x better
TWA	USA	203	623	15	35	2 x better
PanAm	USA	139	557	14	31	2 x better
SAS	Sweden	69	54	3	7	2 x better
Air Canada	Canada	110	305	8	14	2 x better
Swissair	Switzerland	52	115	3	5	2 x better

*No crash since January 1966.

Source: 'How Safe are the World Airlines?', The *Age*, 12 January 1977, adapted from P. Eddy, E. Potter and B. Page, *Destination Disaster*, Quadrangle, New York, 1976, Appendix C.

drive down to the newsagent to pick up a newspaper. People are fearful of the safest ways to travel and blissfully confident about the most dangerous. This is another strange characteristic of the motor car.

Accidents on the roads are normally categorized into two groups: 'vehicle occupants' and 'other road users'. Fatalities and injuries involving vehicle occupants have not increased at the expected rate during the 1970s – during 1974 fatalities in Australia were 38 per cent lower than the level predicted four years earlier and injuries were 21 per cent lower, although over the past two years the results

Table 8.1b Airline Safety Statistics for the Years 1950-74
Airlines Close to World Average

Airline	Nationality	Passengers flown (millions)	Passengers killed	Fatal crashes	'Expected' crashes based on world average
National	USA	72	139	6	8
Braniff	USA	87	185	6	8
Alitalia	Italy	60	293	7	8
KLM*	Holland	38	274	7	8
British Airways	UK	155	691	21	21
Northwest*	USA	90	357	13	12
All Nippon	Japan	79	358	5	5
SAA	South Africa	19	158	4	3

*No crash since January 1966.

Source: 'How Safe are the World Airlines?', The *Age*, 12 January 1977, adapted from P. Eddy, E. Potter and B. Page, *Destination Disaster*, Quadrangle, New York, 1976, Appendix C.

have not been as good. Dr Michael Henderson of the N.S.W. Traffic Accident Research Unit ascribes this drop to seat belt legislation which was first introduced in Victoria in December 1970, with all Australian states and territories enacting similar legislation by 1 January 1972. But no such drop has occurred in fatalities and injuries to the other road users – pedestrians, cyclists and motor cyclists.

When considering the effect of road accidents on vehicle occupants and particularly for occupants of passenger motor vehicles, two basic options exist for improving the situation. The first option covers a range of ways by which accidents can be avoided more often (this is frequently called 'primary safety') and the second option is for improvements in the protection of the occupant of the car if an accident does occur ('secondary safety').

Accident avoidance is increased with improved responsiveness of the car and its increased visibility. Responsiveness is the ability of

Table 8.1c   Airline Safety Statistics for the Years 1950-74
Worse than World Average

Airline	Nationality	Passengers flown (millions)	Passengers killed	Fatal crashes	'Expected' crashes based on world average	Fatal crash record *cf.* world average
Air France	France	91	829	19	14	1½ x worse
Iberia	Spain	66	317	9	6	1½ x worse
CP Air	Canada	17	168	6	4	1½ x worse
Varig	Brazil	24	284	5	3	1½ x worse
Allegheny	USA	67	152	5	3	1½ x worse
Sabena	Belgium	23	193	7	4	2 x worse
Mexicano	Mexico	27	124	5	2	3 x worse
PIA	Pakistan	13	218	7	2	4 x worse
Aer Arg	Argentina	17	282	12	2	5 x worse
LOT	Poland	12	95	4	1	6 x worse
Garuda	Indonesia	13	130	7	1	6 x worse
Avianca	Colombia	35	310	16	2	8 x worse
Cubana	Cuba	11	104	6	1	9 x worse
JAT	Yugoslavia	14	92	7	1	9 x worse
CSA	Czecho-slovakia	19	212	10	1	9 x worse
IAC	India	29	322	19	2	9 x worse
Cruzeiro	Brazil	15	146	11	1	10 x worse
THY	Turkey	16	473	10	1	11 x worse
PAL	Philippines	24	254	17	2	11 x worse
Egyptair	Egypt	7	328	13	1	13 x worse
Aviaco	Spain	11	166	7	0	17 x worse
Tarom	Rumania	7	173	8	0	20 x worse

Source: 'How Safe are the World Airlines?', The *Age*, 12 January 1977, adapted from P. Eddy, E. Potter and B. Page, *Destination Disaster*, Quadrangle, New York, 1976, Appendix C.

the vehicle to react precisely to the driver's requirements and is dependent upon the vehicle's steering and handling, brakes and tyres and wheels. Braking ability is obviously important because braking usually precedes a crash. Differences in braking ability can be extremely important as shown by the illustration of two cars travelling side by side on the same road at the same speed of 100 km/h, but the braking system of the first car can stop it in 50 metres, while the second car can stop in 60 metres. If the first car stopped just before hitting a stationary truck the second car would hit it at well over 50 km/h. As a head-on crash at 50 km/h is usually the limit of survivability the driver of the second car would probably be killed. Tyres are also critical safety items in a car because they provide the sole contact of the vehicle with the road. An English study has shown that over 10 per cent of all traffic accidents are due to tyre failure and subsequent loss of control of the vehicle, and this figure rises to 32 per cent when single vehicle accidents are considered. Tyres are important components of a car in that they are subject to sudden shock and to penetration by sharp objects on the road and in any case deteriorate over time through wear. The House of Representatives Standing Committee on Road Safety when investigating passenger motor vehicle safety found that new tyres did not present a significant safety problem although concern was expressed about the quality of some retreaded tyres and, for example, with the little known fact that a tyre once retreaded is not suitable for use on a car with top speed exceeding 110 km/h. Problems also exist with the strength and durability of aluminium alloy or 'mag' wheels.

The interior design of the car is important in terms of both the visibility of the driver and the responsiveness of the car. If the driver has difficulty in reaching and operating the controls of the car (for example the foot brake in relation to the accelerator), this difficulty, even if very slight, may be the difference between having and avoiding an accident.

In addition to the driver having a wide field of vision it is important that his car is visible to other drivers. Proper lighting as well as the colour of the car itself is important in this regard. Several overseas studies have shown that there is a direct relationship between car colour and accident involvement. A Swedish study of over 30 000 collisions found that black cars were involved in 22 per cent of them while only 5 per cent of all vehicles on the roads were black. This study found pink to be the safest colour. In the U.S. a study was performed using two groups of 3500 U.S. mail vans, one group painted in red, white and blue and the other in olive drab. The brightly coloured vehicles had 27 per cent fewer accidents in total and 52 per cent fewer rear-end collisions. Light colours such as white, off-white, ivory and yellow are certainly much more conspicuous colours than dark red, dark blue and black. Although Australians do favour light-coloured cars, probably the main reason that the Australian car manufacturers retain black in their colour range is because of government demand for cars of this colour.

Secondary safety or occupant protection is concerned with reducing fatalities and the severity of injuries in accidents which do occur. It is dependent upon the crash-worthiness of the car (its ability to withstand and absorb impact), the restraint system, the design of the interior of the car and the windscreen design. From an examination of accident data in the U.S. it was established that the overall cost to society from head-on collisions was far greater than from accidents occurring in other directions. It is now possible to construct a relatively normal, but expensive, car in which humans can survive an 80 km/h head-on collision. This is a considerable advance on the current survivability limit of 50 km/h. Although side impacts are less important in terms of the total cost of that type of accident to society, it is very difficult to design for protection against them because the crash structure (the part of the car which deforms and absorbs energy upon impact and its associated supporting structure) is less able to withstand impact and the distance to the passenger compartment is much shorter. Also, with impact from the side, seat belts are far less effective and human tolerance to lateral impact is less. Despite the difficulties associated with minimizing the effects of this type of collision the Standing Committee on Road Safety felt that every effort should be made, starting with increasing the stiffness of the side structure of the car.

Greatest publicity has been given to the restraint system as a means of secondary safety, because the seat belt has proved to be the only simple idea which has had considerable effect on occupant protection. All other safety improvements involve engineering modifications to the car and the somewhat cloudy management decision by the manufacturer as to whether the additional expense of the safety modification will place their car at a competitive disadvantage. Seat belts, as mentioned, are required by legislation to be worn in all states and territories in Australia and have had a significant effect on reducing fatalities and injuries to car occupants. One problem associated with this legislation has been the relatively high rate at which seat belts are not worn. This rate is around 20 per cent for all capital cities with the exception of Adelaide where it is almost 40 per cent and Hobart where the rate is just over 30 per cent. And seat belts are more often not worn at night when the need to wear them is greater but, of course, the chance of being detected is much smaller. Young male drivers have been found to have significantly more road accidents than other community groups but surprisingly a study done by the Australian Department of Transport showed that this group wore seat belts at a rate at least equal to the average. Males did, however, wear seat belts less than females and the front left passenger had a lower wearing rate (despite being in the most dangerous position in the car) than did the driver. No differences occurred on the basis of age. Dr Michael Henderson in his evidence to the Standing Committee on Road Safety said that he believed there was a hard core of deliberate non-wearers who were also those who drove badly, drank too much and were a high crash risk in any case. He felt there was probably no practical way of getting them to wear the belts although the Committee felt an outside light or indicator which showed an unconnected seat belt was desirable. Children under eight, among certain other groups such as aged passengers, delivery people, when driving in reverse and those with certain medical conditions, are often exempt from the seat belt legislation, although some states, such as Victoria, have passed legislation requiring children to be adequately restrained when riding in the front seat. A child weighing 13.6 kg (30 lb) becomes a force of 272 kg (600 lbs) in a typical head-on collision at 50 km/h. If the child is not properly restrained but is being held by a parent, it will be catapulted about the car on impact – data collected show that children under eight suffer major injury at a greater rate than other vehicle occupants.

Interior design of the car is also an important safety consideration, because even with the compulsory wearing of seat belts, some contact with the car interior will probably be made on crash impact. Progress in this area for production vehicles has not been satisfactory in relation to the advances already made on experimental safety vehicles. Laminated windscreens are available, but only as an option at additional expense; collapsible steering columns used by General Motors-Holden are of a design superseded by their U.S. parent company as far back as 1968; heavily padded intruding dashboards are a recent feature of Australian cars but padding should be more widely used; further development should occur on the head restraint as part of an integrated seat without causing greatly reduced driver visibility or claustrophobia for the rear seat passengers.

Australian car manufacturers when giving evidence to the Standing Committee on Road Safety painted a picture of an industry with dropping vehicle sales, declining profitability, a high level of industrial difficulties, wage and cost increases and increasing competition from imported vehicles. The Committee, however, felt that these problems should not restrict or prevent safety-consciousness in design and development. In fact concern was expressed at the car manufacturers' attitudes to safety. Until recently safety design was a minor consideration which was usually compromised by style and cost considerations. Sir Brian Inglis, General Manager of Ford Australia, expressed current attitudes on vehicle safety when he told the Committee: 'By and large we like to ship our cars with the full safety features. This seems sensible, but if a person specifically asks us to delete something for competitive reasons, or as a matter of choice we will do it.'[1]

Safety features are provided in Australia under two conditions: if the manufacturers are forced by legislation to provide a particular feature or if the manufacturers are sure that the customer will be willing to pay for it (the easiest way to ensure this second condition is to provide the safety feature as an optional extra). Manufacturers have also shown a certain reluctance to recall vehicles when a defect is discovered, have forced the responsibility for warranty work on to their dealers rather than accept it themselves and have also shown a reluctance to pool knowledge and resources on safety-related matters. An example of the reluctance to recall defective vehicles concerns the ignition lock on the HQ and LJ Holdens. If the engine was turned off it was possible to lock the steering column while the car was still in motion. General Motors-Holden had resisted a recall on this (because of the estimated cost of over $5 million) and when told of a fatality which had occurred due to the ignition lock told the Committee 'anyone who switches off the ignition when driving a car is wrong and should not be driving a car'.

Despite the fact that General Motors-Holden employs over 1000 people and spends over $10 million per year on quality control the overall quality of new Australian-made cars is not particularly high. Department of Defence inspections of new vehicles averaged over nine faults per Ford vehicle and over eight faults per Holden vehicle which included a large number of brake faults. The Australian Automobile Association stated to the Committee that they have never inspected a vehicle which has been completely free of faults. The Committee recommended that independent inspectors be sent into the automobile assembly plants to oversee quality control and that an effective system of annual inspections be set up to establish the road worthiness of existing vehicles.

Overall the findings of this Inquiry were that Australian car manufacturers in general are not willing to put in the effort and money needed to build a safe car, and customers do not demand a safe car. Legislation is the only effective means because then all manufacturers are on an equal footing and no manufacturer feels that sales will be lost beause of concentration on safety – the 'dirty word' of the industry.

It is feasible to build a car which is safe within certain speed limits, but how much is the consumer willing to pay to guard against the small chance of being involved in an accident? (The odds against being killed on a given 16-kilometre trip are estimated at two million to one). While control over the form of the vehicle is possible it is much more difficult to control the behaviour of the human driver of the car. Two different directions can be taken in trying to tackle this problem: the first is to implement a system of licensing which will restrict the young, inexperienced or proven deviant drivers; the second direction is to improve the training received by drivers.

When a driver's licence is issued it is formal recognition that the holder has reached a certain minimum age, that he has demonstrated that he has acquired the skills required to control the vehicle and that he has adequate knowledge of the road and traffic laws. Although a driver's licence is officially regarded as a privilege for the holder rather than a right, in practice it is widely recognized that for many people a licence is a necessity, and it is only withdrawn on clear evidence of unfitness.

The Australian Road Research Board examined the conditions under which a licence may be granted in Australia in relation to the road accident situation. The study found that there was no evidence to suggest that car drivers or motor cycle riders of sixteen years of age were any more likely to be involved in accidents than were seventeen-year-old or eighteen-year-old drivers, if experience and distance driven were accounted for. It was also found that drivers of advanced age do not represent a serious risk to the community – over 70 there is an increased accident risk but the contribution to the total number of road accidents is small. Annual eye tests are warranted but compulsory medical examinations are not in terms of cost when related to influence on road accidents. A stringent written objective test of local traffic regulations should be included as part of the testing process for a driver's licence.

In addition to this case for changing licensing conditions overall in Australia, there is probably also a case for the use of restrictive licensing provisions according to the power of the vehicle to be driven in relation to the age, experience and driving record of the licence holder.

A companion study by the Australian Road Research Board into driver training in relation to road safety established three objectives for driver educational and training courses. Training programmes can aim to improve the individual's skill, to provide relevant background information or to change attitudes.

Commercial driving courses, defensive and advanced driving courses and training courses for professional drivers all emphasize improvement of the individual's skill. The study showed that formal courses from a commercial driving school have no benefit in terms of increased road safety over informal methods for learning to drive. In general it is difficult to teach the complex perceptual skills required for safe driving at the same time as teaching vehicle-control skills. Defensive driving courses which teach safety skills to the driver with at least some experience are effective in reducing accident involvement by as much as one-third. Advanced driving courses which concentrate on the skilful handling of the car, on the other hand, have no effect on accident involvement. Professional drivers, drivers of buses, trucks, taxis, police cars and the like, are subject to a wide variety of training methods. The Australian Road Research Board's study indicated that none of these methods were effective with the exception of the Smith–Cummings–Sherman method. This method emphasizes the perceptual aspects of driving (the information being received by the driver) and it can be reduced to five rules:

1. *Aiming high in steering.* Looking as far ahead as possible of the intended path both when going straight ahead and when turning around corners and bends.

2. *Comprehensive viewing.* Avoiding staring at objects in sharp detail, and continuously trying to perceive the whole traffic situation as fully as possible.

3. *Scanning.* Keeping the eyes moving at least every two seconds, including a look in the rear view mirror every five seconds.

4. *Positioning.* Always looking for and trying to take up positions in the traffic with a safe way out, should an emergency appear. This includes a stopping margin ahead and possible exits to the side.

5. *Being seen.* Not to engage in a manoeuvre which requires that other drivers or pedestrians stay put, until (you are) certain that they have seen you.[2]

Driver education courses in high schools emphasize the provision of background information although some training in actual driving is provided. These courses do not improve the learner's subsequent accident record over other teaching methods, but there is some evidence that subsequent violations of the traffic laws are reduced. This type of training would be of very limited benefit in Australia because of the time lag between taking the course and being eligible to hold a driver's licence.

Changing general community attitudes to safe driving is a difficult, if not impossible, task that must be accomplished through the normal mass-media channels. Evidence to date on road safety campaigns suggests that expressed attitudes may be modified by a variety of methods but there is no link with behaviour modifications as a result of this attitude change.

One of the most encouraging conclusions of the study was that safe driving is a skill which can be learned, although complete learning may take up to eight years. Exactly what is learned has not yet been identified with sufficient specificity to set up effective methods of instruction.

In Australia one-half of all drivers killed on the road have blood alcohol concentrations greater than the legal limit. A young man, aged twenty-four, of Coburg, a working-class Melbourne suburb, was lucky not to be included among these statistics one night in 1976 when he was arrested while driving his Morris Mini home 'swerving violently' with smoke and sparks coming from the driver's side of the car. The front tyre on his side of the car had disintegrated but because of the youth's condition with a blood alcohol level of 0.235 (compared with the 0.05 legal limit in Victoria) he was unaware he was driving on his wheel rim. He was fined $200 and disqualified from driving for a year. Half the drivers killed, a quarter of the pedestrians killed, a quarter of the motor cyclists killed and one fifth of the passengers killed on Australian roads also have blood alcohol concentrations above the legal limit.

Not only does the drinking driver become involved in a far greater proportion of traffic accidents than does the normal driver but his ability to survive is lower. Julian Waller, Professor of Epidemiology and Environmental Health, when addressing the International Conference on Alcohol, Drugs and Traffic Safety held in Melbourne in January 1977 said that alcohol acted as an extremely effective cough depressant so that badly injured drinking drivers can easily choke on their own blood or vomit. He said that drivers who drank were forty times more likely to be involved in a fatal road accident than were drivers who did not drink. Smoking also provides problems for the driver. Although this is a new direction of research, Professor Waller had found that drivers who smoke were twice as likely to be involved in crashes as were non-smokers; smoking two packets of cigarettes was equivalent to drinking two or three glasses of alcohol. Because a heavy smoker has replaced up to 10 per cent of the oxygen-carrying capacity of his blood by carbon monoxide, difficulties can occur if a blood transfusion is required for this type of driver after a road accident. Drivers who smoke and drink heavily are almost fifty times more likely to be killed or injured on the roads than drivers who do not.

Over 20 000 drinking drivers are detected each year in Australia. This is certainly an underestimate of the true size of the problem.

Professor Bob Borkenstein, the American inventor of the breath-alyser, said at the Conference on Alcohol, Drugs and Traffic Safety that in the United States the average police officer on patrol makes only two arrests a year for drunken driving, with other drinking drivers detected being let off or given lesser charges. This situation indicates the general high level of community acceptance of the use of alcohol despite the relatively severe penalties which exist for drink-driving. In spite of the obvious direct relationship between drink-driving and traffic accidents, Laurie Newell, the Victorian Police Assistant Commissioner for Traffic, replied to Borkenstein's comments, presumably with a straight face, that no inference could be made about the Australian situation from this as the Victorian figure was three bookings, an increase of 50 per cent on the U.S. figure. Three bookings! 'Are we to stop looking for other traffic offenders and concentrate on drunk driving infringements only?' Newell said in justification of the situation.

A common reaction to the drunk driver is one of horror considering the amount of damage he does not so much to himself but to those who share the road with him and do not drink. These attitudes have led some countries to introduce unconditional prison sentences for drink-driving: Sweden, for example, has had an unconditional one month prison sentence since the 1930s. But more recently there has been a trend towards treating the drink-driving problem as a medical or community health issue as well as a road safety issue. Anne Raymond, formerly with the Australian Road Research Board and now with the St Vincent's Alcoholism Clinic in Melbourne, has classified drinkers into two groups, excessive drinkers and responsible drinkers. Excessive drinkers average the equivalent of ten 7-oz glasses of beer per day, reach a blood alcohol concentration of 0.10 or higher and drink ten or more beers at one sitting. Responsible drinking is indicated by an average of the equivalent of eight or fewer 7-oz glasses of beer per day, a blood alcohol concentration rarely as high as 0.08 and only rarely drinking more than eight 7-oz glasses of beer on a single occasion. With the present detection procedures in Australia the drinking driver is virtually only apprehended if he draws attention to himself by erratic driving. In essence it is the excessive drinker who will draw attention to himself in this manner, the responsible drinker usually will not. Anne Raymond, Michael Henderson and others make a strong case that the group of excessive drinkers who drive have particular characteristics. First almost all of them are male. Raymond found that of all drivers stopped in Melbourne and asked to take the breathalyser, 98 per cent are male. Similar results have been found in other Australian cities and overseas in Holland, Sweden and Canada. The excessive drinker not only has problems with his driving, but he has problems with many other aspects of his life. He has medical, psychological and economic problems. If the excessive drinker is young he will in time develop the physical signs of alcoholism: delirium tremens, cirrhosis of the liver, brain damage. If he is older he will probably already be an alcoholic. About one-third of the drivers apprehended and breath-tested are under 25 years of age and 70 per cent of them are blue-collar workers. These drivers have ten times as many previous convictions for serious traffic offences as does the general driving population and they have about three times the rate of criminal convictions as that found in the whole adult male population. Eight per cent of Australian males are excessive drinkers.

As it is relatively easy to identify the segment of the community that is primarily responsible for the drink–driving problem what can be done about it? Treating the problem merely as a traffic offence and issuing fines, prison sentences and suspending licences will only temporarily remove the offenders from the road. Sooner (most drive anyway during periods in which their licences are suspended) or later they will again be drinking and driving. Young offenders should be treated for alcoholism before they reach middle age and develop the physical symptoms. Only proper medical treatment will have a chance of turning an excessive drinker into a moderate or non-drinker and so remove the prime menace from the road.

While the excessive drinker is the major menace on the road the responsible drinker is also accident prone because of the little known fact that a distinct deterioration occurs in driving performance before the appearance of outward signs of intoxication. This is why blood and breath tests have become so important.

Another important aspect of the whole question of alcohol and road safety is brought up by Anne Raymond:

There seems to be more resistance to accepting and applying scientific evidence relating to the alcohol aspect of road safety than to most others. This may be due partly to the fact that the decision-makers, on the whole, are involved in the situation not as observers but as participants. This makes an objective view almost impossible. While most road safety measures affect drivers in general, those relating to alcohol affect only certain sections of the driver population, mainly drinkers and males. . . . It was perhaps not entirely coincidental that the decision to introduce stricter drink-driving legislation, which brought such a marked decrease in alcohol-related accidents in Great Britain, was made by Mrs Barbara Castle who does not drive.[3]

This point certainly is embedded in the widespread social acceptance of excessive drinking in Australia. Sporting heroes are often shown in newspaper photographs celebrating victory with a few beers. Win or lose, Victorian Football League Clubs provide unlimited beer to players and friends after each game. Mateship is at its zenith in the drinking school at the pub during lunch or after work. Police are lenient on drinking drivers as are judges and the decision-making politicians. An example of this Australian cultural problem occurred when Peter Nixon the federal Minister for Transport, when opening the International Conference on Alcohol, Drugs and Road Safety, suggested that all states might like to follow Victoria's lead and introduce random breath-tests as they had a 'strong deterrent effect'. Queensland's Deputy Premier accused Mr Nixon of meddling in state affairs, the South Australian and Western Australian Transport Ministers stated that existing laws were quite sufficient and P. F. Cox the N.S.W. Minister of Transport said random tests would not be introduced there 'even if they prove successful in Victoria'. The right of the Australian drinker to kill or injure himself as well as others appears to be one of the few non-partisan issues of Australian politics.

A relatively new problem is the effect of drug-taking on driving ability. Research has shown that after smoking marijuana drivers are aware that their reaction speed has been impaired and tend as a result to drive more slowly. But when alcohol and marijuana are both taken, this awareness disappears and the individual drives with increased speed and with increased danger to all on the road due to the slowed reaction times. Possibly of greater concern is the growing use of anti-anxiety drugs such as chlordiazepoxide (Librium) and diazepam (Valium). Each of these interacts with alcohol and has a direct effect on the driver's motor skills, co-ordination and discrimination. Barbiturates, travel-sickness preparations and many other commonly taken drugs can also have significant effects on driving ability. It is obvious that an urgent need exists to establish precisely and publicize widely the exact nature of these effects.

Use of the motor car for social needs rather than as a means of transportation has been another source of deviant drivers over the past two decades. This is a particular problem of young male drivers. Many believe that the young man sees in the car a symbol of his independence, sexual potency and aggression. For the young man, especially from a lower socio-economic background, the competitiveness and aggression of modern society is difficult to cope with and often leads to frustration, cynicism and feelings of inadequacy. In his car, however, he is independent, making the decisions and being responsible for his actions. But these actions are often not guided by the needs of safety. If the individual cannot follow the values of a competitive and aggressive society in his work role, then it is easy to transfer the aggression to the road. On the road he is not a relative failure, he is at least as good as anyone else – given the right car and extras he is indeed 'better' than most. Of course the problem with this fantasy world is the high chance of a traffic accident.

On a Saturday night in August 1976, a sixteen-year-old boy took the keys to his sister's car from her handbag and picked up a friend and two girls for a ride. Driving down Mahoneys Road, Forest Hill (an eastern suburb of Melbourne) a group of boys aged between twelve and fifteen years ducked out from behind some pine trees by the side of the road and 'brown eyed' (pulled down their pants and exposed their bottoms) the car. The sixteen-year-old boy drove at one of the other boys in order to 'stir' the group. One boy aged twelve was hit by the car and 'flew through the air in a crouched position . . . about 2 feet (0.6 m) off the ground. He landed under a wire fence and ended up about 30 feet (9 m) or so away from where he was hit' said one of the group of boys That boy died from the injuries he received.

Many traffic accidents caused by young male drivers are a direct result of such 'big noting'. The young male driver is a considerable safety problem and it is not clear how the size of this problem can be reduced.

Several other groups share the use of the road with the motor car but come off decidedly second best in any collision which may occur.

During 1975 almost 9000 pedestrians, 2500 bicycle riders and 11 000 motor cyclists were injured on Australian roads; 700 pedestrians, 85 bicyclists and 400 motor cyclists were killed. Most of these bicycle and motor cycle riders were young and male, the pedestrians were mostly either under ten or over sixty. In essence the problem is that modern western society has built during the twentieth century a travel environment that suits the car. Motor cycles, bicycles and pedestrians have not been designed into the system and consequently are very vulnerable. Recent measures such as bike paths, bike lanes and pedestrian shopping malls represent an effort to separate these modes from the car but extensive use of any of these measures is rather expensive.

During the first half of this decade the number of motor cycles registered in Australia has more than doubled in comparison with about a 20 per cent increase in the numbers of other vehicles. Although riding a motor cycle now is safer than it was five years ago and is far safer than it was before the Second World War, the fatality rate per 100 million motor cycle kilometres is seven or eight times as high as the fatality rate per 100 million car kilometres.

From a federal Department of Transport study it was established that a higher rate of accidents is associated with motor cycles with an engine capacity above 250 cc, with riders younger than 25 years and with riders with less than two years experience. The study concluded that a licensing scheme should be introduced which would restrict the use of motor cycles above 250 cc engine capacity to riders aged over 25 years. New licensing schemes may have some impact on motor cycle accidents but the effect will never be spectacular because the exposed motor cycle rider shares the road with the protected car driver. Because it is impracticable to provide motor cycles with a separate road network a higher motor cycle accident rate must be accepted.

Heavy commercial vehicles, including semi-trailers or articulated vehicles, pantechnicons or large vans, low loaders and buses, are another group of road users with accident characteristics different from those of the normal passenger car.

The National Association of Australian State Road Authorities (N.A.A.S.R.A.) conducted an extensive examination into the economic effects of the great variety of limits on road vehicle dimensions which exist in Australia. Part of this study was an evaluation of the number and severity of traffic accidents experienced by heavy commercial vehicles. It was found that these vehicles were over-involved in accidents on a numerical basis, but that when the far greater distances travelled by trucks was taken into account the situation changed. For highway travelling articulated vehicles were over-represented in fatal accidents. These vehicles were more likely to be involved in accidents while being overtaken than were rigid trucks. Of all articulated vehicle accidents, 45 per cent involved no other vehicle compared with 29 per cent for all vehicles, and 27 per cent involved mechanical faults compared with 9 per cent for all truck accidents. Brakes, tyres, couplings and steering were most commonly involved in the failure. Collisions in urban areas most often involved a truck running into the back of a car and this fact together with an examination of truck braking systems led the study group to conclude that many truck brakes are deficient. Somewhat contrary to expectation, vehicle length was estimated to be a causal factor in less than 6 per cent of truck accidents, although this low level might not be retained if longer vehicles (such as the 20-metre double bottom) were introduced.

An earlier study by the Traffic Accident Research Unit of the N.S.W. Department of Motor Transport also found trucks to be over-represented in all reported accidents. In a truck-and-car collision the truck driver was less likely to be killed than was the car driver, although if the truck driver was ejected or jumped from his cabin his chances of survival were less. This study recommended a seat restraint system for truck occupants and the fitting of crash guards to trucks to prevent smaller cars running under the tray of the truck on impact.

Accidents involving trucks could be reduced if all truck drivers were trained by the Smith–Cummings–Sherman method described earlier. A less chaotic relationship between cars and trucks would exist if trucks were forbidden to travel in the right-most lane of a three-lane highway and were encouraged to only use the right lane of a two-lane highway when passing. Some education, even if rudimentary, for car drivers about the operating characteristics of heavy vehicles would also improve the relationship between car and truck drivers.

Transportation accidents of a different kind are a current matter of great concern. Oil tankers have increased in size at an astonishing rate: at the end of the Second World War the largest tanker was 18 000 deadweight-tonnes; currently the Shell Oil Company operates several 550 000 dwt tankers and Harland and Wolff, Belfast shipbuilders, have a patent on a design for a 1 000 000 dwt tanker.

The effect of an oil tanker accident can be devastating. Early in 1970 a 50 000 dwt tanker carrying a full cargo of crude oil ran aground on the Spanish Atlantic coast near the town of Virgo. The tanker, the *Polycommander*, spilled about a third of its cargo into the sea where it caught alight. The heat of the burning oil was so intense that it created hurricane force winds which lifted huge amounts of oil into the atmosphere in a fine mist. Several days later the mist condensed and came down as black rain on Spanish coastal farmland and villages. Extensive damage was done to homes, gardens, crops and cattle.

Nor are tanker accidents isolated occurrences. In the month of January 1975 the 236 000 dwt *Showa Maru* spilled 4000 tonnes of oil when she grounded in the Malacca Straits near Singapore; the 88 000 dwt Danish tanker *Jacob Maersk* ran aground while entering the harbour at Oporto, Portugal, exploded and caught fire; the *Michael C. Lemos*, a 250 000 dwt Greek tanker spilled 500 tonnes of oil in the Virgin Islands; while en route for Los Angeles the 50 000 dwt tanker *British Ambassador* sank in the Pacific with a full load of crude oil; two tankers spilled oil into the Atlantic off the U.S. coast; two more tankers collided in the Malacca Straits; and off the South African coast a 13 000 tonne tanker the *Scapbay* caught fire.

Tanker size increased most rapidly after the Arab–Israeli war of 1967 and the closure of the Suez Canal. Oil now had to travel south from the Persian Gulf around the Cape of Good Hope and back up the Atlantic to Europe. In 1967 it cost $3.30 per tonne to ship oil in a 80 000 dwt tanker from the Gulf to Europe through the Suez, but it cost only $2.40 per tonne to move the oil the far greater distance to Europe via the Cape in a 200 000 dwt tanker. This was really the key to the tanker boom between 1967 and the October war of 1973. Oil tankers can operate under long-term contract or on voyage charter. Operating on a single voyage charter can be risky but it certainly proved to be profitable during the period 1967 to 1973. In 1970 Aristotle Onassis gained early delivery of a 200 000 dwt tanker and chartered it to Shell for a single voyage, Europe to the Gulf and back, on which he made an estimated $4 million profit or about one-third the cost of the tanker. More recently for a 300 000 dwt tanker costing around $80 million to build and between $30 000 to $50 000 per day to operate, the profit made can be as much as $7 million per voyage.

Noel Mostert in his extremely interesting book *Supership* puts forward a whole list of reasons why modern tankers are so accident prone. Supertankers are built with a ten-year write-off life; most are built with the dominant aim of making a considerable profit for the owner (most are owned by tycoons such as Onassis and Niarchos, C. Y. Tung and Y. K. Pao of Hong Kong, Hilmar Reksten of Norway and the Indian Ravi Tikkoo – the major oil companies own only about 35 per cent of the world's tanker tonnage). Many economies are often taken in tanker construction. Most have only one high-pressure boiler, a situation unheard of on a passenger liner; most are built with single screws, again never done on a passenger ship; evaporators to provide fresh water to keep the boilers going are normally under capacity; reserve supply tanks of distilled water are inadequate as is the auxiliary power unit. The development of these giant ships has been so fast that adequate design tests have not yet been carried out – the strains and stresses placed on a hull of this size under all sea conditions have not been properly measured. Despite this, many attempts have been made to economize by reducing the amount of steel used in the tanker construction. This situation is made even worse by the fact that many tankers operate under flags of convenience. These countries have shown a general lack of responsibility regarding tanker operations and have a higher accident rate than other countries. Trying to pin the responsibility for an oil spill on a tanker carrying a flag of convenience is a difficult process as Mostert points out:

The *Torrey Canyon* was owned by the Barracuda Tanker Corporation, a financial off-shoot of Union Oil Company of California, which leased the ship and had, in turn subleased it to British Petroleum Trading Limited, which was a subsidiary of the British Petroleum Company. The ship, built in the United States, and rebuilt in Japan, was registered in Liberia, insured in London, and crewed by Italians.[4]

In order to receive compensation for the *Torrey Canyon* accident the British and French resorted to arresting a sister ship of the *Torrey*

Canyon and held it until the insurers paid the $7.5 million settlement for damages.

Not only are the tankers themselves of doubtful quality so too are many of the masters and crews. Because of their immense size tankers are not like the previous generation of vessels to operate: the bridge is 400 metres from the bow and 30 metres above the water, stopping is a very slow process and general manoeuvrability is rather poor. But only two training facilities are available for super tanker masters. Esso Oil Company has an exact-scale set up on an eight-acre (three-hectare) lake near Grenoble, France: exact-scale tankers, loading berths and channels. The other facility is a simulator, similar to those used to train flight crews, at Delft in Holland. But most masters do not use these facilities, they learn on the job with very mixed results.

Even when these tankers are not splitting open or exploding and disgorging their contents into the sea they are still a major source of pollution. Between each voyage tankers clean their tanks. After unloading, as much as 2000 tonnes of oil remains on the sides of the tanks of a 200 000 dwt vessel and more often than not this oil is flushed out into the sea. Although some progress is being made to ensure that tankers use the Load-on-Top method which separates most of the oil from the water expelled into the sea, the cumulative effect of these flushings and the resulting slicks is at least as damaging as the accidents.

Mostert describes the sinking of the 206 000 dwt Shell tanker *Metula* in the Magellan Straits in 1974. The accident poured more than 50 000 tonnes of crude oil on the exact spot where almost two centuries before Darwin had praised the abundance and diversity of the marine flora and fauna. No clean-up of the oil was attempted although a considerable effort was made to salvage the ship. Scientists estimate that the oil will remain as a constant source of pollution for at least ten years.

Oil tankers converge at the Cape of Good Hope on the outward voyage from Europe to the Gulf and again on the return voyage. The waters of the Southern Ocean are among the roughest in the world and naturally take their toll of oil tankers. Thousands of birds and penguins have been killed. Oil in cold waters takes a very long time to break down and currents in the Southern Ocean sweep the oil down towards Antarctica. No one is sure of the extent or the longevity of the damage being done.

Despite the fact that with the October war in 1973 and the subsequent increase in oil prices, world-wide economic depression and greatly reduced demand for oil and as a result greatly reduced demand for tankers, the overall problem of oil transportation will not decrease in the near future. Vast tonnages of super tankers have already been built or are under construction. Even though this shipping has an expected financial life of ten years it will undoubtedly still be operating twenty or even thirty years from now.

World transportation of oil presents problems which are extremely difficult to solve - nobody can force all tankers to operate under any desirable code of rules. A handful of tycoons reap the major benefits from these gigantic vessels; developed countries burning large volumes of oil as a primary source of energy also benefit; the rest of the world and all future generations bear the incalculable cost.

Transportation accidents are quite discriminatory in their nature. The strangest thing about these accidents is that most of the community, by choice in the main, travels most extensively by the mode that is by far the most dangerous. In a way the lower socio-economic groups are at an advantage with respect to traffic accidents because they are forced to travel by safer means, by bus, train or tram, rather than in the dangerous car. But in other circumstances this group is placed in a much more hazardous position. The lower socio-economic group typically forms the non-car-owning segment of the community and while travelling by bus, train or tram is much safer than travelling in a car, walking or riding a bicycle is much more dangerous.

The young are particularly discriminated against. Many cannot afford a car and most of these choose to travel by foot or bicycle (if below licensing age) or motor cycle rather than by public transportation. As a result they are subjected to a far heavier fatality and injury rate.

On the roads the sober are discriminated against. The responsibility of the drinking driver to others than himself has not been recognized by the politicians who make the decisions. Mr P. F. Cox, the New South Wales Minister of Transport, is reported to be against random breath tests for drunken driving because if a person was stopped it would make him look a fool in front of his family. Attitudes such as this are very hard to understand because if the man fails the test he is a fool to be driving and if he passes the test he should feel proud that he is acting responsibly toward his family. The sober driver must suffer greater driving safety risks because he is sharing the road with drinking drivers. He must also pay higher base insurance premiums because of the large number of accidents caused by drinking drivers.

Everyone pays the immediate and long-term costs of bulk oil and chemical tanker accidents at sea, but a higher relative cost is borne by underdeveloped countries and future generations.

Notes

1. The House of Representatives Standing Committee on Road Safety, The Parliament of the Commonwealth of Australia, *Passenger Motor Vehicle Safety*, Australian Government Publishing Service, Canberra, May 1976, p. 50.
2. Cameron, C. and Macdonald, W. A., *A Review of Driver/Rider Training in Relation to Road Safety*, Australian Road Research Board, Report No. 3, Melbourne, January 1975, p. 24.
3. Raymond, A., *Alcohol in Relation to Road Safety*, Australian Road Research Board, Report No. 2, Melbourne, November 1974, pp. 12-13.
4. Mostert, N., *Supership*, Penguin, Harmondsworth, 1974, p. 76.

Chapter 9
Subsidies

The Australian taxpayer outlays a vast amount of money to keep the transportation system afloat. Latest figures show that Qantas made a $14 million loss, A.N.L. a $9.4 million loss, all state railway systems lost money: New South Wales $243 million; Victoria $162 million; Queensland $89 million; South Australia $42 million; Tasmania $18 million; Western Australia $3 million, road building in Australia cost $788 million, capital investment in the railways was $220 million, shipbuilding was subsidized to the tune of $43 million and the subsidy equivalent of tariff protection for the car industry was $342 million. Some transportation odds-and-ends paid for by the taxpayer have not been included in this list, but even so these costs come to over $140 per person or over $600 per family per year.

Are the benefits gained from this considerable expenditure worthwhile when all possible alternative uses of the money are considered? Much of this subsidization has just 'happened' over a period of many years and the worth of the expenditure as part of a government's overall expenditure programme has never been considered. It is certainly time the New South Wales government, for example, decided as a matter of policy whether the $243 million is best spent on railways and buses or whether it would be better used building schools and hospitals or retraining retrenched workers from the Newcastle State Dockyard.

Shipbuilding in Australia has had a mottled history. It was not until the first world war that a definite shipbuilding programme was established with the opening of the facilities of Walkers Ltd in Maryborough, the New South Wales State Dockyard at Newcastle, and Poole and Steele in Adelaide. Before this the only facilities were at Cockatoo Island in Sydney and at Williamstown in Melbourne. Between the wars, shipbuilding declined and several yards closed or diversified into heavy engineering. With the Second World War Evans Deakin established a shipyard in Brisbane and B.H.P. opened their yards at Whyalla, South Australia.

When the Tariff Board examined the shipbuilding industry in 1971 six major commercial shipyards were operating: B.H.P. at Whyalla; the N.S.W. State Dockyard at Newcastle; Evans Deakin in Brisbane; Cockatoo Island in Sydney; Adelaide Ship at Port Adelaide; and Walkers in Maryborough. Since then, Adelaide Ship, a division of Adelaide Steamships Pty Ltd closed in 1973, Walkers withdrew from shipbuilding in 1974, and in 1976 Evans Deakin ceased shipbuilding.

By world standards Australia's shipbuilding activities are not significant. Since the Second World War Australia has constructed vessels totalling around 1.3 million dwt; during 1975 alone Japan produced nine times this amount and it was exceeded by the 1975 annual output of Spain, the United States, Sweden, France, the United Kingdom and Germany. The Netherlands shipbuilding production in 1974 exceeded Australia's post-war effort.

But despite this small size, there have been some notable firsts. In 1964 the N.S.W. State Dockyard at Newcastle completed the 6500 dwt *Kooringa*, the world's first cellular container ship. The *Ocean Digger*, one of the world's largest semi-submersible oil drilling rigs was built at Whyalla in 1967 as were the 14 400 dwt *Iron Duke* and *Iron Monarch*, completed in 1973 to carry finished steel products for B.H.P., and of interest because they were the first vessels to be powered by marine gas turbines. The Australian-built 62 000 dwt oil tanker *Amanda Miller* is fully automated and requires no men in the engine room.

The beginning of the energy crisis in 1973 had a severe effect on the world shipbuilding market. Virtually no new orders for tankers have been placed since then and some existing orders have been cancelled. Estimates of world shipbuilding capacity range between 40 million and 50 million dwt with contracted work standing at 60 million dwt of tanker construction, down from a peak of 95 million dwt in late 1973, and 28 million dwt of bulk carrier and general cargo ship construction. Many countries, particularly Japan and the Republic of Korea, undertook massive shipbuilding capacity expansion programmes to cope with the expected heavy demand for super tanker construction which did not eventuate. This has been a prime cause of the serious current excess at around 50 per cent. Japan and Sweden are currently attempting to redirect their excess capacity towards the construction of smaller non-tanker vessels, a move which will result in substantial employment reductions in the industry.

Overseas shipbuilding operations are based on large-scale production and high degrees of specialization and mechanization. The Australian Shipbuilding Study Mission when it visited major shipbuilding countries late in 1974 found that sixteen yards in Japan could build ships of over 200 000 dwt in size and that four yards in West Germany employed between 2 500 and 15 000 people – the largest vessel built in Australia is the 83 500 dwt bauxite carrier *Clutha Capricorn*, and the N.S.W. State Dockyard and Whyalla, Australia's two biggest yards, employ 2000 and 1900 people respectively.

Nor is size the only problem of the Australian shipbuilding industry. Overseas shipyards of a size similar to those in Australia have a productivity rate three to four times greater, when productivity is measured in terms of the rate of steel erected per man hour. This poor productivity performance is due to two major factors, lack of economies of scale and industrial problems. There is not sufficient shipbuilding demand to justify the additional capital equipment needed to bring local yards into line with Japanese facilities. Both the N.S.W. State Dockyard and Whyalla estimate they need between $40 million and $50 million in additional modern equipment. But the Industries Assistance Commission, in their 1976 evaluation of the Australian shipbuilding industry, predicted that about twenty-four medium to large ships will be built by Australian yards over the next decade. This would just be sufficient demand to keep both the yards going at present rates of productivity. New equipment and increased productivity would mean that only one yard would be kept operating at this level of demand.

Industrial disruptions are also a major problem of Australian shipbuilding. A basic cause of this is the large number of different unions that are represented in Australian yards: fifteen different unions are at Whyalla and the N.S.W. State Dockyard, and twenty-two different unions are at Cockatoo. This compares with one union in shipbuilding yards in Japan, West Germany and Sweden and, as might be expected, eight different unions in United Kingdom yards. With this large number of different unions present, demarcation disputes are common and result in overmanning of many aspects of the work. The unions also oppose interchangeability of work which results in a significant increase in the number of non-skilled support workers required. As the Australian Shipbuilding Study Mission put it: 'Unions at times react to situations by sustaining what is thought to be in the interest of union principles rather than what is best for the establishment as a whole.'[1]

Poor productivity naturally leads to higher costs. Labour and overhead costs of producing medium to large ships in Australia are three to four times greater than in Japan. This is, in the main, not due to differences in wage rates, but to differences in productivity. This type of ship can be purchased from Japan or from the Republic of Korea at contract prices which are only 40 to 50 per cent of the local price before subsidy (and which are still considerably lower than the local price after the subsidy has been paid).

To keep the Australian shipbuilding industry viable, subsidies have been paid under the *Ship Construction Bounty Act 1975* and preceding legislation, which amounted to $18 million in 1969–70 and have steadily increased to $43 million in 1975–6. In 1971 a Tariff Board Inquiry was held into the shipbuilding industry. Before this Inquiry ships exceeding 200 dwt were eligible for a subsidy which equated the cost with that of ships built in Britain and delivered to an Australian port. This subsidy had a maximum of one-third of the lowest Australian tender. The government bought the ship from the builder and then sold it at the subsidized price to the owner. Vessels under 200 dwt could be imported at 30 to 40 per cent duty, while vessels over this size could only be imported with the written permission of the Minister for Shipping and Transport. After the inquiry the government accepted most of the Tariff Board's recommendations and introduced a sliding subsidy scale, depending upon the ship's size (for example a minimum subsidy of 25 per cent of the local contract price for a 1000 dwt vessel and a maximum of 45 per cent for a ship over 9000 dwt for the period to the end of 1975), which would be reduced to a flat 25 per cent subsidy after 1980. New ships of over 200 dwt would gain import approval if no Australian yard tendered to build them or if the Australian price after subsidy exceeded the delivered price from overseas. In December 1973 some minor changes were made to the policy in addition to extending the subsidy scheme to ships to be used by Australian flag operators in international trade. On 13 August 1976 Peter Nixon, the Minister for Transport, announced that the basic policy detailed by the Labor government in 1973 would be followed by his Liberal–National Country Party government and that under this policy he was allowing A.N.L. to place an order for four 15 000 dwt bulk carriers with Japanese yards. Later in the same month Mr Nixon announced that the signing of contracts for two of these ships had been deferred. If Neville Wran, the Labor N.S.W. Premier, could secure a moratorium on industrial disputes at Newcastle, then these ships would be built there. A non-strike undertaking and a wage freeze proved unacceptable to the unions and despite a much publicized visit to Japan by Bob Hawke, the Australian Council of Trade Unions' President, the A.N.L. signed the contract for the other two bulk carriers with Mitsubishi Heavy Industries on 21 February 1977. Federal maritime and shipbuilding unions since then have criticized the A.C.T.U. for not implementing bans on all overseas-built coastal shipping operating in Australian waters. But even such action would only have a remote chance of altering government policy on Australian shipbuilding.

In the report of its 1976 investigation of shipbuilding the Industries Assistance Commission is rather critical of the actions of the major Australian dockyards in light of the 1971 recommendations made by the Tariff Board (who became the Industries Assistance Commission in 1973). These recommendations had been for the dockyards to move away from the construction of the larger ships and to concentrate on smaller, more specialized vessels on which Australian builders could effectively compete on the world market. The Tariff Board also encouraged the industry to improve its labour productivity and to improve administrative, marketing and technical efficiency. None of these things occurred during the period 1971 to 1976, in fact the relative cost disadvantage of Australian shipbuilding with overseas shipbuilding increased, and increased by as much as 40 to 50 per cent with Japan. These changes in 1976 were much harder to implement than they were when suggested by the Tariff Board in 1971 when conditions were buoyant and world demand for shipbuilding was high.

Cessation of building large ships at Whyalla and the N.S.W. State Dockyard will almost certainly mean the closure of these two yards.

The Industries Assistance Commission estimated the closure of the N.S.W. State Dockyard would result in the loss of 3500 jobs in the area or 2.5 per cent of the Newcastle workforce. Although this would cause considerable short-term difficulties, the diverse and stable industrial character of Newcastle would ensure the relatively easy long-term accommodation of the Dockyard closure. But Whyalla is a very different situation. Closure of the shipyard would mean the loss of 3200 jobs or 26 per cent of the Whyalla workforce. Whyalla is much more isolated than Newcastle and the only other major employer in the area is the B.H.P. steel works. With a much younger population, a large migration out of Whyalla would occur with the closure of the shipyards.

The Industries Assistance Commission recommended that the 1973 policy continue with the subsidy continuing to decline from the 45 per cent established in 1973 to 25 per cent by the end of 1980. This would mean the end of Whyalla and the N.S.W. State Dockyard as even in 1975-6 the subsidy required to remain competitive with overseas builders was $65 million rather than the $43 million actually received. But closure of these yards is justified in economic terms and the redundancy problem should be short-term and eased by adequate adjustment assistance. (At the N.S.W. State Dockyard the severance payment is two weeks pay for each year of service up to ten years.) Import restrictions should be removed on vessels above 6000 dwt and duties of around 25 per cent continued to be paid on vessels below 150 dwt. Efficient smaller shipbuilders such as Carrington Slipways Pty Ltd in Tomago, N.S.W. and any of the major yards capable of making the switch to smaller vessels will form a restructured Australian shipbuilding industry – more efficient, more able to compete world-wide and much less reliant on large government handouts.

Another transportation-related industry in Australia that is highly protected is the production of motor vehicles and components. As with shipbuilding, this industry operates at far higher cost than does its counterpart overseas. A medium-sized motor car (such as a Chrysler Valiant, Holden, Ford Falcon or Toyota Crown) built in Australia costs 40 to 50 per cent more than does its equivalent built in the U.S. Wage levels and the cost of raw materials are not significant causes of these differences. The major causes are the inability of Australian manufacturers to generate high volumes of production and resulting efficiencies of economies of scale, and the relative inefficiencies of production processes and methods in Australia. When the component industry is included with the vehicle assembly and manufacture industry, the tariff protection for this lack of ability to compete with the rest of the world is more than $500 million a year.

Five manufacturers produce motor cars in Australia: General Motors-Holden, Ford, Chrysler, Toyota and Nissan. Toyota and Nissan have only recently begun manufacturing in Australia, while Leyland ceased manufacturing operations in 1974. In addition, Australian Motor Industries assemble Triumphs and Ramblers, Motor Producers assemble Datsuns, Volkswagens and Volvos, and Renault assembles Renault and Peugeots. Components for motor cars are manufactured by the vehicle manufacturers, to a limited extent by the assemblers, and by over 150 specialist companies. In all, the industry accounts for around 7 per cent of manufacturing value added and 6 per cent of employment in manufacturing industries, providing about 90 000 jobs.

Australian production of motor cars began at the beginning of the century and involved fitting locally produced bodies to imported chassis. During the 1920s a tariff was introduced which discriminated against this procedure and this led the Ford Motor Company in 1925 and General Motors Corporation in 1926 to begin operations in Australia. Tariffs also encouraged the growth of a domestic parts and components industry during the 1920s and 1930s. An agreement by General Motors-Holden in 1945 to increase the local content of its assembled vehicles led to the production of the first Holden three years later.

From 1957 the duty on fully imported cars was set at 35 per cent. This rate was increased to 45 per cent in 1966 and remained in force until the 25 per cent across-the-board tariff cut in July 1973. Although Australian governments had long expressed an interest in increasing the local content of locally assembled motor cars it was not until May 1964 that local content plans were formally introduced. These plans enabled the car manufacturers to import components at reduced import duties on condition that they would raise the local content of their production. Four plans were established in 1966. The first plan required the manufacturer to reach 95 per cent local content within five years; in return the manufacturer could import the remaining components and parts duty free or at very low duties. The other three plans were called 'small-volume plans' and related import duty concessions to three levels of local content which depended on the manufacturer's volume. Many changes have been made to these plans over the succeeding years. For small manufacturers of less than 25 000 units per year an optional 85 per cent local content scheme was introduced. Then the 95 per cent plan was modified so that the manufacturer had only to reach an average of 95 per cent over all cars produced, although no car could fall below 85 per cent local content. In December 1971 it was decided to phase out the small-volume plans but to retain the 85 and 95 per cent local content plans until the end of 1979. In 1972–3 the total payment which would have been made to the industry to provide the same amount of assistance as the tariff protection (called the net subsidy equivalent of the tariff) was $215 million, while the duty concessions were valued at $18 million. The net subsidy equivalent of the tariff had risen to $342 million by 1975–6.

The motor vehicle industry also receives government assistance in the form of research and development grants, export incentive grants, export market development allowances and, until 1973, investment allowances. Protection from imports is provided to the industry because of the great distance from Japan, Europe and the United States and the addition of freight costs to the price of cars brought in from overseas. Also only about 18 per cent of all vehicles in the world are right-hand drive which means that many imported cars must undergo expensive conversion.

In retrospect, the local content plans have been the cause of the major problems with the Australian automobile industry. One direct effect of these plans has been to encourage small-scale operation. Under the small-volume plans, duty concessions were greatest for low-volume vehicles with the lowest local content. For example, in the year 1968–9 at the height of these plans, each car produced under the small-volume plans received import duty concessions averaging $262, while cars produced under the 85 per cent plan received $75 and under the 95 per cent plan $27 worth of concessions. This situation had the effect of promoting a wide variety of different models

all with small sales volume. It was better to import parts and components to assemble in Australia than it was to import complete cars.
Small-volume, relatively low local content cars, took market share
away from the high local content cars which were under the 85 and
95 per cent plans. With the proliferation of models came a greater
proliferation of parts and components and in turn local suppliers of
these items.

Although volume limits were placed on the small-volume plans
and they were later phased out, the damage had been done. Without
rather drastic government action, there are already too many car
manufacturers in Australia for the industry ever to gain the economies
of scale needed to compete with overseas manufacturers.

But the high-volume plans, the 85 and 95 per cent local content
plan, also have undesirable effects. Because of the very high local
content specification, the local supplier of parts and components quite
often has gained a level of protection far in excess of that offered
by the tariff – no matter how much more expensive the component
is from a local source, the manufacturer is unable to obtain it from
overseas. Another undesirable aspect of the local content plan is that
the taxpayer is providing a direct subsidy to the industry in the form
of import duty concessions. This is public revenue that otherwise
would have been collected. But the amount of this benefit is difficult
to establish and a direct policy decision on the extent of this assistance
cannot be made. The plans also have been changed in detail rather
frequently making forward planning difficult for the manufacturers.
A final problem with the plans has been the rather arbitrary way
in which the government has administered the procedural rules that
are associated with them.

In 1974 the Industries Assistance Commission examined the industry and recommended that the local content rules be abolished and
that the import duty for vehicles and components be reduced by steps
to 25 per cent by 1982. These recommendations were not accepted
by the government and the situation exists as it was prior to the investigation.

The *Age* newspaper printed a three-part series on the Australian
automobile industry in 1977. As part of their report they detailed
the price escalation which occurs on a $2000 Japanese small car on
its way to the Australian consumer. This is shown in Table 9.1. As

Table 9.1 Price and Tariff Components of a Small Japanese Car

Item	Cost	Tariff component
Price loaded on to ship	$2000	nil
Insurance and freight – Japan to Australia	$70	nil
Handling charges	$40	nil
Tariff: 45 per cent of cost – including insurance and freight	$931.50	$931.50
Landed, duty-paid cost	$3041.50	$931.50
Distributor's margin at 13 per cent of landed duty-paid cost	$395.40	$121.10
Sales tax at 27.5 per cent	$836.41	$256.16
Price to dealer	$4273.31	$1308.76
Dealer's margin on 18 per cent of above price	$769.20	$235.50
Freight, cleaning and pre-delivery service by dealer	$140	nil
Total price to consumer	$5182.51	$1544.34

Source: 'The Cars that Ate Australia', The *Age*, 24 February 1977.

the *Age* investigators state: 'It is plain from this table that although the nominal tariff is 45 per cent it is effectively about 75 per cent of the cost of the car when it reaches Australia.' The reporters conclude the article with the estimate that if all cars entered Australia tariff-free every worker in Australia would benefit to the extent of $2.80 per week.

Although the price of petrol seems high in Australia, it is in fact subsidized below the world price. If the price of Australian crude was raised to that charged by the Organization of Petroleum Exporting Countries (O.P.E.C.) in mid-1976, then the price of super-grade petrol in metropolitan Sydney would rise about 40 per cent to around 23 cents per litre or $1.05 per gallon.

The Kingfish and Halibut oil fields were discovered off the Gippsland coast in Victoria by Esso and B.H.P. in 1967. These fields in 1975 accounted for 90 per cent of all production of crude oil in Australia, which represented 71 per cent of total Australian demand.

Together, the Moonie field in Queensland, which was the first commercial oil operation in Australia, and the Barrow Island field in Western Australia, account for less than 10 per cent of Australia's production.

Because of the ability of Australian fields to provide enough indigenous crude to satisfy a sizeable proportion of the local demand, the federal government has set low prices for domestic crude. For example, in mid-1976 crude from the Gippsland fields was priced at $2.33 per barrel while its value on the free market was estimated to be at least $11 per barrel.

This situation is slightly different in nature from shipbuilding and motor car production but again transportation, as a major user of light petroleum products, is being subsidized. But the cost of the subsidy in this case is being borne by the petroleum exploration and producing companies, although government taxation and royalty revenue is being passed up as well.

Government-set low prices for indigenous crude have a significant effect on the amount of exploration undertaken. Although a decision has been made to price all local crude from fields discovered after 14 September 1975 at import parity, B.H.P. made the following case to the Industries Assistance Commission Inquiry into Crude Oil Pricing for an immediate increase in the price of crude from existing fields:

The best available opinion is that most of the oil yet to be found in Australia is likely to be offshore in deep water, probably in depths below 150 metres, and the investment required to finance such exploration and development could be several times that experienced in Bass Strait.

A significant part of this investment must be financed from income generated within the existing industry.[2]

Esso and B.H.P. both argued at this inquiry that an immediate increase in the price for current oil production would provide confidence in the stability of the government's long-term plans for crude oil pricing and this would allow companies in the industry to plan substantial exploration activity.

Another disadvantage of the pricing policy is that it encourages increased consumption of a scarce resource. The low price is a direct subsidy to the consumer, which was worth an estimated $1000 million in 1976. Petroleum products are used more extensively than they would be if priced at world market prices. In the extreme, plants may be set up on the basis of using petroleum as a cheap energy source, when with higher energy costs these plants would not be viable. At a low price the extent of development of existing fields is limited for financial reasons – the Industries Assistance Commission estimated that over 400 million barrels of oil (two years' supply of Australia's crude oil requirements) will not be recovered at existing prices but would have been recovered at import parity or world market prices.

Because all domestic crude oil requirements cannot be met from indigenous production, a system for allocating the cheaper local crude to refiners exists. This procedure was originally set up so that local crude was allocated in proportion to sales of a group of specified petroleum products which were mainly derived from Australian crude. Although some changes have been made to this list of products it still favours light petroleum products such as motor spirit, aviation fuels, kerosene and heating oils. This means that these products are more highly subsidized than are the heavier products – industries which use light petroleum products are subsidized to a greater extent than those which do not. Other inequities exist with this allocation process. International aviation bunkers and international diesel fuel are included among the products which draw a local crude allocation. This means that these fuels are much cheaper in Australia than elsewhere in the world and some of the cost benefits associated with Australian crude oil production are being lost overseas. Another example is that imported diesel fuel has been sold at discounts of up to 35 per cent because its sale generates greater allocations of indigenous crude. This is rather a serious misallocation of resources.

Australian crude oil resources will increasingly fail to meet local demand. The Royal Commission on Petroleum forecast that crude production would plateau around 156 million barrels per year between 1977 and 1980 and then fall to around 120 million barrels in 1985. This represents a drop from meeting 70 per cent of local demand to being able to meet less than 40 per cent. B.H.P. is more pessimistic and estimates that only 20 per cent of Australian demand for crude oil will be provided locally in 1985. These estimates of course depend on the amount of exploration which takes place in the next few years. Known reserves are small. The Mackerel field in Gippsland will be in full production in 1978, the Tuna field is being developed and several other development areas in Bass Strait have been identified. Prospects for other areas are not so bright: the Moonie field is 90 per cent depleted and high expectations of the north-west shelf of Australia have not been fulfilled.

The Industries Assistance Commission recommended that Barrow Island and Moonie crude be priced at import parity less the $2 excise per barrel from the beginning of 1977, while crude from the Gippsland fields be progressively increased in price until it reaches import parity by 1985. Such a progression would be less inflationary and would also enable industries which cannot easily pass on any of the increased price (such as rural industries and mining which are supplying overseas markets to fixed contracts) to minimize their difficulties with the move to world pricing for crude. The Industries Assistance Commission argued that free world pricing would remove inequities between producers and consumers and also remove the unplanned market distortions brought about by the allocation system. Additional revenue to the producers would enable them to mount a worthwhile exploration effort and to fully develop existing productive fields. During 1977 to 1980 the I.A.C. estimated that the producers and the government would each receive an additional $625 million. If the government considers this additional revenue to the producers to be excessive, royalties and taxes can be increased and this extra revenue used within the framework of an explicit government spending programme.

Transportation is a prime area where non-economic reasons are used to justify financial and operating conditions which are inequitable, while in most cases the non-economic reasons could be satisfied in another simpler and less expensive fashion.

Australian shipbuilding is an example. The fact that it received $43 million in subsidies in 1976 means that the industry has to rely on non-economic grounds for its justification. These grounds include: defence considerations; the necessity for an island continent with a high dependence on international trade to have shipbuilding and repair facilities; and the social and regional implications of closing down the industry. Examining these reasons in turn: First, existing naval dockyards can carry out refits, repairs and modernizations and could construct warships if required. The Air Force imports its planes so why can't the Navy import its ships. Second, it is important for an island continent to have repair facilities and these can be provided by the smaller, more competitive yards which will remain viable. Large ships built in Australia are in themselves no different from large ships built overseas, except for the much higher cost. Third, closure of the N.S.W. State Dockyard and B.H.P.s yard at Whyalla will mean a loss of over 6000 jobs in the two cities, but will also save subsidy payments of almost $32 million ($8000 per worker for 2000 workers at the N.S.W. State Dockyard and 1900 workers at Whyalla). Nothing would be lost by using this finance to set up two manufacturing operations, one in Newcastle and one in Whyalla, which could well be worker-controlled. These manufacturing facilities would employ the same skills used in the yards and could even be involved in building small ships. They may even make money.

Car production in Australia also needs to undergo some radical changes. Such changes would not be difficult to undertake from an economic point of view because, as the Industries Assistance Commission points out, from the introduction of the local content plans until mid-1973 $1500 million was paid out under the plans, while during the same period total wages paid by the industry were $2400 million, and this $1500 million does not include the subsidy equivalent of the tariff protection received during the period. Australian car production provides jobs for Australians, but this is the only value – all car manufacturers in Australia are owned by overseas multinational companies which retain in Australia just sufficient resources to keep production going. Since the jobs are the only benefit, almost the same result would be obtained by paying those working in the industry the protection money for doing nothing. All other Australians would benefit by being able to buy much cheaper cars. A more satisfactory solution would be to remove all government constraints and aids from the car manufacturers operating in Australia. At the same time the government should encourage the setting up of one or two Australian manufacturers who would concentrate on one or two models of a particular class of car. As the existing manufacturers fold, the Australian operations would increase production volume and provide employment opportunities for many of the workers made redundant. Even if only half or less of the 600 000 cars bought in Australia each year were locally produced, it would still mean high-volume production and economies of scale for the few Australian models. Australia would then have a domestic automobile industry structure similar to Sweden. Success similar to that experienced by Volvo and Saab would provide Australians with lower cost, better cars and would provide Australia with increased export earnings.

It is interesting to examine what benefits Qantas provides Australians in return for the $14 million paid out of taxation revenue in 1976. If international airlines are losing money it would seem to be far more sensible to close Qantas and have U.S. or British airlines service Australia and then the American or British taxpayer would subsidize international trips for Australians. If the reason is national prestige, then equal national prestige and better value-for-money would be obtained by using the $14 million to build a hospital in India outside which could fly a large Australian flag.

Railways have similar problems. Politicians believe that passengers and freight travelling by rail should be subsidized. For some reason it seems preferable to have huge losses paid for by the general public rather than have the users of rail services pay the full cost of those services. Certainly there is benefit in encouraging the suburban commuter to travel by rail rather than by car, but the benefit of having freight and passengers travel on low-volume high-cost rural train journeys rather than by road is not so clear. Indeed for many of these rural trips it would be cheaper for the railways to use taxis for passengers and taxi trucks for freight than it would be to run the train. Politicians have limited the amount of depreciation provisions as one way to keep fares and freight charges down. This means that often routine repairs and replacements cannot be met from revenue and have to be financed by interest-bearing loans with the result that rolling stock becomes steadily more antiquated and railway operating losses become steadily larger. The only solution to this problem is to allow railway management to close or restructure any aspect of the operation in an attempt to make it a break-even venture. If the politicians want a particular non-profitable operation or service to continue for social reasons a specific subsidy should be paid so that this service also breaks even. Railways operate under what is called a 'common carrier obligation' which means that they have to carry any freight offered to them. This obligation will cease to be a burden if the railways have wide rate-making powers. A final requirement for a more efficient rail service is to give the railways the option of operating road vehicles instead of trains if the circumstances warrant.

Most of the $600 paid by every Australian family each year for transportation subsidies could be avoided. There is no need to subsidize shipbuilding, car production or airline operations. Certain railway operations and certain A.N.L. services may justify subsidy, but certainly not all. Roads have to be built, but more use of tolls could be made on expensive restricted-access roads. Transportation should not be allowed to continue as an area where widespread inefficiencies are unquestioningly paid for by the taxpayer.

Notes

1. Australian Shipbuilding Industry Study Mission, *Shipbuilding Productivity and Industrial Relations in Australia*, Australian Government Publishing Service, Canberra, 1975, p. 20.
2. Industries Assistance Commission, *Crude Oil Pricing*, Australian Government Publishing Service, Canberra, 1976, p. 15.

Chapter 10
Energy

It has become common to measure the well-being of a society on the basis of per capita consumption of energy, although with the energy crisis of the early 1970s the primary focus switched from an emphasis on high amounts of per capita usage to an emphasis on high efficiency of energy transformation. Ivan Illich, the founder of the Center for Intercultural Documentation in Cuernavaca, Mexico, believes that neither high-energy consumption nor thermodynamic thrift leads to well-being. Both require huge public expenditure and increased social control. General well-being will only be attained by the least possible use of mechanical energy. Illich argues that a high-energy policy will lead to social relations which are dictated by technology while a low-energy policy will provide a wide choice of possible life styles and cultures.

There is a threshold up to which energy consumption and equity increase simultaneously – increased energy consumption allows the underprivileged sectors of the community to be relieved of much of the drudgery and burden of oppressive physical work. But beyond the threshold increased energy consumption does not bring greater equity – with this increase in energy consumption control over the energy becomes vested in fewer hands. Early in the twentieth century the motor car brought greater mobility to a few together with vastly increased rates of energy consumption. Today, 20 per cent of Australian families do not own a car, but the urban environment has adapted completely to the car. Those without a car are at a considerable disadvantage. Urban congestion has reduced the benefits of the car and the next step has already been taken by Sir Reginald Ansett who rides to work in a helicopter each day consuming vastly increased energy resources. Even at the level of the motor car, access or lack of access to energy provides a great source of social inequity.

This threshold is at a much lower level than that required to arouse concerns of pollution. Illich believes it is possible for societies to establish quite accurately the energy consumption rate at the threshold and that this level of minimum feasible power will provide a basis for a variety of social orders which are modern and desirable.

As transportation is a prime user of energy the threshold beyond which energy consumption leads to social inequity can be expressed in terms of speed. Illich set this speed at 24 km/h, the speed of a bicycle. He justifies his selection by the following reasoning:

The model . . . male spends more than 1500 hours per year on his car; driving or sitting in it, parking or searching for it; earning enough to pay for the vehicle, the tolls, the tyres, the insurance or the highway taxes. These four hours per day for gathering his resources for it do not include his transport-related dallying in hospitals, traffic courts, and garages, his sitting time before the TV to be sold a new model, or the time needed to earn or enjoy the travelling on his vacation. In terms of lifetime invested, the average (driver) attains four miles per hour. In countries without any transport industry, people walk at this rate wherever they want to go.

Man, unaided by any tool, is quite efficient when he moves. He carries one gram of his weight over a kilometre in 10 minutes by expending 0.75 calories, which makes him thermodynamically more efficient than any motorized vehicle and most animals, such as rats or oxen. He is still less efficient than horses or sturgeon.

A century ago, however, the bicycle appeared. It lifted man's self-powered mobility into a new order, beyond which there can be no further progress. On flat ground he can travel faster than on foot and do so using only one-fifth of the calories he would have expended walking. He can now carry one gram of his weight over one kilometre expending only 0.15 calories. Equipped with a bicycle, man does better not only than any machine but also than any animal.[1]

But despite the new insights and compelling originality of Illich's argument it is unlikely that people will willingly break down the technology that has been built up. The physical and social infrastructure of today's society is firmly embedded and it is for this reason that the energy requirements of transportation* are dealt with in this chapter in terms of present structures and equipment.

---

*Energy is measured in kilo-joules (kJ) with 1 kJ approximately equal to 1 British Thermal Unit and 1 litre of motor spirit providing approximately 38 000 kJ of fuel energy. One thousand kilo-joules are equal to 1 mega-joule (MJ).

The earth's main source of energy is the sun. But man is very inefficient in diverting solar radiation for his own use: of an annual total of $5\,400\,000 \times 10^{12}$ MJ of energy provided by the sun, man uses only 200×10^{12} MJ. Most of this energy man uses not as direct solar radiation but from the several natural energy cycles which store part of the incoming solar energy. The most important of these to man is the chemical energy cycle. Carbon compounds are fixed by photosynthesis into plant structure, and when plants and animals die a very small proportion of the total remains become converted into coal, oil or natural gas – long-lived fossil fuels. Also important is the water cycle which is based on evaporation and precipitation processes generated by the sun. Man has diverted some energy from the water cycle by converting water flow into hydro-electric power. Another natural energy cycle is based on wind power, and man derives a small amount of his energy from this source.

But fossil fuels are at present by far the major supplier of man's energy needs – in Australia over 90 per cent of the energy requirements are supplied by fossil fuels. As these fuels are being used up at a rate 10 000 times faster than they were deposited this situation will change around the turn of the century. Nuclear energy from uranium is a possible replacement for energy from fossil fuels. Fusion reactors using deuterium, a heavy hydrogen isotope which occurs naturally in all forms of water, is an encouraging possibility for the longer term. More extensive use of the renewable energy resources is another possible direction for development. Hydro-electric power is a cheap and clean form of energy but the few suitable areas in Australia (notably Tasmania) have already been rather extensively developed. It is unlikely that hydro power will ever become a major source of energy in Australia. Neither will tidal power or geothermal power because of the special circumstances required for power generation by these means. Solar energy, although extremely plentiful, is still expensive to collect, store and deliver, although this situation may change over time.

Data on the consumption of fuel for energy generation, as collected and predicted by the Department of Minerals and Energy for the period 1962 to 1985 in Australia, are shown in Figure 10.1. For the year 1971–2 half of Australia's energy requirements were provided by petroleum products with another 30 per cent coming from black

Figure 10.1   Consumption of primary fuels in Australia

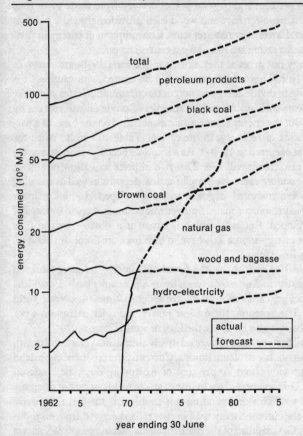

*Source Australia's Fuel Requirements to the Year 2000: A
Preliminary Report,* Department of Minerals and Energy, Fuels
Branch, Melbourne, 1973

coal and another 10 per cent from brown coal. Natural gas provided about 4 per cent and bagasse (a fuel derived from waste sugar cane pulp), hydro-electricity and wood each provided around 2 per cent of Australia's energy requirements. Consumption of energy in Australia is increasing at a rate of 6 per cent each year.

Energy resources as they existed in the early 1970s are shown in Table 10.1. This information should be treated with caution. It is tempting to divide energy resources by consumption rates and make statements such as: 'Australia's reserves of crude oil will run out by 1990.' But the energy resources are established on the basis of a particular cost of recovery, in the case of Table 10.1 up to twice the cost that occurred in 1970-1. As a resource becomes more scarce the world price for it will rise. This rise in price will allow producers to make a more extensive search for new deposits as well as enabling what were marginal deposits to be developed. In this manner additional resources many times current estimates could eventually be developed. But even with this caveat it is obvious that in time another energy source will have to take over the dominant position held by fossil fuels.

Table 10.1 also shows the favourable energy resource situation which exists in Australia, especially on a per capita basis. Fossil fuel resources per capita in Australia are about six times the overall world figure. The potential for nuclear power and solar energy on a per capita basis is also far above the U.S. or world figure.

Fossil fuels in Australia are relatively abundant as black and brown coal, but not as petroleum liquids. Currently the off-shore Gippsland fields provide about 70 per cent of Australia's domestic crude oil needs. This is expected to decline to less than 40 per cent of domestic needs by 1985. Compounding this problem is the fact that nearly half of the current energy used in Australia is derived from oil products. R. G. Chapman of the State Electricity Commission of Victoria predicts that only ten years' reserves are left in proven oil fields in Australia and that future discoveries will not extend this period of crude oil availability by much. In contrast he points to coal reserves which are relatively abundant and will be available as a fuel source for electricity generation until nuclear power takes over at the end of the century.

In addition to having differing energy reserves, fuels also have dif-

Table 10.1 Primary Energy Resources in Australia 1970-1* Compared with World Figures

Fuels	World		U.S.A.		Australia		Victoria	
	MJ x 10^{12}	MJ x 10^6	MJ x 10^{12}	MJ x 10^6	MJ x 10^{12}	MJ x 10^6	MJ x 10^{12}	MJ x 10^6
Fossil								
Coal (black and brown)	29 900	(8.3)	7 200	(36.0)	827	(65.5)	158	(45.1)
Petroleum liquids	6 100	(1.7)	1 100	(5.4)	11	(0.7)	11	(3.2)
Natural gas	5 000	(1.4)	1 100	(5.4)	62	(4.7)	11	(3.2)
Total	41 000	(11.4)	9 400	(46.8)	900	(70.9)	180	(51.5)
Nuclear								
Current reactors	2 000	(0.7)	610	(3.2)	306	(26)		
Breeder reactors	173 000	(48.2)	57 600	(288)	28 800	(2270)		
Fusion	10^6							
Renewable								
Hydro (average annual)	110	(0.04)	11	(0.04)	014	(0.011)	0.014	(0.004)
Solar (total annual on 10 per cent of land area)	101 000	(27.8)	5 000	(26)	5 000	(400)	140	(40)

*Based on recovery at up to twice current costs.

Note: Values shown in brackets are energy resources on a per capita basis.

Source: R. G. Chapman, 'Electricity Generation and Supply', in Bureau of Transport Economics, *Electric Cars: Their Future Role in Urban Transport*, Australian Government Publishing Service, Canberra, 1975, p. 141.

fering energy conversion rates. Before it can perform any useful work the raw fuel material must be processed and converted into a suitable form. Motor spirit, diesel oil and electricity are energy sources for transportation and all have been converted from a primary energy source. During this conversion process some energy is lost and the loss rate differs between fuels. Figure 10.2 shows the conversion processes and energy losses as they occurred in Australia at the end of the 1960s. Overall at the oil refineries, gas works, briquette factories and power stations, 27 per cent of the primary energy entering the conversion process is lost as heat. Although technological advances have been made in these processes since the late 1960s the basic situation is still the same.

Further losses are incurred when the secondary or processed energy source is used to drive a transportation vehicle. Motor spirit is not efficiently converted into propulsion energy by the normal motor car. In a car averaging 30 km/h and 5.5 km/litre in city traffic less than 10 per cent of the energy contained in the crude oil will be used. In contrast a similar car, but battery electric powered, has over twice the energy conversion efficiency of the petrol driven car.

The transport sector of the Australian economy uses over a quarter of the total national consumption of energy. This use of energy by transportation is split between modes and between personal travel and goods movement as shown in Table 10.2. It is interesting to note the heavy energy demands of personal travel by cars and station wagons. As over half of this energy demand is not for business trips or the journey to work, it means that around 30 per cent of all energy used in transportation is used for social, recreational and shopping trips. Road transportation certainly dominates energy consumption, although goods movements by sea also consume a reasonable amount of energy. International sea freight consumes energy heavily, using 200×10^{12} kJ of energy in 1970–1 while air freight used 5×10^{12} kJ, a relatively large amount of energy when related to the relatively small amount of goods moved.

This consideration brings out the point that Table 10.2 provides only the total energy usage of the various modes of transport. It does not provide any data on the relative efficiencies of the use of energy by the different forms of transportation. This information is shown in Table 10.3. For personal travel, air requires over twice the energy

Figure 10.2   Conversion processes for Australian energy

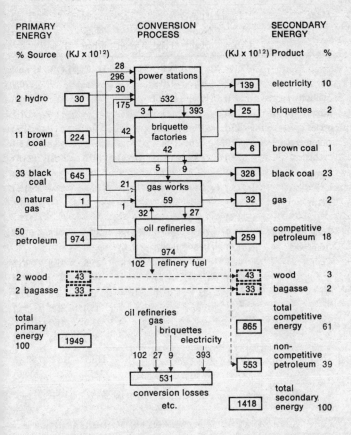

Source J.J. Fryer, *Energy for Australia's Future and its Implications for Marine Waters,* Proceedings of the Thermo-Fluids Conference on Thermal Discharge, Institution of Engineers, Sydney, December, 1972

Table 10.2 Energy Consumption on Australian Transportation, 1970-1

Mode	Personal travel			Goods movement			Total
	Urban	Non-urban	Total	Urban	Non-urban	Total	
	kJ x 10¹²	kJ x 10¹²	kJ x 10¹²	kJ x 10¹²	kJ x 10¹²	kJ x 10¹²	kJ x 10¹²
Cars and station wagons	188.8 (38%)	82.0 (16%)	270.9 (55%)	–	–	–	270.9 (55%)
Motor cycles	1.0 (<1%)	0.5 (<1%)	1.5 (<1%)	–	–	–	1.5 (<1%)
Commercial vehicles	9.0 (2%)	5.6 (1%)	14.7 (3%)	51.8 (10%)	47.0 (9%)	98.8 (20%)	113.4 (23%)
Buses	4.4 (<1%)	2.7 (<1%)	7.1 (1%)	–	–	–	7.1 (1%)
Tram	0.7 (<1%)	–	0.7 (<1%)	–	–	–	0.7 (<1%)
Total for road transport	203.9 (41%)	90.8 (18%)	294.9 (59%)	51.8 (10%)	47.0 (9%)	98.8 (20%)	409.0 (82%)
Train	11.5 (2%)	6.4 (1%)	17.9 (4%)	–	21.8 (4%)	21.8 (4%)	39.7 (8%)
Air	–	23.1 (5%)	23.1 (5%)	–	2.8 (<1%)	2.8 (<1%)	25.9 (5%)
Sea	–	–	–	–	41.9 (8%)	41.9 (8%)	41.9 (8%)
Total	215.5 (43%)	120.3 (24%)	335.9 (67%)	51.8 (10%)	113.5 (22%)	165.3 (32%)	501.2 (100%)

Note: Figures in parentheses represent percentage of the total transport energy consumption.

Source: J. A. Lee and N. Clark, 'Energy Consumption by Categories of Australian Transport', in Bureau of Transport Economics, *Electric Cars: Their Future Role in Urban Transport*, Australian Government Publishing Service, Canberra, 1975, p. 117.

per passenger-kilometre of the private car or tram. Trains and buses are even more energy efficient on a passenger-kilometre basis. For moving goods, rail and sea are considerably more efficient than road or air: moving one tonne-kilometre by air requires about 60 times

Table 10.3   Energy Intensiveness of Australian Transportation 1970-1

Mode	Personal travel kJ per passenger-kilometre	Goods movement kJ per tonne-kilometre
Car	2155	–
Commercial vehicle	–	4167
Bus	1675	–
Tram	2123	–
Train	1792	559
Air	5618	34 483
Sea	–	586

Source: N. Clark, J. A. Lee and K. W. Ogden, 'The Use of Energy for Personal Mobility', *Transportation Research*, Vol. 8, 1974, p. 402.

the energy of moving by rail. Both for moving goods and for moving people electric powered transportation is much more energy efficient than transportation powered by petroleum products. The only exception is the bus which can achieve high utilization for most of its trips while a train even in peak hours is vastly underutilized on the return trip. Moving people by these mechanical means should also be compared with the 150 kJ person-kilometre of energy used for walking and the 85 to 140 kJ per person-kilometre for cycling.

But the energy used directly for the propulsion of the transportation vehicles is not the only use of energy for the transportation network. For example Jim Beck, when at the University of Melbourne, estimated that it took about 54×10^6 kJ of energy to manufacture a car in Australia. For 1970-1 this meant that the total amount of energy devoted to car manufacture in Australia was 17×10^{12} kJ. Besides car manufacture, energy is consumed in the manufacture and sale of tyres and spare parts, in selling cars, in repairing cars, in petrol and oil refining and sales, in the construction and maintenance of parking facilities and in highway construction and maintenance. This indirect energy consumption is greatest for road and air and less for rail and sea; for air it is estimated to be as high as 60 per cent of the total energy requirements of the mode and as high as 40 per cent for commercial road vehicles.

Virtually all (98 per cent) the energy used for transportation is derived from crude oil, which in turn means that the transportation sector consumes just over half of all the oil-derived energy produced in Australia. This places transportation in a particularly vulnerable position with the uncertainty that exists about crude oil resources and about the future price for crude oil. Also the use of petroleum products as energy sources for transportation (and in particular the internal combustion engine) has come under strong criticism for its high pollution levels.

It is government policy that any new crude oil developments in Australia will be priced at import parity. At current prices this would mean an increase in the retail price of super-grade petrol of around 40 per cent. Even if the Industries Assistance Commission recommendations on crude oil pricing are accepted and the price of Gippsland crude is slowly increased to reach import parity in 1985, there will still be substantial price increases over the next decade for the Australian motorist. How will the motor car, with the gasoline internal combustion engine, cope?

The Petroleum Information Bureau points out that while average weekly earnings, in money terms, increased by over 400 per cent from 1949 to 1972, during the same time the price of petrol rose by less than 70 per cent. Ten gallons of petrol cost 15 per cent of average weekly earnings in 1949 but only 5 per cent of average weekly earnings in 1972. But this situation is due to the fact that indigenous crude in 1972 was selling at about one-fifth of the price of imported crude. The world price of crude is controlled by the O.P.E.C. countries and during recent years the O.P.E.C. price has increased fivefold and many serious dislocations of oil supplies from the Middle East have occurred. It appears that O.P.E.C. pricing policy is to establish a price for crude which will increase at a rate about 1½ per cent greater than the average inflation rate of the major oil importing countries. This fact, together with Australia's intention to move towards import parity pricing for local crude, ensures a large increase in the price of petroleum products in Australia in the near future.

Two characteristics of the motor car indicate that even quite large increases in the price of crude oil might not have a great influence on the level of use of the car. First, because motor spirit is a highly processed product, the cost of the original crude oil forms only a relatively low percentage of the cost of the final product. For example, if the price of crude oil rose from $2.50 to $11 a barrel, a rise in excess of 300 per cent, the price of super-grade petrol would only increase by about 40 per cent. The second characteristic relates to the value that the car driver places on his own time. This value is currently estimated to be between 25 and 30 per cent of the individual's wage rate. So while the cost of the petrol used on a 10-kilometre trip might be around 30 cents, the perceived time cost for the driver might be $1.50 to $2. The value of the extra travelling time on public transportation, for example, is sufficient for most people to absorb quite large increases in the price of petrol.

One way to combat the rising price of petrol is to find ways of using less of it. This can be done by either increasing the average number of people riding in a car on any trip, or by reducing the fuel consumption rates of cars. Car pooling is the obvious way to increase the occupancy rate for car trips. Although this does spread the vehicle operating costs over several people, an individual travelling in a car pool has lost some of the flexibility which is the greatest advantage of car travel. Also a car pool can only operate on the regular trip to work which comprises much less than half of the total number of car trips. Design changes are the key to lower fuel consumption. A lighter car, with increased use of aluminium in the body and engine and with a less powerful engine, will have a lower fuel consumption rate. A continuously variable transmission, supercharging and aerodynamic changes to the body design would also reduce fuel consumption. The Commonwealth Bureau of Roads in its *Report on Roads in Australia 1975* quotes studies done in the United States which show that these changes in vehicle design could provide a car owner with up to 50 per cent savings in total energy consumption and with a 30 per cent reduction in operating cost.

While it appears that the motorist in his private car will absorb the coming price rises in petrol quite easily (although most likely not with good grace), the situation is somewhat different for the movement of goods. As with moving people, moving goods by road has the advantage that there is no change of mode required during the trip. Like people, goods have a value of time spent on the trip. But unlike people this value is either very large or very small. If an entire manufacturing process is waiting the delivery of a spare part the cost of time spent in travel is very high, but if the item being delivered is only adding to already adequate inventories of like items then the cost of travel time is very low. In addition the transfer of goods between modes can easily be organized so that it is much more efficient than the transfer of people between modes. This has resulted from containerization and an example is the container train which runs daily between Sydney and Melbourne. So that while people are quite strongly tied to their cars, goods are not quite so strongly tied to road transport. An increase in the price of fuel will have the effect of transferring freight between the transportation modes according to the modes' energy intensiveness (see Table 10.3), and according to the proportion which fuel costs are of the total operating costs of the various modes.

Air is by far the most energy intensive mode. Increases in the price of aviation fuels will have a significant effect on the ability of air freight to compete with the other modes. Fuel costs for both domestic roll-on roll-off shipping and rail are about 3 per cent of operating costs. But the effect of fuel price rises is quite different for these modes because ship's bunker fuel undergoes little processing from crude oil while locomotive diesel fuel undergoes considerable processing. The full effect of an increase in the price of crude oil is felt by shipping but only a portion of the increase is passed on to rail. Fuel costs for road are 6 per cent of total operating costs and this relatively small percentage has the effect, as shown by John Taplin, of a 30 per cent rise in fuel costs resulting in a loss of only 2 per cent of road freight to rail on competitive routes. For international shipping, fuel price increases will result in lower vessel speeds to reduce fuel consumption – down to the theoretical design optimum of 25 knots. Taplin also predicts that for the bulk trades the relatively higher proportion of fuel costs to total operating costs compared with that for general cargo will mean that importing countries will concentrate on nearer sources of supply. For example, over the next few years Japan might find it increasingly attractive to enlarge its iron-ore purchases from Australia, its nearest supplier.

The net effect of crude oil price increases on the transportation of goods will be a slight re-allocation from road to rail and a larger shift between sea and rail on coastal routes. Air freight will experience competitive problems with land modes on domestic services and international trading relationships may alter due to increased shipping costs.

Crude oil shortages will mean increased prices in the first instance but eventually there will be shortages. John Taplin estimates that Australia has about twelve years of proven oil reserves at the present rate of production and O.P.E.C. oil is expected to be nearly depleted by the end of the century. Recently there has been much public interest in the electric car. Can the electric car compete with the internal combustion engine or will it have to wait until there are severe shortages of crude oil before it becomes widely accepted?

Electric vehicles are already in use in some specialized areas of transport such as milk delivery vans and fork-lift trucks. Currently there is no commercial production of electric vehicles and imports are few. The Bureau of Transport Economics established the characteristics of an electric passenger car which could presently be built to compete with a conventional four cylinder internal combustion car. This electric car would have a maximum speed of 102 km/h, acceleration from rest to 50 km/h in 10.9 seconds and a range of 100 kilometres compared with an unlimited range for the conventional car, acceleration from rest to 50 km/h in 6 seconds and a top speed of 150 km/h. These characteristics of the electric car limit its usefulness to urban driving. Although urban driving accounts for almost two-thirds of the total distance driven by Australian cars and station wagons, this does not represent the true upper limit of the potential market for the currently developed electric car. The potential market is much less because most car owners at least once or twice a year take long trips through rural areas for which the electric car would be unsuitable. Unless the range of the electric car is extended or the re-charging time is reduced (even below the current best of about an hour) it will only be truly competitive with the conventional car as the second family car. The Commonwealth Bureau of Roads estimated that just under 30 per cent of all households owned two or more cars in 1971 and predicted that this figure would increase to over 35 per cent by 1981. From these data the Bureau of Transport Economics estimated that the electric car could reasonably expect to compete for about a 10 per cent share of the current automobile market. Its ability to compete will be greatly influenced by a purchase price estimated at 25 per cent higher than that of a conventional car, but fuel costs will be as low as one-third of those for the internal combustion car.

Electric cars have the prime advantage that they are almost pollution free. In effect the total pollution will be greatly diminished and transferred from thousands of ground-level sources to a handful of high-level sources at the power station stacks. While the pollution at power stations is much easier to control and is normally located away from population centres, even this problem may be overcome with the eventual introduction of pollution-free methods of electrical energy generation anticipated for the 1990s.

Some safety problems do exist with the introduction of electric cars, however. A mixture of relatively low-performance electric cars and relatively high-performance internal combustion cars will increase road congestion and create a situation where accidents are more likely to occur. In the event of an accident the occupants of an electric car experience some danger from the possibility of electric shock and also from the hazardous contents of the batteries. If an electric car and a petrol-driven car collide the chance of a fire resulting is increased. Another potential hazard of the electric car is for the pedestrian. Because of its very low noise levels the electric car gives virtually no warning that it is about to start moving, which is obviously rather dangerous for pedestrians and the problem may have to be overcome by artificial means.

If from a governmental policy point of view the reduction in urban pollution more than compensates for the lower performance characteristics, the safety problems and the threat to the established automobile industry, then positive steps should be taken to promote the development of the electric car. A lower sales tax rate on a new electric car than on a new petrol-driven car would enable the purchase price for both vehicles to become about the same, while provision of low off-peak electricity tariffs for battery car use would increase the advantage in running costs. Certain central areas of the major cities could be closed to all except electric vehicles – besides encouraging the use of electric cars for urban travel this measure would also reduce inner-city pollution levels. In addition cheaper parking rates in all urban areas could be provided for electric cars. In order to help the electric car break into the one-car-family market, concession fares on long-distance public transportation could be offered to families owning electric cars.

From this examination of the situation it seems unlikely that the electric car will capture any sizeable segment of the automobile market in the near future, even with large increases in petrol prices. But two factors could change this: the development of an electric car with range and performance characteristics to match the internal combustion car; and government measures to promote the electric car and to limit the conventional car.

One possible direction of development for the electric car is to move away from sole reliance on a battery. A captive system where the car is permanently connected to a current rail under the road is limited in geographical coverage and is very expensive to provide. But a semi-captive system offers considerable scope for future development. Normally the electric car would run on batteries, but when driven on freeways or major arterial roads, one lane could have a current rail embedded beneath it and the car could connect into this system. The power level provided through the current rail could be sufficient to propel the car at normal freeway speeds as well as simultaneously charging the batteries. Eventually this type of system could be operated under automatic control with the advantages of greater safety and increased road capacity.

Another alternative fuel to petrol for use in motor cars is liquified petroleum gas (L.P.G.). At the present rate of extraction there are eighty years' domestic supply of L.P.G. Use of L.P.G. in motor cars can provide a moderate reduction in air pollution, but if a car operating on L.P.G. is tuned to minimize pollution it suffers from reduced power and increased fuel consumption and so it is unlikely that many car owners would tune their cars in this way. L.P.G. has a current cost advantage over petrol solely on the basis that it is free of excise. It appears most unlikely that L.P.G. will ever become a major fuel source for the motor car.

Bicycles have a number of considerable advantages when used as urban transportation vehicles. Many trips made by cars in urban areas are under 8 kilometres in length and rarely average greater than 30 km/h. This type of performance can be matched by a bicycle. In addition bicycles consume very low amounts of energy per person-kilometre and are pollution free. Two major disadvantages are associated with bicycle riding in urban areas: lack of protection in any form of accident and particularly in a collision with a motor car; and, exposure of the rider to the weather.

Increased safety for the bicycle rider can be provided by exclusive right-of-ways or bike paths. A bike path can take one of three different forms. It can be built as a separate path along a road but separated from it or it can be built entirely apart from the existing road. A second way to set up a bike path is to mark a lane down the edge of an existing road and to prohibit car parking from the area at all times. The final way is to erect signposts stating that the road is also a bikeway but do nothing else. The first way, a separate bike path, is obviously the safest but, except for limited recreational situations, it is too expensive. Signposts do nothing to protect the bike rider and are merely an empty gesture. Lane markings are effective if parking is prohibited although some problems still exist at the intersections.

Exposure to the weather is a problem that nothing can be done about. If bicycle riding became very popular in an urban area the problem might become how to transport all the riders when they leave their bicycles at home on a wet day.

From a social point of view bicycles also have considerable advantages. Bicycles provide very inexpensive mobility to those adults who cannot afford a motor car and to all children and teenagers who are too young to hold a driver's licence.

Although bicycles and bike paths are receiving a lot of recent public attention it is still questionable whether they will become a major means of urban transportation in Australian cities. Separated bike paths are generally not feasible in the inner areas of large cities, while it would take major impetus to have municipal councils prohibit parking and mark bikeways down existing roads and on service roads of major arterial routes. For the bicycle to become a major urban transportation mode, facilities would have to be provided to enable bicycles to be carried on other modes. This would enable the cyclist to ride to a bus stop or train station, load the bike on the bus or train for the line-haul portion of the journey, and then ride again to the final destination. Research has been done in the United States to develop a trailer for bikes which could be towed behind an express bus. The public transportation system in general, and particularly the railway, should be encouraged to provide facilities to carry bicycles at all times of the day. This type of development would allow the bicycle rider to cover much larger distances and to have access to all parts of widely spread Australian cities such as Sydney and Melbourne.

Energy has a peculiar relationship with personal mobility – beyond a certain level small increases in mobility consume quite large amounts of additional energy. This is shown rather clearly in a study done by Nick Clark, John Lee and Ken Ogden. They established a standard of personal mobility which is equal to the annual number of kilometres of personal travel per head of population. This encompasses all modes of travel including walking and cycling. The average Australian was estimated to have travelled 6500 kilometres in 1959–60 and over 12 000 kilometres eleven years later in 1970–1. Domestic and international air travel and motor car travel had more than doubled during the period, while walking, bicycling, bus, train and tram travel declined somewhat. The standard of mobility is increasing with time, and increasing in relation to standards of living. Also of interest is the fact that the travel modes which are increasing over time are the faster modes with the greatest energy requirements.

A relationship between the standard of mobility and the standard of living is confirmed by examining the estimated standard of mobility for a range of countries which is given in Table 10.4. As expected the countries with more developed economies experience a greater level of personal mobility. A country's economic development is directly related to its economic wealth and to the level of salaries and wages paid to its workforce. As wage and salary levels become higher so too does the value placed by the individual on time saved in travelling. This fact justifies the switch to faster modes of transportation as living standards rise.

Clark, Lee and Ogden postulate that there is a constant factor in the standard of mobility calculation and that is the amount of time that a person is willing to spend travelling each day. This limit is set at just under two hours a day or about 500 hours per year. With this limit it then becomes an easy matter to establish a rough maximum and minimum value for the standard of mobility – 2500 kilometres can be covered at 5 km/h by foot in 500 hours, while at the other extreme 150 000 kilometres can be flown in a jet aircraft averaging

Table 10.4   Standard of Mobility for Selected Countries*

Country	Rail	Bus†	Air	Car	Walk/cycle‡	Total
		km of personal travel per head of population				
U.S.A.	80	200	1010	12 750	500	14 540
Australia	790	340	660	9960	500	12 250
Canada	160	(200)	1000	9680	500	11 540
U.K.	640	990	370	6100	750	8850
France	800	390	270	5560	750	7700
Japan	2740	980	160	1730	1000	6010
Poland	1140	990	20	340	1500	3990
India	210	190	10	20	2000	2430
Brazil	120	(200)	50	490	1500	2360
Thailand	110	(200)	30	80	1750	2170
Indonesia	30	(200)	10	40	1750	2030

*These figures refer to the year 1969 or to a year close to 1969.

†Values in brackets assumed.

‡Walk/cycle is wholly estimated from a scale ranging from 2000-5000 km of personal travel per head depending on the level of motorized mobility.

Source: N. Clark, J. A. Lee and K. W. Ogden, 'The Use of Energy for Personal Mobility', *Transportation Research*, Vol. 8, 1974, p. 404.

300 km/h. While this minimum value might reflect the situation in a country with an economy based on subsistence agriculture the maximum value is unrealistic; as shown in Table 10.4 the standard of mobility for the United States is around 15 000.

The considerable difference in energy consumption at different levels of personal mobility is shown in Table 10.5. Average personal mobility in India, Brazil, Thailand or Indonesia consumes only one-thirtieth of the energy used for average personal mobility in the United States. The average Australian consumes twice the energy that the average Frenchman or Japanese does for personal mobility, and almost twice that of the average Englishman.

Of course averages are deceptive and within Australia itself great variations in energy usage for personal mobility occur. Twenty per cent of Australian families do not own a car, many more do not travel by air. For these Australians a standard of mobility of 5000 or 6000

Table 10.5   Transport Energy Consumption and Personal Mobility

Standard of mobility	2500	5000	7500	10 000	12 500	15 000
Energy usage by mode						
Car	0.54	3.23	10.78	16.16	21.55	26.94
Bus/train	0.43	3.23	2.55	2.04	1.28	0.85
Air	0	0.56	1.40	3.09	7.02	8.43
Walk/cycle	0.29	0.20	0.11	0.10	0.07	0.07
Total	1.26	7.22	14.84	21.39	29.92	36.29

Energy usage by mode measured in 10^6 kJ per person per year

Source: N. Clark, J. A. Lee and K. W. Ogden, 'The Use of Energy for Personal Mobility', *Transportation Research*, Vol. 8, 1974, p. 406.

would be quite likely. These people are using only one-fifth of the transportation energy of the average Australian and a much smaller fraction of the energy used by the most mobile community groups. If energy is a scarce commodity should such inequities in consumption rates be allowed to continue? Should a serious commitment be made to implementing, at least on a pilot project basis, such schemes as Ivan Illich's radical proposal to reduce energy consumption and increase social equity?

Note

1. Illich, I., 'Energy and Social Disruption', *The Ecologist*, Vol. 4, No. 2, February 1974, p. 51.

Chapter 11
Decision Making

Important participants in the process of transportation development can be split into five groups: taxpayers, travellers, businessmen and women, public instrumentalities and planning authorities. These groups interact to provide the infrastructure, vehicles and service that together form the transportation system. Some idea of the extent of this interaction can be gained from Figure 11.1. Transportation is an unusual area of economic activity because some modes are operated by private enterprise (with some government control), some modes have public instrumentalities providing service in competition with private enterprise, and some are exclusively operated by public instrumentalities. Urban and line-haul road services are provided solely by private enterprise. Ansett, the private carrier, competes with T.A.A. the public instrumentality for domestic air passengers and freight. A.N.L., a public instrumentality, competes with private enterprise shipping lines on coastal and international service. Line-haul rail services are provided by the state government railways and the Australian government controlled Australian National Railways as well as by private enterprise, although the private and public services do not compete. Pipelines are operated by private enterprise and government instrumentality, but these services also are not competitive. Route bus operations are another service provided both by the private and public sectors. Qantas, the government owned airline, is the only international air carrier. Metropolitan rail, tram and ferry services are also operated by public instrumentalities without competition.

Although operating a transportation service and providing the vehicles needed involve large capital outlays, this investment is relatively small when compared with the cost of the infrastructure – the roads, the railway lines, the shipping wharves, the air terminals, the pipeline network. While private enterprise is quite heavily involved in transportation operations, provision of the infrastructure (with the

Figure 11.1 The decision–making structure for Australian transportation

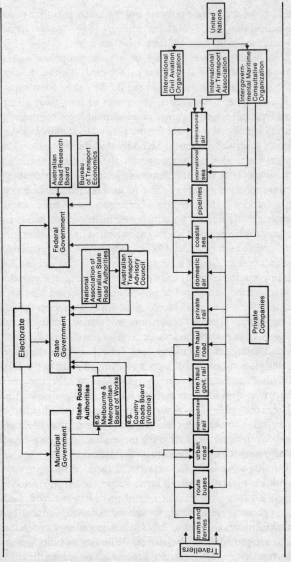

exception of the private railways linking mines with ports and also some pipelines) is beyond the capabilities of private enterprise and has remained in the hands of the public sector.

John Pickett when examining the influence of public authorities on the development of Melbourne put forward two main reasons why urban service authorities were in the public sector. Firstly that it is inefficient to have many sellers of services such as water, electricity and telephones which require massive capital investment, but a private monopoly could exploit the market and so the single seller was the public service authority. Secondly that the provision of urban services (particularly education and health care) is often considered as an appropriate way to redistribute income. It is interesting that for transportation neither of these reasons is particularly important. Air operations is the only area where private enterprise would like to enter but is being kept out by government control, and even this constraint is being eased slightly as indicated by the Fraser government's decision in February 1977 to grant I.P.E.C. permission to import and operate freight aircraft across Bass Strait. All other areas of transportation either already have private enterprise operators or else are so unprofitable that no private operator would want to enter. Transportation is not considered as an important means of redistributing income. Typically concessions are given to certain community groups (such as students and pensioners) for travel on public transportation. Although more could be done along these lines, the perceived benefits of motor car travel are a major impediment to the effective redistribution of income through transportation. Direct government control over the motor car is slight and limited to sales tax, fuel tax and registration fees. So government action in the current context can do little to make motor cars more widely available, while greater access to public transportation for those who do not own a car does not adequately compensate them for this lack.

In contrast to other urban services all forms of transportation are provided at highly subsidized rates: neither the private motorist nor the truck owner pays the full cost of providing the roads he uses; railway passengers and freight are subsidized by huge annual deficits; annual subsidies are paid to A.N.L. and enormously expensive terminals are provided for the airlines. Why has mobility become so important that a sizeable portion of the cost of providing this mobility is met by the taxpayer? Has this situation developed as a conscious series of steps taken by the decision makers concerned with transportation policy or has it just evolved in a haphazard fashion? What are the goals of the decision makers?

Looking again at Figure 11.1 it can be seen that major decisions for the transportation system are made by politicians. They decide whether to build roads or to build railways or to build something else. They decide whether certain rural railway services will be discontinued or not. They decide who can operate air services. They decide where shipping lines can purchase ships. On the other hand the private enterprise decision maker cannot change the structure of the transportation system. He can decide how he wants to operate his trucking fleet on the existing road network, his shipping line between the existing dock facilities, his airline within the constraints of the terminals provided and the conditions of the two-airline policy. The enormous impact of the motor car on urban structure in the twentieth century is vivid proof of the fact that the private enterprise decision maker can radically change the structure of the transportation system – but he can only do it by applying pressure and influencing the governmental decision maker, he cannot do it directly. Hence it is of value to consider what goals lie behind the actions of the governmental decision maker.

The public sector decision making process is carried out on two levels. Overall the federal, state and to a much lesser degree municipal governments make the important policy decisions. Within this policy framework, decision makers at the public instrumentalities (the public organizations which operate that segment of the transportation system – the government railways, T.A.A., A.N.L., Qantas) must operate.

Without a doubt the major goal of any politician is to keep his seat in parliament. An individual may enter parliament with naive expectations of being able to make particular changes to the social system and to implement certain programmes. But with the party system as it operates in Australia the new politician must simply stick to the party line. By the time he has been in parliament long enough to have any say about what the party line will be, he has long forgotten the bright ideals he first brought with him – he has absorbed the traditional party policies. This process has the great advantage that it is difficult for any individual to corrupt the system; it would be difficult to have a Richard Nixon in Australia. But on the other hand the great disadvantage is that the whole system is very conservative and very unwilling to change. More of the same becomes almost a standard operating procedure for any government in power. As an example of this phenomenon look at the transport policy which was a plank of the winning Liberal platform in 1975. In part it states:

We acknowledge that travel by motor car will continue to dominate people's travel habits and road networks will remain the chief link between people.

With the great majority of workers in Australian cities living in one suburb and working in another not connected by fixed line public transport, the states are anxious to provide increased modern bus services to relieve congestion and pollution on suburban streets.

We will assist the states both in a long-term plan to replace non-standard gauge railway with standard gauge railway, and more immediately, in programmes for the modernization and rationalization of state rail systems.

Acknowledging [the] key role for overseas shipping we will encourage fast and economic services to and from Australia.

We recognize also that Australian coastal shipping and the Australian ship-building and repair industries are important to Australia.

Australia has earned a high international reputation for the safety and efficiency of its civil aviation operations. We will ensure that this high reputation is maintained.

We will continue the two-airline policy. We will encourage our international carrier Qantas to continue its proud role in international aviation and to take new initiatives in the development of tourist travel.[1]

These words sound as if action is to be forthcoming. But they are just words; it means just more of the same – no exciting initiatives, no efforts for greater transportation equity. The Labor government was no different. Transportation is a mess now but if stirred up could become even a greater mess – it is best left alone. Nor are federal governments alone in this attitude to transportation. These are several points from the thirteen in the Victorian Liberal government's platform on transportation:

Retention of the railways under state control, development of modern rail services capable of fast and economical freight handling by means of modern specialized rolling stock, and the establishment of fully equipped freight centres at appropriate locations.

Careful planning of an adequate freeway and road system to cater for the increasing volume of motor traffic consistent with the preservation of existing communities and environmental assets.

Recognition that the reduction of road congestion and the threat of pollution of the environment requires that public transport be developed rapidly and cater for an increasing share of the public need for transportation services.[2]

Again words with a ring of action about them but sufficiently vague to make accountability for results difficult to demand. In the long period of Liberal government in Victoria no progress has been made on these points; why should the public now expect a sudden change?

Politicians aim to create no waves. In the final result they are responsible to the electorate, but they perform to win votes rather than to provide a more equitable society. Labor has its solid ground in the trade union, working class vote while the Liberals also have a strong hold on a voting block – the business and to a lesser degree the professional segment. It is the middle ground which will swing and put a government into or out of office. It is also very difficult to determine exactly what actions and policies will bring support from this voting block. Often the safest approach for the politician is to offer more of the same – it is always risky to propose radical change.

So for the transportation system nothing changes. More roads are built, more cars are built that are essentially the same as the first T model Ford but with a few extra trappings, railway systems continue despite staggering losses each year, the two airline policy drags on without proper evaluation, car traffic remains unconstrained in urban centres. As usual it takes a crisis to precipitate even the smallest change in the system. Even administrative changes to improve traffic movement in the inner suburbs and central business district will not be made until there is a traffic jam of major proportions.

Despite the same shortcomings of the transportation system continuing on, there seems to exist a strange sense of false confidence that somehow things will just get better by themselves. For example, Ron Hodges, General Manager of the Victorian Railways, when questioned about the record-setting half-year deficit of $85 million achieved by VicRail during June to December 1976, said he was confident the deficit for the full year would not exceed the $129 million predicted in the State Government's Budget papers. This was despite a continuing fall in the number of rail passengers and the fact that in recent years the loss in the second half of the financial year has always exceeded that of the first half.

Another strong reason for the continuation of the status quo is that any sensible politician plans for at most only the next three years. Recently in federal politics planning on the basis of three years has been rather optimistic. Any significant change in the transportation system will almost certainly take much longer than three years and before it is completed the generally perceived disadvantages will probably outweigh the value of future promised advantages. This type of situation does not win votes. The transportation plans which have been developed for all major Australian cities certainly suffered from a planning horizon which was too long. Most of these plans were initially adopted, but the time needed to implement them was longer than three years and election promises destroyed any semblance of long-range planning they may have contained.

Politicians avoid substantial change but they are often willing to spend vast amounts on extending the existing system. The astounding thing is how willingly the voting public accepts outrageously escalating costs on more of the same projects: West Gate bridge was to cost $42 million when proposed in 1968 and will now cost $200 million; a jump from $80 million in 1970 to $300 million in 1976 has occurred in the estimated cost of Melbourne's underground loop. Far more public outrage is expressed when Telecom announces an annual trading profit than when a transportation operation or project ends up costing the taxpayer several times the amount of Telecom's profit. The Australian people have become numb – the railways are expected to lose money, bridges always cost more than originally planned. Inefficiency, sloppiness and mismanagement have become accepted characteristics of the transportation system.

Recently, public instrumentalities and other organizations not guided by the profit motive have used a technique called 'social benefit–cost analysis' to help them to choose between various alternative courses of action. The Bureau of Transport Economics, for example, has used this method to evaluate urban public transport investment proposals in a series of reports over the past five years. In their analyses the

Bureau of Transport Economics considered all the costs associated with travel under the existing conditions and all the costs associated with travel when the project under consideration has been undertaken. 'The costs cover not only such direct costs as purchase of public transport vehicles, public transport operation, road construction and the operating costs of cars and trucks, but also the value of travel time and traffic accident savings.'[3] When the existing costs are higher than the costs associated with the proposed project the difference measures the benefit of the project. These benefits, taken over a specified planning horizon, are then related to the initial capital cost of the project. If the ratio of benefits to costs exceeds one, then the project is worthwhile, otherwise it is not.

Two additional points should be noted about these analyses. The first is that the capital costs of the existing system are ignored. This is because these costs have already been incurred, they are sunk costs and nothing can be done to change that. The second point is that all costs and benefits which occur in future time periods are discounted or brought to present values. If the current interest rate is 15 per cent, a dollar invested today will be worth $1.15 in one year. In a similar manner if a dollar is to be received in one year's time it is worth less than a dollar received today because it cannot earn income during the year – at 15 per cent interest a dollar received one year from now will be worth 87 cents today.

The benefits from any transportation project should be calculated for all sectors of the community whether they are users or non-users of the facility. The most obvious benefit is the difference in operating and maintenance costs between the existing system and the proposed system for the operating authority. Of course the new system may cost more to run, in which case the benefit would become a negative benefit. Benefits to existing users of the system would most likely be the value of travelling time saved and increased travel comfort. If the project improved public passenger transportation facilities, some passengers hopefully would switch from car travel to public transportation. The benefit in this case is the value of the resources saved by the switch. Some passengers may also change over from other public transportation – this may affect passenger comfort and travel time on the other system as well as the operating costs. Remaining road users would receive substantial benefits if a large number of travellers switched from private cars to public transportation. These benefits would be mainly time savings, reduced operating expenses and reduced accident costs. New passengers attracted by the improved public transportation service are counted by the Bureau of Transport Economics to benefit at a rate of one-half of the difference between the total travel cost for the existing system and the total travel cost of the improved system. Finally the community in general might benefit from the improvement if lower noise levels, less air pollution and less environmental disturbance result.

The proposal for a central Sydney tramway was evaluated using social benefit–cost analysis. This tramway was to connect Central Station and Circular Quay either forming a loop going up Castlereagh Street and back down Pitt Street or else forming a bone shape with both northbound and southbound trams using Pitt Street. Three-section articulated trams with about 100 seats and a total capacity of just under 300 were proposed to move the expected large volumes of passengers.

Costs for this project were the construction costs and the cost of the rolling stock. Benefits would accrue from the removal of buses in George Street, Pitt Street and Castlereagh Street. Air pollution in the central city would be reduced but the congestion on neighbouring George and Elizabeth Streets would increase. Most people riding on the trams would be former bus riders and these passengers would enjoy more regular, faster and more comfortable transportation. For the no-fare evaluation of the project, those tram passengers who otherwise would not have made the trip or who would have walked also benefit – the walkers by the value of the travel time saved and the new riders by the amount of the fare plus the value of the time spent travelling (if this were not the case the new rider would continue to stay at home). Also the Public Transport Commission of New South Wales would benefit by saving the operating cost of the bus service replaced by the tram.

When all these costs and benefits were added up and discounted at a rate of 7 per cent for the time value of money, then in the case where a 10-cent adult fare was charged, the benefit–cost ratio was 1.3, and it was 2.4 for a no-fare system. Either system would seem on the basis of this evaluation to have been worthwhile, but the New South Wales Ministry of Transport and Highways decided that:

After careful consideration of the recommendation [and] . . . having regard to the cost involved and other factors, the tramway proposal was not one to be supported.

However, it was felt that alternative ways of improving inner-city transport warranted examination and that the Public Transport Commission should continue to carry out investigations in this area.[4]

Benefit–cost analysis is certainly an improvement over previous decision making methods used in the public sector, but it still should be used with care. In most cases the costs are rather straightforward, easily identified and easily quantified. Many benefits, however, are not easy to identify and even when identified are difficult to quantify. What is the appropriate dollar value to attach to reduced pollution levels or improved road safety? Also what is the appropriate discount rate to be used? When a favourable or an unfavourable result of a benefit–cost analysis is dependent upon such subjective evaluations the responsibility rests with the decision maker to ensure that he understands the assumptions contained in the report presented to him.

A cost–benefit analysis (now more fashionably called benefit–cost analysis) was used in 1961 as a justification for the beef roads programme in northern Australia. J. K. Johnson was critical of the analysis because all relevant costs were not included. Also not all feasible alternatives were evaluated – better alternatives to the beef roads programme existed but were not considered.

Benefit–cost analysis is a considerable aid to decision making but it does not provide all the information and analysis needed for the best decision. The decision maker must add sound judgement.

Several other unusual circumstances seem to characterize transportation decision making.

It seems that a problem situation can lie dormant for many years but when it becomes a public issue the government department or instrumentality concerned demands a report on the matter with the utmost haste. Federal and state departments of transport are quite adept at this. At the meeting of the Australian Transport Advisory

Council* in July 1971 it was decided that the Bureau of Transport Economics should prepare 'as a matter of urgency . . . a report on the overall need for investment in urban public transport services and prospective finance for that purpose, in the years to 1979'.[5] By November of that year the Bureau of Transport Economics had managed to convert these broad sweeping statements into a specific plan of study, and in June 1972 the report appeared. A little over six months was given to establish and evaluate the needs of urban public transportation. Another example concerns freeways. When it became obvious that a large segment of the public was not in favour of extensive freeway construction the then Minister for Urban and Regional Development, Tom Uren, directed the Commonwealth Bureau of Roads to assess 'the need for the freeway systems currently proposed or being developed, in the capital cities and larger provincial cities of Australia'.[6] He made the request in March 1973 and this seemingly mammoth task was completed in less than five months.

This places the staff assigned to conduct these studies and prepare the reports under considerable time pressure. It is quite common to find statements such as the following in the forewords of reports prepared for governmental bodies: 'It is almost certain that some work has been overlooked, particularly in the field of counter-measures, this being one of the drawbacks of a rushed job.'[7] Another report foreword opened with the quote from Chesterton: 'If a job is worth doing, it is worth doing badly.' This quote presumably related to the fact that 'the time available for the present review has been so limited that it has been impossible to do full justice to many of the studies examined'.[8]

After much haste and burning of midnight oil the report is finished and provided to the government decision maker. Often the heat is

---

*As of mid-1976 the membership of the Australian Transport Authority Council (A.T.A.C.) was: federal Minister for Transport; federal Minister for the Capital Territory; federal Minister for the Northern Territory; Minister for Transport and Highways, New South Wales; Minister of Transport, Victoria; Minister for Transport, Queensland; Minister for Local Government and Main Roads, Queensland; Minister of Transport, South Australia; Minister for Transport, Police and Traffic, Western Australia; Minister for Transport, Tasmania; Minister for Tourism and Works, Tasmania; Minister for Transport, New Zealand (observer).

off this particular issue by that stage and so the report is exiled to the departmental files.* Even if the report is used in the decision-making process better information could have been assembled if more time had been provided. It is common for the majority of these reports not to be available to the public, or else made public so long after preparation that conditions have changed so much that the report is now irrelevant.

This whole process has two undesirable effects on decision making for transportation: the governmental decision maker does not receive the best and most considered advice and the public is unable to obtain information as to the basis for many transportation decisions.

The availability of data relating to transportation operations in Australia also proves to be a problem. Few data are available, and those which are often are of poor quality. For example, two main sources of data on inter-capital city freight movements exist: the Australian Bureau of Statistics document *Interstate Freight Movements* and the truck traffic figures reported in *Truck and Bus Transportation* magazine. The Australian Bureau of Statistics figures include only those freight forwarders or road transport operators or both who engaged in interstate freight movements for hire or reward and who moved a total of 2500 tonnes or more during the quarter under consideration. The user of the figures is cautioned that the collection is constructed on 'a limited basis providing partial coverage'[9] and that 'it is not possible at this stage to assess reliably the precise proportion of total interstate freight tonnage falling within the scope of this collection'.[10] Data given in *Truck and Bus Transportation* are a little more representative of the true overall movement of freight by road. But the collection is limited to certain routes and it is constructed by assigning an average load to all trucks stopping at certain checking stations. So the source of these data cannot be considered to be very accurate either. A supply of adequate data is a primary requirement for effective decision making – it is not generally available for decisions about the Australian transportation system.

---

*One report I prepared for a government instrumentality was urgently required within two months. Now over two years later I still have no idea about the fate of the report. It is not available to the public.

All these impediments to the transport decision-making process have had the effect of turning transportation planners' thoughts away from the long-term. The urban transportation plans of the 1960s and early 1970s did not work, essentially because of the long period needed for implementation. Short-term low-capital projects stand a much better chance of being approved and implemented. Therefore the productive and worthwhile role for the transportation planner is to concentrate on these short-term low-capital projects and to resist the temptation of flirtation with future technological prognostications.

This type of thinking has formalized itself at the Commonwealth Bureau of Roads where it is given the name 'incremental planning'. Small, achievable, low-cost projects are proposed and implemented as incremental steps toward some broad long-term objective. Planning of this type is at best pragmatic. Long-term planning does not seem to work, so give short-term planning a try.

But it is not the plans which are necessarily at fault; it is the decision making process. Long-term plans will never work if they are open to radical change every year or two. What is best for society in the long run usually does not correlate with the voters' hip pocket nerve just prior to an election. The electorate is too fickle to have a continuing influence over the essential components of long-term transportation plans.

The most difficult task concerns developing the long-term plan in the first place. Obviously all sections of the community should be given an opportunity to participate in the formulation of long-term plans. But these plans should contain basic elements which then cannot be altered by politicians prior to an election. Certain tangential areas of the plan may well be left flexible to react to changing circumstances, but the central core of the plan must remain unaltered. This is the only way that any timely forward planning will be properly implemented for transportation projects in Australia.

Long-term planning and politics are incompatible. In the long-term it is desirable for the Victorian Railways to build up a fleet of modern rolling stock. Politically it is desirable to maintain low fares and freight rates. In Victoria in an attempt to keep fares and rates down the government over a long period has not allowed the Victorian Railways to allocate sufficient funds for depreciation. This means that replacement of worn out rolling stock and repairs and maintenance of equipment is mostly financed from borrowings from the government. These loans are interest bearing and have reached the massive level of $1237 million. But this does not even keep VicRail's head above water – the average age of rolling stock is still increasing. Short-term political considerations will never allow VicRail to be viable.

Somehow transportation planning and politics should be divorced. One way is to set up a commission with control over the whole area depicted in Figure 11.1. Planning documents produced by this commission would be subject to political approval but no political influence would be imposed on operating decisions including pricing. Government subsidies should be provided to specific unprofitable operations if considered worthy of this support; otherwise these operations should be pruned.

Notes

1. *Transport Policy*, Liberal and National Country Parties, Canberra, November 1975, pp. 3, 4, 6, 8, 9.
2. *The Official State Platform*, Liberal Party of Australia Victorian Division, South Melbourne, November 1975, pp. 23, 24.
3. Bureau of Transport Economics, *Economic Evaluation of Capital Investment in Urban Public Transport*, Bureau of Transport Economics, Canberra, June 1972, p. 6.
4. New South Wales Ministry of Transport and Highways, personal communication, February 1977.
5. Bureau of Transport Economics, *Economic Evaluation of Capital Investment in Urban Public Transport*, op. cit. p. 3.
6. Commonwealth Bureau of Roads, *Report on the Need for Freeway Systems in Australian Capital Cities*, Commonwealth Bureau of Roads, Melbourne, August 1973, p. 7.
7. Raymond, A. *Alcohol in Relation to Road Safety*, Australian Road Research Board, Report No. 2, Melbourne, November 1974, p. 1.
8. Cameron, C. and Macdonald, W. A., *A Review of Driver/Rider Training in Relation to Road Safety*, Australian Road Research Board, Report No. 3, Melbourne, January 1975, p. i.
9. Australian Bureau of Statistics (then Commonwealth Bureau of Census and Statistics), *Interstate Freight Movements*, Australian Bureau of Statistics, Canberra, 1972, p. 1.
10. Ibid p. 2.

Chapter 12
Greater Mobility

Energy and politics will have the greatest influence on the development of transportation in Australia for the rest of the century. The influence of energy depends on science and good luck: the rate and nature of technological advances, and the rate and extent of discovery of additional energy resources. The influence of the political process is much more controllable and it is the electorate's responsibility to ensure that the proper controls are applied. The wide-ranging effects of two only moderately dissimilar sets of policies are illustrated in the following two scenarios.

Scenario 1

The Labor government during its brief interlude in power in the early seventies injected considerably increased funding into the Australian transportation system and also tried to improve overall coordination of the system by attempting to increase the extent of federal control. Opposition from Liberal/National Country Party state governments limited the effectiveness of these moves and the subsequent federal government of Mr Fraser quickly reversed their direction. The new federalism programmes returned the responsibility for control and primary funding for most aspects of transportation back to the individual states.

But despite the low key approach to transportation issues taken by the Fraser government it is now history that a transportation-related issue forced Malcolm Fraser out of politics. The decision taken in 1978 to price indigenous crude at import parity by 1985 had proved to be disastrously unpopular by the months just before the 1984 federal elections. The O.P.E.C. countries, by forcing their price of crude up to $25 per barrel, had caused the price of petrol for the Australian motorist to leap to 45 cents per litre (or over $2 per gallon). Mr Fraser took a particularly hard line on this issue and lost the party leadership to Andrew Peacock on the resulting ballot. A Liberal/National Country Party win in the 1984 election was due entirely to the fact that Peacock re-introduced the artificially low price for domestic crude on the basis of the significant new finds in Bass Strait and at Barrow Island.

This action essentially turned the tide for the Liberal/National Country Party Coalition which remained in power for their second twenty-three year period of the century.

But by 1998 the true implications of this transportation policy were really being felt. Low crude prices had kept the price of petrol relatively low which encouraged people to own and use cars. In addition continued state control of the urban public transportation networks had resulted in decades of mounting deficits and a continuing decline in the standard of equipment and service offered. Hardening of conservative attitudes during the 1980s and 1990s had enabled all state governments to construct comprehensive urban freeway networks. But now these networks were clogged during rush hour. Up to 1998 the political muscle of the motor car driver had overcome all – no significant curbs had been placed on the use of the car.

Subsidization of the motor car manufacturers in Australia had continued during the previous two decades and by the end of the century the cost of an average car was even relatively higher than it was in the mid-1970s. One direct effect of this was that even though the number of cars per capita in Australia had increased significantly during this period, the number of families not owning a car had also increased – from 20 per cent of all families in 1975 to 30 per cent in 1998.

In June 1998 the federal Minister for Transport, Tony Staley, introduced a plan at the A.T.A.C. meeting by which the state Transport Ministers could reduce the congestion on urban roads. The essence of the plan was to issue permits (at a charge of $200 per month) for cars using the city freeways during rush hour. This plan appears likely to be implemented by the various states prior to the 1999 federal election. In a survey conducted by the *Bulletin* in September 1998 most large companies operating in Australia indicated that in addition to providing two company cars for each of their executives they would be willing to pay the permit fees. Although not often publicly admitted, most companies now pay all parking fines and fines for other traffic offences committed by drivers of company cars.

Public transportation to country areas offers a very poor service and is highly subsidized. Private bus operations in rural areas would certainly fold without the current high levels of public support.

Interstate passenger services are almost entirely provided by the private car and air. While cars move at high speeds along the National Highway system, T.A.A. and Ansett continue to provide high-cost low-standard air services. The relative cost of international air travel has increased mainly due to the fact that the most profitable customers, those paying first class fares, have been diverted to money-losing Concorde services. As a result economy fares have risen dramatically, and even so in 1997–8 Qantas made its seventeenth consecutive annual operating loss.

Movement of goods fared no better during the last two decades of the twentieth century. The only change for urban goods delivery during the period was the increase in congestion – no government initiative has been forthcoming and the individual private organizations concerned have been unable to integrate or co-ordinate their activities on a voluntary basis. Considerable economic benefits still lie with the relatively few large organizations for the line-haul movement of goods.. Often irrational union reaction to the conservative government policies has led to inefficiencies and rapidly increasing costs in the handling and transportation of goods.

A Monash University study completed in March 1998 estimated that the average Australian family was subsidizing the transportation system to the extent of $3000 per year.

Scenario 2

The Liberal/National Country Party Coalition won the election in 1977 but economic conditions continued to deteriorate over the next three years and in 1980 a Labor government was returned. Gough Whitlam had retired after failing to win in 1977 and Bill Hayden became Prime Minister in 1980.

By 1985 Labor had re-introduced the Inter-State Commission and had taken over all of the country's government railway systems. During the next decade most branch railway lines were closed and vast amounts were spent on providing the railway system with modern rolling stock and upgraded track. In May 1995 the Australian National Railways Commission was advised that they would now have to operate Australia's government railway systems on a break-even basis and that they would be unconstrained in the way they chose to do this. Any operations that were justified from a social rather than an economic viewpoint would be fully subsidized to a break-even level by the federal government.

Strong financial deterrents were imposed on the use of the car for commuting into the central business district. These varied from city to city but included such measures as very high parking charges, tolls for driving into the central city area and complete bans on cars in specified central areas. These measures were combined with the provision of suburban car parking stations with express bus services to the central city.

Import parity pricing of domestic crude and the resulting high petrol prices had encouraged a strong move to electric cars. In 1991 a price-competitive dual-fuel electric–petrol car was released by Australian Automobile Manufacturers (the only motor car manufacturer operating in Australia). This car was effective for commuting under electric power and for long trips under petroleum power.

From the start given them by the Fraser Government in 1977 I.P.E.C. blossomed into an efficient third airline in Australia using a range of S.T.O.L. aircraft for fast door-to-door service for freight and for passengers. The Inter-State Commission when formed in 1985 immediately started to remove the financial advantage that Ansett had enjoyed under the two-airline policy (which Labor had rejected in principle two years earlier). Looking back from the present situation in 1998 a considerable improvement in domestic air services has resulted from the competition between T.A.A., Ansett and I.P.E.C.

The Fraser government in the late 1970s had watched while the inefficient shipbuilding industry slowly disintegrated. The Howard Liberal/National Country Party government which came to power in 1996 dismantled A.N.L. and allowed both coastal and international freight to be carried by the shipper offering the most competitive rates regardless of national origin.

An important early step taken by the Hayden Labor government was to remove all government assistance from the car industry and to set up the worker-controlled Australian Automobile Manufacturers. By 1990, eight years after this action was taken, Australian Automobile Manufacturers was the only car producer operating in Australia.

A Monash University study completed in March 1998 found that while 30 per cent of Australian families did not own a motor car, over 80 per cent of this group chose not to own one. The price of a motor car was within the financial means of almost all Australian families, but the comfort and frequency of public transportation had improved to the point that there was a realistic choice not to own a car. The study also found that the average Australian family was subsidizing transportation by only $100 per year.

Neither of these two options involve any significant technological development, or even any significant change by applying already developed technologies. Basically all they involve is different management philosophies by the politicians and bureaucrats concerned. One set of philosophies provides a good chance of getting us all out of the 'transportation problem'; the other set of philosophies provides no chance at all. Obviously the two scenarios described are only two of a wide range of possible developments. A wise use of technology will provide even better results; unwise reliance on a purely politically motivated process will provide even worse results.

It rests with us all to become knowledgeable of the transportation options available and to influence the developmental process in a desired direction – a direction to reduce the present inequities of mobility.

Bibliography

To increase the readability of the book direct reference has only been made to quotations. This bibliography includes other sources used.

A National Program for Urban and Regional Development, Department of Urban and Regional Development, Canberra, 1974.

Allan Pattison and Associates, *Central Business District Parking in Australian State Capital Cities*, Commonwealth Bureau of Roads, Melbourne, June 1973.

Anderson, M. C., Crook, K. A. W. and Diesendorf, M. O., *The Concorde SST and Australia*, The Society for Social Responsibility in Science, Canberra, 1974.

Atkins, A. S., Kuczera, G. A. and O'Brien, W. T., *Assessment of Land Transport Alternatives for Webb Dock*, Port of Melbourne Environmental Study, Centre for Environmental Studies, University of Melbourne, Melbourne, December 1976.

Atkins-Meinhardt, *Modal Interchange Facilities at Moorabbin and Glen Waverley Stations: Feasibility Study*, Victorian Railways, Melbourne, 1974.

Australian Bureau of Statistics, *Bus Fleet Operations Survey Twelve Months Ended 30 June 1971*, Australian Bureau of Statistics, Canberra, 1974.

Australian Bureau of Statistics, *Household Expenditure Survey 1974-75*, Australian Bureau of Statistics, Canberra, 1976.

Australian Bureau of Statistics, *Journey to Work and Journey to School*, Australian Bureau of Statistics, Canberra, August 1974.

Australian Bureau of Statistics, *Motor Vehicle Registrations, 1975*, Australian Bureau of Statistics, Canberra, 1976.

Australian Bureau of Statistics, *Rail, Bus and Air Transport 1974-75*, Australian Bureau of Statistics, Canberra, 1976.

Australian Bureau of Statistics, *Road Traffic Accidents Involving Casualties*, Australian Bureau of Statistics, Canberra, 1976.

Australian Bureau of Statistics (then Commonwealth Bureau of Census and Statistics), *Survey of Motor Vehicle Usage Twelve Months Ended 30 September 1971 (Preliminary)*, Australian Bureau of Statistics, Canberra 1973.

Australian Department of Labour and Immigration, *Manpower Training Needs of the Road Transport Industry*, Australian Government Publishing Service, Canberra, 1975.

Australian Road Research Board, *Acquisition of Land for Roads*, Australian Road Research Board, Special Report No. 7, Melbourne, 1971.

Australian Road Research Board and Commonwealth Department of Transport, *Motorcycles and Safety Symposium*, Australian Road Research Board, Melbourne, 18 June 1976.

Australian Road Research Board, *Road User Cost Manual*, Australian Road Research Board, Special Report No. 9, Melbourne, 1973.

Australian Shipbuilding Industry Study Mission, *Shipbuilding Productivity and Industrial Relations in Australia*, Australian Government Publishing Service, Canberra, 1975.

Australian Transport Research Forum, *First Forum Papers, Sydney 1975*, Australian Government Publishing Service, Canberra, 1976.

Australian Wool Board, *Wool Transport in Australia*, Australian Wool Board Development Division, Melbourne, August 1971.

Balmer, C. J., 'Melbourne's Metropolitan Transportation Plan: A Sociological Viewpoint', Australian Institute of Urban Studies (Victorian Division), Occasional Paper No. 2, Melbourne, 1974.

Bence, R., *Patterns of Public Transport Use in the Melbourne Metropolitan Area*, Australian Road Research Board, Report No. 22, Melbourne, December 1973.

Bendixson, T., *Without Wheels*, Indiana University Press, Bloomington, 1975.

Blainey, G., *The Tyranny of Distance*, Sun Books, Melbourne, 1966.

Board of Review, Eastern Suburbs Railway, *Report to the Government of New South Wales*, Board of Review, Eastern Suburbs Railway, Sydney, October 1976.

Boughton, C. J., *Fatal Road Accidents – Victoria 1968*, Australian Road Research Board, Report No. 36, Melbourne, March 1975.

Brogden, S., *Australia's Two-Airline Policy*, Melbourne University Press, Melbourne, 1968.

Bureau of Transport Economics, *An Assessment of Tasmania's Interstate Transport Problems*, Australian Government Publishing Service, Canberra, March 1973.

Bureau of Transport Economics, *A Review of Public Transport Investment Proposals for Australian Capital Cities, 1973-74*, Australian Government Publishing Service, Canberra, August 1973.

Bureau of Transport Economics, *A Review of Public Transport Investment Proposals for Australian Capital Cities, 1974-75*, Australian Government Publishing Service, Canberra, April 1975.

Bureau of Transport Economics, *A Study of Intersystem Railway Freight Rating Practices*, Australian Government Publishing Service, Canberra, November 1976.

Bureau of Transport Economics, *Brisbane Airport: Economic Evaluation of Alternative Development Strategies*, Australian Government Publishing Service, Canberra, July 1975.

Bureau of Transport Economics, *Consumer Preferences in Urban Buses and Bus Services, Part A, Main Report*, Australian Government Publishing Service, Canberra, December 1975.

Bureau of Transport Economics, *Economic Evaluation of Capital Investment in Urban Public Transport*, Bureau of Transport Economics, Canberra, June 1972.

Bureau of Transport Economics, *Electric Cars*, Australian Government Publishing Service, Canberra, July 1974.

Bureau of Transport Economics, *Electric Cars: Their Future Role in*

Urban Transport, Australian Government Publishing Service, Canberra, 1975.

Bureau of Transport Economics, *Freight Transport to North West Australia 1975 to 1990*, 1973 – Parliamentary Paper No. 100, The Parliament of the Commonwealth of Australia, The Government Printer of Australia, Canberra, 1975.

Bureau of Transport Economics, *Liquefied Petroleum Gas as a Motor Vehicle Fuel*, Australian Government Publishing Service, Canberra, April 1974.

Bureau of Transport Economics, *Port Authority Cargo Movements 1972-73*, Australian Government Publishing Service, Canberra, 1976.

Bureau of Transport Economics, *Port Pirie: Economic Evaluation of Harbour Improvements*, Australian Government Publishing Service, Canberra, October 1975.

Bureau of Transport Economics, *The Economics of an Australian Landbridge*, Australian Government Publishing Service, Canberra, July 1975.

Bureau of Transport Economics, *Transport and Energy in Australia, Part 1 – Review*, Australian Government Publishing Service, Canberra, 1975.

Bureau of Transport Economics, *Transport and Energy in Australia, Part 2 – Consumption by Categories*, Australian Government Publishing Service, Canberra, 1975.

Bureau of Transport Economics, *Transport and Handling of Australia's Wool Production*, Australian Government Publishing Service, Canberra, December 1971.

Bureau of Transport Economics, *Transport Outlook Conference 1975: Papers and Proceedings*, Australian Government Publishing Service, Canberra, 1976.

Cameron, C. and Macdonald, W. A., *A Review of Driver/Rider Licensing in Relation to Road Safety*, Australian Road Research Board, Report No. 1, Melbourne, January 1975.

Cameron, C. and Macdonald, W. A., *A Review of Driver/Rider Training in Relation to Road Safety*, Australian Road Research Board, Report No. 3, Melbourne, January 1975.

Chappell, C. W. Jr. and Smith, M. T., *Review of Urban Goods Movement Studies*, U.S. Department of Transportation, Federal Highway Administration, Highway Planning Technical Report, No. 20, April 1971.

Cities Commission, *A Recommended New Cities Programme for the Period 1973-1978*, Canberra, 1973.

Clark, N. (ed.), *Analysis of Urban Development: Proceedings of the Tewksbury Symposium*, Transport Section, Department of Civil Engineering, University of Melbourne, Special Report No. 5, 1970.

Clark, N., Lee, J. A. and Ogden, K. W., 'The Use of Energy for Personal Mobility', *Transportation Research*, Vol. 8, 1974, pp. 399-407.

Cleaves, R., *Chrome, Concrete and Crowds: Living in Cities*, Penguin, Ringwood, 1974.

Cole, D. E., 'The Wankel Engine', *Scientific American*, Vol. 227, No. 2, August 1972, pp. 14-23.

Colman, J., *Planning and People: An Introduction to Urban Planning in Australia*, Angus and Robertson, Sydney, 1973.

Commission of Inquiry into the Maritime Industry, *Report on Adequacy of Australia's Ports*, Australian Government Publishing Service, Canberra, February 1976.

Committee for Urban Action, *Public Transport*, Committee for Urban Action Melbourne, 1972.

Committee for Urban Action, *Transport in Melbourne: The Inner Areas Crisis*, Committee for Urban Action, Melbourne, 1970.

Committee of Inquiry into the National Estate, *Report of the National Estate*, Australian Government Publishing Service, Canberra, 1974.

Committee of Senior Representatives of Commonwealth and State

Road Authorities, *Report on a National Highways System*, Australian Government Publishing Service, Canberra, 1974.

Commonwealth Bureau of Roads, *An Approach to Developing Transport Improvement Proposals*, Occasional Paper No. 2, Commonwealth Bureau of Roads, Melbourne, 1976.

Commonwealth Bureau of Roads, *Assessment of Freeway Plans, State Capital Cities*, Commonwealth Bureau of Roads, Melbourne, 1974.

Commonwealth Bureau of Roads, *Australian Roads Survey, 1969-74: Summaries of Results - Inventory, Improvement Projects and Costs*, Commonwealth Bureau of Roads, Melbourne, August 1973.

Commonwealth Bureau of Roads, *Australian Road System Perceived Performance - Melbourne and Sydney 1973-1974*, Commonwealth Bureau of Roads, Melbourne, October 1974.

Commonwealth Bureau of Roads, *National Highways Linking Sydney, Melbourne and Canberra, 1975 (First Report)*, Commonwealth Bureau of Roads, Melbourne, 1975.

Commonwealth Bureau of Roads, *National, State and Regional Forecasts - Population, Motor Vehicles and Traffic*, Finance Division, Commonwealth Bureau of Roads, Melbourne, August 1973.

Commonwealth Bureau of Roads, *Report on Roads in Australia 1975*, Commonwealth Bureau of Roads, Melbourne, 1975.

Commonwealth Bureau of Roads, *Roads in Australia 1973*, Commonwealth Bureau of Roads, Melbourne, 1973.

Commonwealth Bureau of Roads, *The Effect of Stopping Freeway Construction in State Capital Cities - 1973*, Commonwealth Bureau of Roads, Melbourne, 1973.

Conference on Electrical Transportation, Institution of Engineers, Australia, Sydney 1975.

Conference on Metropolitan Transport - The Way Ahead?, Institution of Engineers, Australia, Sydney, 1975.

David Holdings Pty Ltd, *David Holdings: The Food People*, Blacktown, N.S.W., no date.

Davis, K. (ed.), *Cities: Their Origin, Growth and Human Impact*, Readings from *Scientific American*, W. H. Freeman, San Francisco, 1973.

de Nevers, N., 'Enforcing the Clean Air Act of 1970', *Scientific American*, Vol. 230, No. 6, June 1973, pp. 14-21.

Department of Capital Territory, *Inquiry into Off-Road Vehicles*, Australian Government Publishing Service, Canberra, June 1976.

Department of Industry and Commerce, *Holiday Peaks: The Social and Economic Effects*, Australian Government Publishing Service, Canberra, 1976.

Department of Tourism and Recreation, *Development of Tourism in Australia*, Australian Government Publishing Service, Canberra, 1973.

Department of Transport, *Australian Transport 1974-75*, Australian Government Publishing Service, Canberra, 1975.

Department of Transport, *Australian Transport 1975-76*, Australian Government Publishing Service, Canberra, 1976.

Department of Transport, *Marketing Urban Transport Seminar March 1976*, Australian Government Publishing Service, Canberra, 1976.

Devery, P. J., Lucas, P., Francis, C. and Hughes, J. L., *Developing the Pilbara Iron Province as a Travel Region*, Australian National Travel Association, Sydney, January 1971.

Dougherty, P., McNiven, D., Moffat, K., Smee, B., Washington, G. and Wentworth, B., *Establishing Port Macquarie/Hastings Region as a Major Travel Destination*, Australian National Travel Association, Sydney, May 1970.

Dyos, H. J. and Aldcroft, D. H., *British Transport*, Penguin, Harmondsworth, 1974.

Eddy, P., Potter, E. and Page, B., *Destination Disaster*, Quadrangle, New York, 1976.

Ellery, R. L. J., Kernot, W. C., von Mueller, F., Neild, J. E., Le

Souef, A. A. C. and Turner, H. G., *Victoria and its Metropolis, Past and Present*, Vol. II, McCarron, Bird and Co., Melbourne, 1888.

First Report of the Task Force on New Cities for Australia, Australian Institute for Urban Studies, Canberra, 1972.

Fisher, N. W. F., 'Financial Analysis for National Programmes', Australian Society of Accounts – Victoria Division, *Lecture Series*, August 1972.

Fitzroy Residents' Association, Brooks Crescent – *A Study of the Current Slum Reclamation Procedures of the Housing Commission, Victoria*, Fitzroy Residents' Association, Fitzroy, 1972.

French, A., 'Energy and Freight Movements', *Transportation Journal*, Vol. 16, No. 1, Fall 1976, pp. 26-41.

Fry, A. T., Easton, G. R., Ker, I. R., Stevenson, J. McL. and Webber, J. R., *A Study of the Economics of Road Vehicle Limits: Concepts and Procedures*, National Association of Australian State Road Authorities, Report R1, Melbourne, July 1974.

Fysh, H., *Qantas Rising*, Angus and Robertson, Sydney, 1965.

Gattorna, J. L., *The Role of Air Cargo in Australia's Domestic and International Distribution Systems*, Productivity Promotion Council of Australia, Melbourne, 1974.

Gilmour, P., *An Analysis of the Modal Choice for Freight Movements Between Melbourne and Sydney*, Commonwealth Bureau of Roads, Melbourne, November 1974.

Gilmour, P. (ed.), *Physical Distribution Management in Australia*, Cheshire, Melbourne, 1974.

Gilmour, P., 'Some Policy Implications of Subjective Factors in the Modal Choice for Freight Movements', *The Logistics and Transportation Review*, Vol. 12, No. 1, 1976, pp. 39-57.

Gilmour, P., 'The Economics of Private Bus Services in Australia', *Traffic Quarterly*, Vol. 28, No. 3, July 1974, pp. 437-452.

Gilmour, P., 'The Use of Nonmetric Multidimensional Scaling in

Transportation Analyses', *International Journal of Transport Economics*, Vol. 3, No. 1, April 1976, pp. 97-108.

Gilmour, P., Borg, G., Duffy, P. A., Johnston, N. D., Limbek, B. E. and Shaw, M. R., 'Customer Service: Differentiating by Market Segment', *International Journal of Physical Distribution*, Vol. 7, No. 3, 1977, pp. 141-48.

Haig, B. D., *The Australian Economy to the Year 2000*, Australian National University, Canberra, 1971.

Halton, C. C., 'Transport Planning', *Australian Transport*, Vol. 18, No. 10, October, 1976, pp. 17-21.

Hammarskjold, K., 'The State of the Air Transport Industry', International Air Transport Association, Annual General Meeting, Montreal, September 1974.

Harding, J. R., Lapidge, S. J., Hutchings, A. W., Dodgshun, A. G., Laurent, L. H. R. and Harris, C. R., *Establishing the South Australian Mid-North, Barossa Valley and Riverland as a Travel Region*, Australian National Travel Association, Sydney, September 1971.

Hawks, E., *The Romance of Transportation*, Thomas Y. Crowell, New York, 1931.

Henderson, J. M., 'Traffic Accidents and Social Deviance', in Edwards, A. R. and Wilson, P. R., *Social Deviance in Australia*, Cheshire, Melbourne, 1975, pp. 111z121.

Henderson, J. M. and Sims, A., *Heavy Vehicle Crash Injury*, Traffic Accident Research Unit, Department of Motor Transport, New South Wales, Sydney, January 1970.

Hensher, D. A., *Urban and Suburban Passenger Transport Policy Options*, Commonwealth Bureau of Roads, Melbourne, October 1973.

Hensher, D. A. (ed.), *Urban Travel Choice and Demand Modelling*, Australian Road Research Board, Special Report No. 12, Melbourne, 1973.

Highway Research Board, *Urban Commodity Flow*, Highway Research Board Special Report No. 120, Washington, D.C., 1971.

Hocking, R., *Some Aspects of Australia's Two-Airline Policy*, Committee for Economic Development of Australia, M. Series No. 35, Melbourne, August 1972.

Holdsworth, J. H., *Social Cost of Displacement in Urban Areas*, Commonwealth Bureau of Roads, Melbourne, March 1972.

Holdsworth, J. H., *Residential Disruption Costs in Urban Areas*, Commonwealth Bureau of Roads, Melbourne, November 1972.

Holdsworth, J. H., *Residential Disruption Costs in Urban Areas: A Brisbane Case Study*, Commonwealth Bureau of Roads, Melbourne, April 1974.

Hughes, A., *A Re-Analysis of Survey Data on Community Attitudes to Roads*, Commonwealth Bureau of Roads, Melbourne, September, 1973.

Illich, I., 'Energy and Social Disruption', *The Ecologist*, Vol. 4, No. 2, February 1974, pp. 49-52.

Increasing Productivity in the Transport Industry, The Chartered Institute of Transport, Victorian Section, Melbourne, November 1973.

Independent Commission of Transport, *Changing Direction*, Coronet, London, 1974.

Industrial Relations in the Transport Industry, The Chartered Institute of Transport, Victorian Division, Melbourne, November 1972.

Industries Assistance Commission, *Assistance to Manufacturing Industries in Australia 1968-69 to 1973-74*, Australian Government Publishing Service, Canberra, 1976.

Industries Assistance Commission, *Commercial Motor Vehicles, Parts and Accessories: Interim Report on Short Term Assistance*, Australian Government Publishing Service, Canberra, November 1976.

Industries Assistance Commission, *Crude Oil Pricing*, Australian Government Publishing Service, Canberra, September 1976.

Industries Assistance Commission, *Railway and Tramway Locomotives, Rolling Stock, Etc.*, Australian Government Publishing Service, Canberra, June 1976.

Industries Assistance Commission, *Passenger Motor Vehicles, Etc.*, Australian Government Publishing Service, Canberra, July 1974.

Industries Assistance Commission, *Shipbuilding*, Australian Government Publishing Service, Canberra, September 1976.

International Air Transport Association, *Agreeing Fares and Rates*, International Air Transport Association, Geneva, Second edition, August 1974.

International Conference on Personal Rapid Transit, University of Minnesota, Minneapolis, 1974.

International Symposium on the Effects of Energy Shortage on Transportation Balance, *Transportation Research*, Vol. 8, No. 4/5, October 1974, pp. 245-501.

Interplan Pty Ltd, *City of Melbourne Strategy Plan*, Melbourne City Council, Melbourne, August 1973.

John Paterson Urban Systems, *A History and Review of Planning Melbourne – Since 1940*, Commonwealth Bureau of Roads, Occasional Paper No. 3, Melbourne, April 1974.

John Paterson Urban Systems, *Transport Services Available to and used by Disadvantaged Sections of the Community*, Commonwealth Bureau of Roads, Melbourne, June 1974.

Johnson, J. K., 'Government Influence on Transport Decision-Making in the Northern Territory', in Linge, G. J. R. and Rimmer, P. J. (eds), *Government Influence and the Location of Economic Activity*, Department of Human Geography, Research School of Pacific Studies, Australian National University, Canberra, 1971, pp. 359-374.

Joy, S. C., 'Railway Track Costs', in Munby, D. (ed.), *Transport*, Penguin, Harmondsworth, 1968.

Joy, S. C., 'Urban Form and Passenger Transport Problems', in *The Economics of Roads and Road Transport*, Commonwealth Bureau of Roads, Occasional Paper No. 1, Melbourne, 1968.

Ker, I. R., *Equity in Road User Taxation and Charges in Australia*, Australian Road Research Board, Special Report No. 14, Melbourne, 1974.

Koenigsberg, E. and Lathrop, D. S., *Transocean Tug-Barge Systems: A Conceptual Study*, Matson Research Corporation, San Francisco, July 1970.

Kolsen, H. M., Ferguson, D. C. and Docwra, G. E., *Road User Charges: Theories and Possibilities*, A Report for the Bureau of Transport Economics, Australian Government Publishing Service, Canberra, July 1975.

Link, P. L., *Future Communications Systems in an Australian Business Organization 1972 to 2000 A.D.*, Unpublished Master of Administration thesis, Monash University, 1973.

Little, F. M., Morozow, O., Rawlings, S. W. and Walker, J. R., *Social Dysfunction and Relative Poverty in Metropolitan Melbourne*, Research and Development Division, Melbourne and Metropolitan Board of Works, Research Report No. 1, Melbourne, May 1974.

Loder, J. L., *Automated Personal Transportation: An APT Solution for Australian Cities*, Loder and Bayly, Melbourne, June 1973.

Loder and Bayly, *FG Corridor Study*, Loder and Bayly, Melbourne, June 1973.

Logan, M. I., Maher, C. A., McKay, J. and Humphreys, J. S., *Urban and Regional Australia: Analysis and Policy Issues*, Sorrett, Malvern, 1975.

Melbourne and Metropolitan Board of Works, *Melbourne Metropolitan Planning Scheme 1954*, Melbourne and Metropolitan Board of Works, Melbourne, 1954.

Melbourne and Metropolitan Board of Works, *The Future Growth of Melbourne*, Melbourne and Metropolitan Board of Works, Melbourne, June 1967.

Melbourne and Metropolitan Board of Works, *Planning Policies for the Melbourne Metropolitan Region*, Melbourne and Metropolitan Board of Works, Melbourne, November 1971.

Melbourne and Metropolitan Board of Works, *Report on General Concept Objections*, Melbourne and Metropolitan Board of Works, Melbourne, February 1974.

Melbourne and Metropolitan Tramways Board, *Central Sydney Tramway: Feasibility Study*, Melbourne and Metropolitan Tramways Board, Melbourne, September 1974.

Metropolitan Transportation Committee, *Melbourne Transportation Study*, 3 Vols, Metropolitan Transportation Committee, Melbourne, 1969.

Meyer, J. R., Kain, J. F. and Wohl, M., *The Urban Transportation Problem*, Harvard University Press, Cambridge, Massachusetts, 1965.

Miller, P. M., 'The Crashworthiness of Automobiles', *Scientific American*, Vol. 230, No. 2, February, 1973, pp. 78-86.

Ministry of Transport, Victoria, *Private Enterprise Bus Services Study* (4 Vols.), P.A. Management Consultants Pty Ltd and Wilbur Smith and Associates Pty Ltd, Melbourne, 1976.

Mostert, N., *Supership*, Penguin, Harmondsworth, 1974.

Munby, D. (ed.), *Transport*, Penguin, Harmondsworth, 1968.

N. Lichfield and Associates, *Stevenage Public Transport*, Vols I and II, Stevenage Development Corporation, Stevenage, U.K., 1969.

National Association of Australian State Road Authorities, *A Study of the Economics of Road Vehicle Limits: Concepts and Procedures*, National Association of Australian State Road Authorities, Melbourne, July 1974.

National Highways Study Team, *Summary Report*, Commonwealth Bureau of Roads, Melbourne, August 1973.

National Materials Handling Bureau, *Pallets and Containerisation in Australia*, National Materials Handling Bureau, Bureau of Transport Economics, Canberra, June 1974.

National Population Inquiry, *Population and Australia*, 2 Vols, Australian Government Publishing Service, Canberra 1975.

Nelson, J. C., 'The Economic Effects of Transport Deregulation in Australia', *Transportation Journal*, Vol. 16, No. 2, Winter 1976, pp. 48-71.

Niall, J., 'Survey of General Aviation Industry, 1973', 14th Agricultural Aviation Symposium, Melbourne, November 1973.

Niall, J., *The General Aviation Industry in Australia*, Institute of Applied Economic and Social Research Technical Paper No. 7, University of Melbourne, Melbourne, 1974.

Noble, K. J., Potts, R. B. and Wood, G. L., *Australia – U.K. Container Service*, Mathematics Department, The University of Adelaide, Adelaide, December 1969.

Ogden, K. W., 'Issues in Urban Goods Movement Planning', *Proceedings of the 7th Conference of the Australian Road Research Board*, 1974, Vol. 7, Part 3, Adelaide, pp. 186-205.

Ogden, K. W., *Transport Implications of Different Forms of Growth of Melbourne*, Transport Section, Department of Civil Engineering, University of Melbourne, Special Report No. 3, Melbourne, August 1970.

Ogden, K. W., *The Effect of Technological Innovation on Future Road Traffic in Australia*, Commonwealth Bureau of Roads, Melbourne, 1973.

Ogden, K. W. and Hicks, S. K., (eds), *Urban Goods Movement*, Commonwealth Bureau of Roads, Melbourne, 1975.

Organization for Economic Co-operation and Development, *The Urban Movement of Goods*, Organization for Economic Co-operation and Development, Paris, October 1970.

Overseas Travel by Australians, 1973/4, Australian Tourist Commission, Melbourne, February 1976.

P.A. Management Consultants and Wilbur Smith and Associates, *Private Enterprise Bus Services Study*, 4 Vols, Ministry of Transport, Victoria, Melbourne, 1976.

P. G. PakPoy and Associates, *Study of the Transport of Goods for Tasmania*, Premier of Tasmania's Department, Hobart, May 1971.

Parliament of New South Wales, *Report by Urban Transport Committee of New South Wales to the Minister for Transport and Highways and the Minister for Planning and Environment*, Government Printer, New South Wales, March 1976.

Pearce, D. W., *Cost-Benefit Analysis*, Macmillan, London, 1971.

Pickett, J. C., *Public Authorities and Development in Melbourne*, Urban Research Unit, Research School of Social Sciences, Australian National University, Canberra, 1973.

Pierce, J. R., 'The Fuel Consumption of Automobiles', *Scientific American*, Vol. 232, No. 1, January 1975, pp. 34-44.

Pike, J. and Conquest, T., *Melbourne Bike Way Plan*, Centre for Environmental Studies, University of Melbourne, Melbourne, 1975.

Planning and Transport – the Leeds Approach, Her Majesty's Stationery Office, London, 1969.

Projections of the Population of Australia 1977 to 2001, Australian Bureau of Statistics, Canberra, 1976.

R.A.C.V. Traffic Engineering Department, *The R.A.C.V. Travel Time Study 1976*, Royal Automobile Club of Victoria, Melbourne, March 1976.

Raymond, A., *Alcohol in Relation to Road Safety*, Australian Road Research Board, Report No. 2, Melbourne, November 1974.

Report of the Board of Inquiry into the Victorian Land Transport System, Government Printer, Melbourne, 1972.

Revised Transportation Models for Melbourne, Proceedings of Workshop, Transportation and Highways Branch, The Institution of Engineers, Australia, Melbourne, May 1975.

Rimmer, P. J., *Freight Forwarding in Australia*, Department of Human Geography Publication HG/4, Australian National University, Canberra, 1970.

Rimmer, P. J., 'Transport Decision-Making and its Spatial Repercussions: Shooting an Arrow at a Moving Target', *Monash Publications in Geography No. 11*, Department of Geography, Monash University, Melbourne, 1974.

Rimmer, P. J., 'Transport', in Jeans, D. N. (ed.), *Australia: A Systematic Geography*, Sydney University Press, Sydney, 1977.

Rothenberg, J. G. and Heggie, I. G. (eds), *Transport and the Urban Environment*, Macmillan, London, 1974.

Royal Commission into Alleged Payments to Maritime Unions, *Final Report*, Australian Government Publishing Service, Canberra, 1976.

Royal Commission on Petroleum, *Fourth Report, Marketing and Pricing of Petroleum Products in Australia*, Australian Government Publishing Service, Canberra, 1976.

Royal Commission on Petroleum, *Fifth Report, Towards a National Refining Policy*, Australian Government Publishing Service, Canberra, 1976.

S.A.T.S.: The Issues and Options, Planning Research Centre, Department of Town and Country Planning, University of Sydney, Sydney, August 1972.

Schaeffer, K. H. and Sclar, E., *Access for All: Transportation and Urban Growth*, Penguin, Harmondsworth, 1975.

Schriever, B. A. and Seifert, W. W. (eds), *Air Transportation 1975 and Beyond: A Systems Approach*, The M.I.T. Press, Cambridge, Massachusetts, 1968.

Smerk, G., *Urban Transportation: The Federal Role*, University of Indiana Press, Bloomington, 1965.

Snowy Mountains Engineering Corporation, *Australian Natural Gas Utilisation and Transportation Study*, The Pipeline Authority, Canberra, October 1976.

Solomon, K. T., *Overseas Study Tour*, Australian Road Research Board, ARR Report No. 6, Melbourne, December 1973.

Special Lectures in Transport: National Transport Policy, Transport Section, Department of Civil Engineering, University of Melbourne, Melbourne, 1968.

Steering Committee from The Commonwealth Department of Transport, The South Australian Highways Department and The Commonwealth Bureau of Roads, *Report on the National Highway Linking Adelaide and Darwin*, South Australian Highways Department, Adelaide, 1976.

Stone, T. R., *Beyond the Automobile*, Prentice-Hall, Englewood Cliffs, N.J., 1971.

Streets for People, Organization for Economic Co-operation and Development, Paris, 1974.

Stretton, H., *Housing and Government*, 1974 Boyer Lectures, The Australian Broadcasting Commission, Sydney, 1974.

Stretton, H., *Ideas for Australian Cities*, Georgian House, Melbourne, 1974.

Survey of Australian Tourism 1973/74, Australian Travel Research Conference, Canberra, no date.

Sydney Area Transportation Study (S.A.T.S.), 4 Vols, New South Wales Planning and Environment Commission, Sydney, 1974.

Taplin, J. H. E., 'Energy and Transport in an Island Continent', *Transportation Research*, Vol. 8, 1974, pp. 259-65.

The Law Reform Commission, Report No. 4, *Alcohol, Drugs and Driving*, Australian Government Publishing Service, Canberra, 1976.

The House of Representatives Standing Committee on Environment and Conservation, The Parliament of Australia, *Environmental Impact of Freeways, The Impact of State Highway 23 on Blackbutt Reserve, Newcastle, New South Wales: A Case Study*, Australian Government Publishing Service, Canberra, 1974.

The House of Representatives Standing Committee on Road Safety, The Parliament of the Commonwealth of Australia, *Passenger Motor Vehicle Safety*, Australian Government Publishing Service, Canberra, May 1976.

The Parliament of the Commonwealth of Australia, Parliamentary Paper No. 102/1976, *North-South Highway Connecting Darwin to Melbourne via Mount Isa and Broken Hill*, Report from the Commonwealth Bureau of Roads, Australian Government Publishing Service, Canberra, 1976.

Tonge, J. I., 'Road Accidents Involving Articulated Vehicles in Queensland (1965-1967)', *Medical Journal of Australia*, May 1971.

Town and Country Planning Association, *Melbourne Transportation:*

Statement of Principles Forming the Basis of the Association's Six Point Transport Policy, Town and Country Planning Association, Melbourne, 1971.

Town and Country Planning Board, *Land Requirements and Recommended Designated Areas*, Town and Country Planning Board, Melbourne, April 1975.

Townroe, P. M. (ed.), *Social and Political Consequences of the Motor Car*, David and Charles, Newton Abbot, 1974.

Trace, K., 'Australian Coastal and Overseas Shipping', in Gilmour, P. (ed.), *Physical Distribution Management in Australia*, Cheshire, Melbourne, 1974, pp. 58-84.

Urban Issues Consultants, *The Social Impact of Major Urban Road Projects*, Commonwealth Bureau of Roads, Melbourne, November 1972.

Urban Freeway Study Project Team, *Report on the Need for Freeway Systems in Australian Capital Cities*, Commonwealth Bureau of Roads, Melbourne, August 1973.

Urban Research Unit, Australian National University, *Urban Development in Melbourne*, Australian Institute of Urban Studies, Canberra, February 1973.

Uren, T., 'Urban Development', in McLaren, J. (ed.), *Towards a New Australia Under a Labor Government*, Cheshire, Melbourne, 1972.

U.S. Department of Transportation and U.S. Department of the Interior, *Bicycles U.S.A.*, U.S. Government Printing Office, Washington, 1973.

Webb, G. R., *Victoria's Transport Problem*, Develop Victoria Council, Melbourne, 1962.

Webb, G. R. and McMaster, J. C., (eds), *Australian Transport Economics*, Australia and New Zealand Book Company, Sydney, 1975.

Wheeler, S. J., *The Rate and Regulation Structures of the Australian Freight Transport Industry and Their Effects on Corporate Freight Movements*, Unpublished Master of Administration thesis, Monash University, Melbourne, 1974.

Wheeler, S. J. and Gilmour, P., 'Road Transport Regulation in Australia: Protection of the Railway?', *International Journal of Transport Economics*, Vol. 1, No. 3, December 1974, pp. 313-322.

Wilson, S. S., 'Bicycle Technology', *Scientific American*, Vol. 230, No. 3, March 1973, pp. 81-91.

Wood, H. T., 'Commercial Vehicles: Weight and Dimensional Limits in Relation to Accident Experience', *Proceedings of the 8th Conference of the Australian Road Research Board*, 1976, Vol. 8, Session 26, Perth, pp. 16-36.

Wood, H. T. and Cowley, J. E., 'A Pilot Study of Truck Accidents in Australia', *Proceedings of the 7th Conference of the Australian Road Research Board*, Vol. 7, Part 5, Adelaide, 1974, pp. 48-68.

Wood, R. T., 'The Urban Freight System: Why it Doesn't Work Better', *Proceedings of the International Physical Distribution Management Conference*, Tokyo, June 1973.

Young Driver Accidents, Road Research Group, Organization for Economic Co-operation and Development, Paris, March 1975.

Index

Trade Unions Australia:
Who runs them, who belongs – their politics, their power

Ross M. Martin

There are two widely held beliefs concerning
Australian trade unions. One is that they are
exceptionally aggressive; the other is that they are very
powerful.

An aggressive image of trade unions is projected
through the news media, where they are seen to be
continually demanding or rejecting, protesting noisily,
or on strike whether for a narrow sectional interest or
for broader issues of social concern. The impression
that they are powerful comes from their numerical
size, their association with the Australian Labor Party,
and their use of the strike weapon. Yet while trade
unions are often in the news, this does not necessarily
help them to be understood: the fierce public
controversies about unions and their power are rarely
well informed.

Trade Unions in Australia offers a real understanding
of these complex and important components of
Australian society. Professor Ross Martin has written
a crisp, clear and straightforward survey of
contemporary trade unions: their past, how they are
organized and run; their achievements within a
constraining legal framework; and finally an analysis
of their real character. Contrary to popular belief, he
argues that they are in fact *dependent* institutions,
reacting to events rather than shaping them.